Trials and Error

Trials and Error

THE AUTOBIOGRAPHY

Dougie Lampkin

with James Hogg

**SIMON &
SCHUSTER**

London · New York · Sydney · Toronto · New Delhi

A CBS COMPANY

First published in Great Britain by Simon & Schuster UK Ltd, 2018
A CBS COMPANY

1 3 5 7 9 10 8 6 4 2

Simon & Schuster UK Ltd
1st Floor
222 Gray's Inn Road
London WC1X 8HB

www.simonandschuster.co.uk

Simon & Schuster Australia, Sydney
Simon & Schuster India, New Delhi

Photography courtesy of Red Bull, Trialscentral, Eric Kitchen,
G2F Media and Lampkin Family archives.

The author and publishers have made all reasonable efforts
to contact copyright-holders for permission, and apologise
for any omissions or errors in the form of credits given.
Corrections may be made to future printings.

A CIP catalogue record for this book
is available from the British Library

Hardback ISBN: 978-1-4711-7061-4
Trade Paperback ISBN: 978-1-4711-7651-7
Ebook ISBN: 978-1-4711-7062-1

Typeset in Bembo by M Rules
Printed and bound by CPI Group (UK) Ltd, Croydon, CR0 4YY

Simon & Schuster UK Ltd are committed to sourcing paper
that is made from wood grown in sustainable forests and support the Forest
Stewardship Council, the leading international forest certification organisation.
Our books displaying the FSC logo are printed on FSC certified paper.

CONTENTS

PROLOGUE

Pateley Bridge, North Yorkshire – 26 September 1993

Trials is a funny old sport. Not funny ha ha. Although it does have its moments. Funny as in it's the only motorsport I can think of where you rarely go above 10 or 15 miles an hour and where things like balletic grace and acrobatic finesse are essential to your success. Not exactly the Isle of Man TT, is it? Also, because trials often take place on hillsides and up streams, etc., you're often very, very close to the spectators. When it comes to offering opinions, advice and support, most spectators aren't backward in coming forward, so if you're sensitive to a lot of noise or to strangers calling you a prat when you make a mistake, I'd probably take up snooker or something.

To those who don't know, trials are split into sections – the sections being natural obstacles such as streams, hills, rooted climbs and muddy banks – and we have to try to ride through each section without putting a foot down. Each time we do put a foot down it's called a dab and the more dabs you get, the higher your score, and the higher your score, the less chance you have of winning. There are usually about fifteen different sections in a lap and we do two laps in a trial.

I'm currently on the last section of the last lap of the British round of the 1993 World Outdoor Championship and am in a forest halfway up a very steep hill. It's been raining, naturally, which means there's mud absolutely everywhere, and directly in front of me there's a climb of about 20 metres. All that's standing in my way is the aforementioned mud, a few tree roots and a succession of moss-covered boulders, some of which are a good 7 or 8 feet high. The majority of these will have to be scaled if I want to complete the section. If I can do it without touching the ground, better still.

Despite the location, there are at least a thousand people within eyeshot and at this very moment in time they all seem to be looking at me. Some are standing on the hill and others are either sitting in, or even hanging out of, the trees. They're an intrepid bunch, trials fans.

Although I know one or two people here, the most important person with regard to what I'm about to attempt, apart from me, is my dad. In trials we have what are called minders – people who advise us on what line to take and who guide us through each section. They're like golf caddies or navigators in a rally, basically, and Dad's mine. Minders are also there to help us when we get into trouble and because of the conditions up here, not to mention the sheer height of some of these boulders, a lot of them have been spending their time trying to catch falling bikes. There's a boulder about 10 metres up and the last three riders have all fluffed it right at the top. They all fell and if it hadn't been for their minders, who were standing at the top of the boulder, their bikes would have fallen on top of them. Coming a cropper's almost inevitable in this sport and the golden rule is to avoid the machinery wherever possible.

This is the tenth and final round of the championship, which started in Luxembourg in April, and I'm currently lying 25th out of 37 riders. Bearing in mind it's my first World Championship and I'm not yet a factory rider, that's not too bad.

I'm actually on the brink of achieving something special here, as if I manage to ride this section cleanly I should finish in the top ten. My God, that'll be good! Especially as it's my home trial. As importantly, though, it will elevate me to 17th position in the 1993 World Outdoor Trials Championship. That's something I wouldn't even have dreamed of at the start of the year. Anyway, I'm not there yet. Far from it!

I've just cleared the first step of this hill, which was a boulder about 6 feet high, and Dad's having a quick word. There's almost no run-up to the next one so it's going to be tight. He's telling me to move over to the left slightly to improve my line. Right, I've done that now. As Dad runs forward and takes his place on top of the boulder he shouts his next instruction: 'Really mek it 'ave it!' he shouts.

This is what my dad always says when he wants me to attack an obstacle, and with no run-up and a 7-foot rock to scale I'm going to have to do just that. It may be only a few feet from where I am to where I want to go, but a million things can go wrong.

'Come on Doug,' Dad shouts again. 'Come on, mek it 'ave it!'

I'm in the right gear, so here goes: one, two, three – *BOOM!*

My line is absolutely perfect and as I clear the brow of the rock the crowd just explode. Next, I have to jump off this boulder on to another one which is about 3 metres away. There's a 10-foot drop between them, so I'd better not cock it up. I suppose the attribute we use most in this sport is balance and, all the time Dad's talking to me and I'm waiting to go again, I'm having to make sure I remain upright and keep my feet on the bike. It's obviously not easy but this becomes second nature very, very quickly.

Right, Dad's helping me sort out my line again. 'Come forward a few inches,' he says. 'You're right there. Couldn't be better.' It may only be 3 metres but when you're landing on a slippery rock that's a tiny bit uneven, you have to concentrate.

'Keep your front wheel high, okay?' says Dad. 'There's plenty of room to land.'

I crouch down into my bike and just as I twist the accelerator towards me I leap forward. The power from the bike, together with my own movement, puts me safely on the adjacent boulder. I've cleared it!

Once again, the crowd go mad.

'Nice one Doug,' shouts Dad.

Now for the big one. The third and final climb.

I reckon this is about 15 metres and it's basically a very steep, muddy bank with a boulder at the top. Dad decides to demonstrate the line he wants me to take by walking it himself. ''Ere, look,' he says, as he sets off up the hill. It's fairly straight and I agree with him. I usually do.

Once again, there's next to no run-up so I'll have to 'Mek it 'ave it!' The crowd can sense what's coming and they're already making a noise.

As I look up one last time I see Dad, who's standing on the boulder, step back from view. That's probably wise!

Okay then. One, two, three – *BANG!*

Although it's muddy it's not too wet at the moment so I'm still getting plenty of traction. Come on, we're nearly there! Dad was right about the line, it's perfect. Up to the boulder and we're over it!

What was probably no more than about four or five seconds seemed like at least twenty and the only thing that almost spoiled it all was the fact that I very nearly took out Dad as I went over that last rock. I think he underestimated how far I'd come in and he had to take drastic action. It's all fine, though.

'You've done it, Doug,' says Dad. 'That's you ninth. Not bad Doug, not bad at all.'

For once, I allow myself a little smile. Pateley Bridge is only a few miles away from where we live, so it's happened in front of a proper home crowd. To be honest, that's not really why I'm smiling, though. I'm smiling because I've just had a clear glimpse of what might be to come.

CHAPTER 1

Lampkins at Twelve o'Clock

Some of you reading this will be aware that I'm not the first member of the Lampkin family to win things on a motorcycle. In fact, I'm way down in fifth position. In that respect, we're often referred to as a motorcycling dynasty. Or, more often than not, a Yorkshire motorcycling dynasty. Let's not forget the important bit.

But regardless of how associated the Lampkins are with God's Own County, that side of my family has actually only been up here since the early 1940s and originally hail from – wait for it – south London. I bet you weren't expecting that. Anybody who's ever had the pleasure of listening to my dulcet tones will realise how weird that sounds, as it's safe to say I've got a bit of an accent on me. It's all true, though.

The how and why of the move from London to Yorkshire leads nicely into the dynasty story so I think it's a good place to start.

When the Second World War broke out on 1 September

1939 my grandparents, Arthur Alan and Violet May Lampkin, were living in a place called Shooters Hill, which is in the London Borough of Greenwich. All four of their parents lived nearby so they were a proper south London family. They were also a big family, with Grandad having nine siblings and Grandma four.

Like many others in the area – about 32,000 – Grandad worked at Woolwich Arsenal where he was an engineer. As one of the main munitions factories in the UK, this was a big target for the Germans and when the factory was bombed in 1940 Grandad decided it was time to act. Grandma, together with my Uncle Arthur, who was 18 months old, and Aunty Janet, who was just a baby, had already spent time away from London after being evacuated, but when they came back Grandad decided to apply for a transfer to another factory.

The two places that were offered to Grandad were Birmingham, and Steeton, which is about 3 miles north of Keighley. Although he'd never heard of Steeton, Grandad decided that it probably had less chance of being bombed than Birmingham and so arranged a visit.

After arriving late in the evening on his BSA Blue Star 400 he went straight to the digs that had been organised by the factory. Unfortunately, the place had been oversub-scribed by the Ministry of Defence and so, after making him a cup of tea, the landlady very kindly set about finding him some alternative accommodation. After making a few enquiries she managed to get him a room for the night with a Mr and Mrs Williams and the following day he reported to the factory. Once Grandad was happy that he'd made the right decision, he found somewhere permanent to live (a small rented cottage in Albert Square in nearby Silsden) and then drove down to London to collect Grandma, Arthur and Janet.

After buying a sidecar for his BSA he then loaded them all up – Grandma riding pillion and Arthur and Janet in the sidecar with their belongings – and headed north. I have no idea how long the journey was but with no motorways it must have taken them at least seven or eight hours. It was obviously worth it, though, and although the vast majority of families who'd moved north during the war went back once peace had been declared, Grandad and Grandma decided to stay put. Years later Grandad claimed that it was the best decision they ever made and I'd be the first to agree with him. London's all right in small doses. A bit like bike racing, really.

Once they were all settled, the Lampkin family were eventually offered a house in Silsden, one of about 30 that had been built specially for munitions workers and their families. Their new address was 5 Windsor Avenue and although it sounds quite grand it was actually a flat-roofed, three-bedroomed council house. Nothing wrong with that, though. It was their first family home, really. About three years later the family started growing again when, on 7 April 1944, my Uncle Alan was born.

Arthur, who was born in May 1938, the same month as the Scottish Six Days Trial (SSDT), had always taken an interest in the BSA and, whenever Grandad was either tuning it or mending it, Arthur would be by his side, taking it all in. According to Grandad, Uncle Arthur's interest in motorbikes skyrocketed one day when a friend of his turned up at the house on a trials bike. Arthur, who was about 12 or 13 at the time, had never seen anything like it and, as well as starting to attend trials as a spectator, he immediately began saving up for his own bike.

About two years later, when he was 15, Arthur was caught riding the BSA on a public highway and he and Grandad were summonsed to appear before the local magistrate in Skipton. Apparently, Grandad was unrepentant for his son's misdemeanour and said to the magistrate, 'He was born on wheels and he wants to be a trials rider!'

Good for you, Grandad.

While Arthur was saving up for his own trials bike, Grandad had said to him that he'd give him half the money. The bike was going to cost £150 (a fortune in those days) so this was welcome news. When Arthur eventually told his father that he'd managed to save up his share of the money, Grandad realised that he was skint. 'I have no idea where he got it [the money] from,' Arthur once said to me. 'But he did.'

The bike Arthur ended up buying was a 197cc James, which today are about as rare as hen's teeth. Because there were no junior trials back then, Arthur had to wait until he was 16 before he could ride competitively, but once he did there was no stopping him. In his very first season Arthur competed in the Scott Trial and the Allan Jefferies – two of the most difficult events in the British trials calendar – and although he had L-plates stuck to his 197cc James, he was obviously a natural. After just five events Arthur had graduated to the expert ranks, which is where he stayed for the rest of his career.

The following year, which was 1955, Arthur managed to get his hands on a 350cc Royal Enfield Bullet and just a few days before his 17th birthday he took part in his first ever SSDT. Once again, Arthur's performance was way beyond what it should have been for somebody of his age and experience, and at the end of the week he was presented with a special newcomer's award. The man who won the SSDT that year was Jeff Smith, who had been riding for the famous BSA factory team since 1953.

About this time Arthur was lucky enough to befriend a well-known Yorkshire-based trials rider called Tom Ellis. Tom was also a member of the BSA factory team and, after taking to Arthur and realising his potential, he asked BSA if they'd give him the use of a bike. Despite still being just 17 years of age, Arthur was duly handed a 500cc BSA Gold Star and in the following year's SSDT he finished fifth overall and won the over-350cc class by some margin.

At the time, the only way you could earn any money in off-road motorcycling was by scrambling and so, with his Gold Star as his weapon, he decided to give it a bash. Arthur made his debut at an event at Post Hill near Pudsey in Leeds. It wasn't the best of starts, though, as Arthur ended up making friends with a bush while in pursuit of the Huddersfield scrambling great Frank Bentham. Not surprisingly, Arthur got the hang of scrambling in no time at all and before too long he was invited by BSA to become a fully fledged factory rider. At 18 years of age Arthur was the manufacturer's youngest ever factory rider and he repaid their faith and support by going out and winning everything in sight, including the prestigious Sunbeam MCC Pinhard

Prize, which was basically the award for the best under-21 competitive motorcyclist in the world. Uncle Arthur would probably play all this down if you ever discussed it with him, but in my eyes it's extremely impressive. It gets better, though.

In 1959, after he'd completed his national service, Arthur was given a 500cc BSA Gold Star Scrambler and that season he won the Cumberland Grand National, the Lancashire Grand National and the coveted ACU Scrambles Drivers' Star. He was just 20.

Back then, scrambling was one of the most popular motorsports in the country and you'd often get tens of thousands of people turning up to watch a race. More importantly, it was also incredibly popular on television, as was trials. Just as Arthur's star began to rise in the two sports, so did the viewing figures and, with televised trials taking place almost every weekend from April through September and scrambling from October to March, he quickly became one of the best-known sportspeople in the entire country. Eventually, the TV bosses decided to ditch trials in favour of scrambling every week and so for most of the 1960s you were able to watch it every single weekend on terrestrial television. There were only three channels back then – two until 1964 – so there must have been millions of people watching. These days, you'd be hard pushed to find anyone who has received, or receives, as much coverage on terrestrial television as the likes of Arthur, Jeff Smith and Dave Bickers. That's why people started calling Arthur 'Mr Television'. He was never off the thing!

By the way, one of the main commentators on trials and

scrambling back in the 1960s was the legendary Murray Walker. Despite being associated with Formula 1, he was probably even more at home commentating on these two sports as he'd had first-hand experience of both. He wasn't at all bad, apparently.

But despite Arthur becoming a big television star, his family back home – which had now grown by two with the arrival of my dad, Martin, who was born in 1950 and my Aunt Veronica, who was born in 1952 – had to relocate to a neighbour's house if they wanted to watch him compete, as for the first few years they didn't own a television set.

Arthur still competed in trials and in 1963 he eventually won the SSDT, having won the Scott Trial in 1960 and 1961. He won the Scott Trial again in 1965, but by then he wasn't the only Lampkin who was associated with off-road motorcycling. Alan, who is more commonly known as Sid, which is how I'll refer to him from now on, had been Arthur's biggest fan. Despite riding from an early age, he'd really got the bug while attending the Ilkley Grand National in 1959. At just 15 years of age Sid wasn't allowed to compete. He was, however, allowed to ride the course and from that day on there were officially two Lampkin brothers doing daft things on two wheels for not very much money. According to Uncle Arthur and Uncle Sid, you used to get £3 for riding in a normal scramble meeting and £5 if it was televised. It's not much, is it? Bearing in mind you were putting your neck on the line.

One of Sid's first big tests on a bike happened when he entered the Scott Trial in 1960. At just 16 he was obviously a bit wet behind the ears and unfortunately, like so many other riders, he failed to finish the trial. What made it special for Sid was that Arthur went on to win it, giving him the belief and the impetus that one day he could emulate his famous older brother.

By 1961 Sid had improved immeasurably and, as well as finishing well at the Scott, he had also joined Arthur and the likes of Jeff Smith, Bill Nicholson and Fred Rist in the BSA factory team. Just like Arthur, Sid repaid BSA's support by winning and in 1963, aged just 19, he won his first national trial. From then on he went from strength to strength and by the mid-1960s he too had become one of the most recognisable sportspeople in the country.

In terms of success, 1966 was definitely Sid's year as in October he achieved something very special indeed. In May he won the SSDT and then in October he won the Scott, beating, among many others, Arthur and the eventual seven-time winner of the Scott, the legendary Sammy Miller. What you have to remember here is that Sid was still only 22 years old at the time. Bearing in mind the strength of the competition back then, which was probably unparalleled, that was a gobsmacking achievement.

Back then, riders used to travel all over the place to compete in scrambles and trials and some of the distances they covered were ridiculous. Arthur once told me that, after arriving on the Russian border one day in his van together with fellow BSA rider and friend, Jeff Smith, they still had another 1,500 miles to drive before arriving at their destination. I think it's about 1,500 miles to the Russian border, so that's a 6,000-mile round trip! British Airways had unfortunately stopped their Silsden to Moscow service by then, which was a pity. There were obviously no satnavs in those days and, I should think, very few motorways. It was a different world.

Incidentally, I'm often asked how my Uncle Sid got his name, so while we're talking about Sid I may as well tell you. Many years ago, Arthur had a bike shop in Silsden and one day he left Sid in charge. Arthur had just taken delivery of a load of second-hand stuff that he wasn't sure he could shift, but by the time Arthur returned Sid had managed to sell most of it. Arthur immediately christened his younger brother 'Sid the Second-hand Super Salesman' and from then on it stuck. Well, the 'Sid' bit.

Unlike Arthur and Sid, Dad was a bit of a latecomer to the world of competitive off-road motorcycling and he didn't enter his first national trial until just turning 19. He made a good start, though, finishing just outside the top ten. By then, scrambling had lost some of its popularity and although Dad tried his hand at it – and at things like speedway – he put the majority of his efforts into trials. In that respect, Dad was the first of the three Lampkin brothers to specialise and, together with one of his best friends, Malcolm Rathmell, and with a rider called Mick Andrews, he went on to dominate the sport in the 1970s and the early 1980s.

The pinnacle of Dad's career, which included three British Championships, three consecutive SSDT wins and four Scott Trial wins, happened in 1975, when he became the inaugural World Outdoor Trials champion. From 1964 to 1974 the competition had always been called the European Championship and Dad had won that in 1973. Then, in 1975, the governing body had started inviting riders from the United States to compete, which meant that from then on it was classed as the World Championship. Bearing in mind he was my dad and bearing in mind the World Championship is what I spent the majority of my competitive career chasing, that was a pretty special carrot to have dangling in front of you.

The only question, apart from whether I was good enough, was could I handle the pressure? Not just the pressure of emulating my dad, but the pressure of emulating the dynasty. By the time I was growing up, Arthur's son, John, had also started winning things, which meant I'd be riding on the coat-tails of four off-road success stories. Four!

Could I handle the pressure?

Of course I could.

I'm a Lampkin!

CHAPTER 2

Put Those Hens Down, Now!

Right then. How many people do you know who were named after a motorbike? There'll be some clever so-and-so reading this who claims to know a Norton Smith or a BSA Metcalf, but I bet most of you don't. Well, you do now, because I, Douglas Martin Lampkin, born at 4.15am on Tuesday 23 March 1976 at Airedale Hospital in Keighley, weighing in at a rather healthy 8 pounds 2 ounces, was named after a 1923 Douglas 350cc that my dad had recently bought. I didn't discover that I was named after a piece of machinery until many years afterwards, but apparently my parents had been undecided as to what they were going to call me and when Dad purchased the Douglas shortly before I was born he suggested it to my mum, Isobel. 'Why not?' she said. 'It's better than anything you've suggested so far.'

My middle name comes from my dad, and when my wife Nicola and I had our son Alfie we decided to follow suit by giving him my name, so he's called Alfie Douglas Lampkin.

The thing is, when our second son Fraiser was born we didn't know how to stop, so he's called Fraiser Douglas Lampkin. It's a good job we didn't have a girl. She'd have been stuffed.

Dad had been competing in the French round of the 1976 World Outdoor Trials Championship just prior to me making an appearance and he arrived back in Lothersdale, which is where we lived, just as Mum was going into labour. Funnily enough, something very similar happened to me and Nicola when she was expecting Alfie, except my timing was a bit out. Anyway, that's for later.

What can I tell you about the very young Dougie Lampkin? Well, apart from having dark-brown eyes and straight brown hair, I was sitting up by September, crawling by October and had four teeth – two top and two bottom – by mid-December. Oh yes, I was also a complete and utter pain in the backside. Mum doesn't like talking about this as it brings back too many bad memories, but in order to get me to sleep back then either she or Dad would have to lie down next to me and hold my hand. Once I'd gone to sleep, they would then have to try to peel my fingers away, but the moment I lost contact with them I'd immediately wake up and start protesting. I honestly couldn't tell you why I was like that, but I've certainly been ribbed about it over the years. I dare say it will begin again now that I've been daft enough to write it down.

While we're on the subject of embarrassing things you did as a small child, I may as well come clean about the dummy. Or should I say, dummies. You see, as well as having a dummy in my mouth at all times I also carried a spare one in my hand just in case. This was of my own doing and was a very early example of doing something belt and braces.

As is often the way, my mum had to resort to bribery when it came to persuading me to give up the dummies and it worked an absolute treat. We were at Bolton Abbey one day and I was looking at some fish in the River Wharfe. Mum came up and said that if I gave up the dummies I'd be in for a new pushbike, and so without hesitation I fed them to the fishes. Because we'd travelled a long distance (well, about 7 miles) I had my entire collection with me that day just to be on the safe side and apparently I chucked the lot in. From then on I was dummy-free and, touch wood, I have been ever since.

The first house we lived in was 2 Dale End in Lothersdale, but I'm afraid I don't remember a thing about it. All I've been told is that it was opposite the local pub and occasion-ally Mum and Dad would operate a tag team and take it in turns to pop over for a sneaky drink.

During that time my dad was a factory rider for the Spanish manufacturer Bultaco. He'd won the inaugural World Championship with them in 1975 and was great friends with the Bultó family who owned the company. Subsequently, when Mum announced that she was preg-nant with me, the Bultó family sent over a motorbike as a gift. Poor Mum was probably expecting a bunch of flowers or something, but instead she got a 50cc Bultaco Chispa, which was actually meant for me. Chispa is Spanish for spark and having a motorbike from birth was obviously meant to spark some interest. It worked, except that instead of trying to ride the thing, which would have been remarkable for a baby or a toddler, I used to crawl up to it, pull myself up and then chew on the seat. Mark my words, motorbike seats make fantastic teething rings. I actually got through the back two corners of the seat in next to no time, so if it had gone on any longer I might have done the whole thing. I've still got that bike, by the way. It's being restored by a friend of mine called Blackie Holden and he's doing a great job. When I was younger, as well as riding the hell out of it, I also decided to paint one of the mudguards a different colour, so it hasn't been easy. We're still missing one or two parts, but we'll get there. I've asked Blackie not to touch the seat, though. That's a bit of history!

When I was about 18 months old we moved to a house in Addingham, which is near Ilkley, called Stegg Holes. The house itself was huge and at the back there was a massive garden and a duck pond. The fact that I'd had a motorbike before I was even born was obviously a good omen, although the Bultaco was meant for a seven- or eight-year-old so it was far too big for me. In the end, when I was about three, my dad bought me a tiny little blue 50cc Italjet and from the moment it arrived I was never off it. Dad also got me a copy of his signature helmet, so I was like a mini-me.

All this went swimmingly for the next year or so and that's pretty much all I remember about my early life: tearing around our garden on my 50cc Italjet pretending to be my dad. Then, one day, Dad came home with a brand-new two-door Range Rover. You know, one of those massive square things that are becoming dead popular again. It was white, which in hindsight was quite a bizarre choice for somebody living in the wilds of North Yorkshire. It was Dad's pride and joy, though, and it was a real head-turner when he was out in it.

About a month after he bought it, I was flying around the garden as usual and just for a change I decided to have a quick blast around the drive. I remember flying off the grass but whatever I was looking at, it wasn't Dad's Range Rover. That was parked, pride of place, in its usual spot and as I rode on to the drive I went straight into the side of the damn thing, completely destroying the passenger door in the process. Within a few seconds Mum and Dad were on the scene. I was quite badly hurt but that was insignificant.

'What the hell have you done? Look at my door. LOOK AT MY DOOR!'

Once Mum had got me to my feet and was satisfied that my injuries weren't life-threatening she gave Dad leave to carry on being furious. He didn't say much, though. He didn't have to. It was all in his facial expression.

That was the first time I remember getting into trouble at home, but it wasn't the most serious offence I ever committed. That happened a few years later and involved my brother, Harry. He's 18 months younger than I am and when he first arrived I was dead suspicious. He had blond curly hair and with me having short brown hair I thought he was an imposter and not to be trusted. Slowly but surely I began to accept the fact that, like Sally, who was our faithful but slightly gormless golden retriever, he was almost one of the family and from then on we've always been very close. When Harry was about five and a half and I was about seven we decided to try to teach some of Mum's hens how to swim. This involved us throwing them on to the duck pond and, I'm ashamed to say, even ducking one or two of them under. My mother, who was born in East Keswick near Leeds and brought up on a pig farm there, is one of the world's biggest animal lovers. In fact, I think she prefers them to humans mostly. When she saw us manhandling her hens she went absolutely ballistic and when she screamed for us to stop we jumped out of our skins.

'WHAT THE HELL DO YOU THINK YOU TWO ARE DOING? PUT THOSE HENS DOWN, NOW!'

Boy, were we in trouble.

First of all, Mum dragged us around the garden and while she was doing it, I remember thinking, *I wish I hadn't done that.* I'd never seen Mum properly lose it before and I don't mind admitting that I was absolutely petrified. She's a formidable woman my mum and in her eyes we'd committed a cardinal sin.

Once we'd been around the garden a couple of times she stopped by the pond and then banged our heads together. God, that hurt! After that she ducked us both under the water, just like we'd done to the hens. I think they call it waterboarding these days? After that, the shouting started and it didn't stop for what seemed like hours. Needless to say, we didn't do it again. Seriously, though, whatever you do, do not cross my mother!

I think Mum was always slightly disappointed that Harry and I never grew up to be animal lovers. It's not that we don't actually like animals, we're just not that fussed really. A few years ago, her faith in the younger generation was restored slightly when my eldest son Alfie announced that he wanted to get himself some sheep and a few hens. Mum was absolutely made up with this and since then she's started dragging him off to Skipton auction mart.

I should point out here that the reason I haven't mentioned either nursery or primary school yet isn't because I didn't go. I did, more's the pity. It's because I wasn't that bothered and to be honest I have very little memory of either. I did have a girlfriend, though, at primary school. A girl called Kim Preston. Where the heck did that come from? My memory surprises me sometimes. I had a teacher called June Crabtree, I remember, and I think I quite liked her. She was very kind. That's about it, though, so apologies if anyone's disappointed.

By 1983 Bultaco were going the same way as so many other Spanish companies and by the time that year's SSDT came along my dad hadn't been paid for months. In an attempt to try to get them to cough up he took his Bultaco and an SWM to Fort William; the idea being that if Bultaco hadn't paid him by the time the trial started he'd ride the SWM instead. He didn't want to do it but at the end of the day he had a mortgage to pay and a young family to support. When the money didn't arrive, Dad stuck to his guns and rode the SWM, and just a few months later Bultaco went into administration. It was a really sad end to a once great company and Mum later told me that Dad had been devastated. He never rode competitively again after that, but he was far from idle. Dad had always been a big car man and after retiring from trials in 1983 he started going to the auctions and buying and selling a few cars. The trouble was that he was far too honest and so when somebody asked him what he'd paid for it he'd tell them the truth. This always prevented him from making a decent profit, so he gave it up as a bad job. He carried on buying them, though, and always had a decent motor or two in the drive. Some of them even had their passenger doors intact!

I remember a few years later he went to a car auction and bought a van for Cousin John. John was just starting to import motorbikes from Beta at the time and Dad decided that he needed a van. It was an old Fiat.

Not long after Bultaco went under, Mum and Dad decided to have a go at being publicans and bought a pub called the Miners Arms in Greenhow. Greenhow is a former lead-mining village about 3 miles west of Pateley Bridge, and behind the pub we had about 12 acres of land. For a kid who was into motorcycling this was a dream come true and, best of all, it mitigated the chance of me ever damaging anyone else's vehicles. In fact, the only damage I could do was to myself. The pub was almost always busy and had a darts team, a pool team and even a couple of dominoes teams. Food seemed to be the biggest draw, especially at the weekends, and on a Sunday Mum would serve anything up to two hundred meals. This was a gargantuan task when you think about it and she'd spend half her week preparing for the onslaught of hungry customers. The food was damn good though and as word got around we just got busier and busier.

The only foreign holiday I remember in any detail from the mid-1980s is when we went skiing to Avoriaz in the French Alps. I remember this holiday for two reasons. First, instead of having skiing lessons at ski school like all the other kids did, Harry and I just put on some skis and got on with it. That was interesting! Second, and as a consequence of that, as we were skiing back into Avoriaz one afternoon Harry lost control and, after ploughing into a nearby café, he completely wiped out around six tables containing about 20 cups of hot chocolate and the same number of people. Dad was absolutely gutted. Not because of the embarrass-ment or because Harry might be hurt. But because he had to replenish the 20 cups of hot chocolate! I've been back to Avoriaz several times as an adult and each time I always have a giggle about what happened. Harry won't go near the place. He's gone off skiing.

The majority of the rest of our holidays were spent either at Staithes, where we had a holiday cottage, or at Grandad and Grandma Hemingway's (Mum's parents') pig farm in East Keswick. These holidays in particular are responsible for a large proportion of my happiest childhood memories, and from the age of about three or four the majority of our school holidays were spent there. Looking after us and a successful pub obviously wasn't easy and so those six weeks between July and September must have been like respite care for Mum. At last, they've gone! Her and Dad used to come and see us at weekends and stuff, but for the other five or six days of the week the Miners Arms in Greenhow was a Dougie- and Harry-free zone.

From about a month before we went to East Keswick I'd start dreaming about what was to come and by the time we broke up I'd be champing at the bit. As soon as we got home from school on that last day we'd load our bikes into the car, pack a few things into a bag and then Mum or Dad would drive us over there. It's about 30 miles from Silsden to East Keswick but it used to feel like three hundred. Never in my life have I been as keen to get from one place to the other, and when we finally arrived at the farm we'd get our bikes out and start exploring.

We had a farm, an outdoor swimming pool, a big house and about 10 acres of land that had streams running through it and even a wood. It was just the best. Each day would go something like this: we'd get up dead early, have breakfast and then go for a swim. After that we'd ride our bikes for a bit up and down the streams and then after a quick session with the airguns we'd do some climbing. All this activity would be interspersed with a few trips to the pantry, as just inside the door was a large bowl that was always full of sweets. The rule was that you could have what you wanted, when you wanted it, but we were still hungry come lunchtime. This was one of my favourite parts of the day as after piling into the kitchen there on the table would be Grandma's speciality. I've no idea what it was called but as far as I know it was a mixture of cheese and tinned tomatoes and it would always be served up in a big frying pan with no handle. We used to ask for this every day we were there and we'd devour it with a big loaf of white bread. My grandparents, who were called Marie and Maurice, were the nicest people on God's earth and as far as Harry and I were concerned they lived in heaven. Mum's brother John was running the farm by this point, so they were always there for us if we needed them.

It's hard to explain just how idyllic my childhood was, really. At home we lived in a nice pub with a pool table and, as well as having a park's worth of land at the back, we also had a couple of motorbikes and a pushbike each. Best of all, though, we had a holiday cottage on the east coast where we'd swim or do some crabbing, and two perfect grandparents who lived in paradise. There wasn't much not to like really and I've always been massively grateful. How could you not be having a life like that?

The only time things ever went wrong at East Keswick was when we started siphoning petrol from Grandma's car. She knew about it – well, some of it – but Harry and I were absolutely rubbish at doing it and nine times out of ten we'd end up with a gobful of premium unleaded. Our cousin Ben, who also spent his summers at East Keswick with his brother Dan, was the master of siphoning petrol and so if he was around we'd get him to do it. I can almost taste that premium unleaded now. Horrible!

While we're here I'd just like to give a quick mention to my other grandparents. I'm afraid I never met Grandma Lampkin as she died shortly after I was born. Grandad Lampkin lived next door to the precision-engineering company he set up in Silsden – which Arthur and Sid eventually took over – until shortly before his death in 2005. He was a real character. Despite living in Silsden since the early 1940s and being a bona fide adopted Yorkshireman, Grandad never lost his London accent, and regardless of what he was doing he always remained immaculately turned out. I remember he used to wear a flat cap almost constantly and always had a tie underneath his jumper. Once he retired from the workshop, his big passion – apart from playing golf at Silsden Golf Club and putting 10p bets on the horses (last of the big spenders!) – was perusing the local second-hand shop. Basically, he'd go in there, buy a spanner or an old petrol container and then sell them to one of his children or one of his grandchildren. Whoever he bought it for had to buy it back. That was the rule! I remember going to see him one day and he said, 'Here you go, Dougie. I've bought you this old petrol can. It was only three quid.' Ever the dutiful grandson, I obviously thanked Grandad very much and handed over the three quid, but because I had no idea what had been in it beforehand I had to chuck it away.

In the mid-1990s Grandad fell ill and, as well as being on oxygen for the rest of his life, he became immobile. This didn't stop him, though. Instead of sitting in an armchair and moaning about it, he got himself a mobility scooter and set about using up a few batteries' worth. We all called it The Chariot and he didn't half do some miles in it. It was a proper grand tourer.

Eventually, Grandad Lampkin had to go into a nursing home and on visiting him he'd always ask me first where I'd been and then what I'd been doing. Finally, once all that was over and done with, he'd get on to the important stuff and, after quietly leaning over to me, he'd say, 'But are you still making a few quid?' That was what he really wanted to know and as long as I said something like, 'Aye Grandad, I'm still making a few quid,' he'd sit back a happy man. They're my fondest memories of Grandad Lampkin. He was a good man.

The first trial I ever took part in happened at the back of the Miners Arms on our land when I was about eight. It was a beginners' trial and, as well as it being my first crack, it was also Harry's, Cousin Ben's, Cousin Dan's and Malcolm Rathmell's son, Martin's. Malcolm Rathmell was one of Dad's biggest rivals back in the day and our two families had been friends for years.

It was quite an easy trial to be honest and with a score of just three I ended up winning it. My weapon of choice that day was a Whitehawk 80, which was basically a TY80 engine in a bigger frame and had wheels that made it about three-quarter size. It was quite a popular step-up bike back then and I used to love it.

From then on Harry and I started badgering Mum and Dad to take us to trials on a weekend. Both days, mind you. If Dad was golfing on the Saturday, which he often was, Mum would take us, and Dad on the Sunday. Mum's family, the Hemingways, are just as involved in motorcycling as the Lampkins, so unlike a lot of other mothers who got roped into watching their kids take part in a sport, Mum actually had an interest in the one we were keen on. This probably helped smooth things along a bit when she was courting my dad, but as she's not keen on me talking about her I'd better shut up now before I get thrown in the duck pond.

To be fair, the trials scene in those days was like one big social gathering, just as it is now. This meant that the majority of parents would be looking forward to it almost as much as the kids, and the moment we all arrived at a trial we'd go off and do our thing and they'd go off and do theirs. We'd all come together once the trial began, but until then it was each to their own.

One question I'm often asked is whether I was competitive

right from the very beginning of my trials career and the answer is always, 'Kind of.' I always rode to win and I always rode to the best of my ability. I didn't really have a hunger back then and without wanting to sound too arrogant I won many of the trials I entered. Had I had that hunger I'd have been gutted at losing but I wasn't really. I just took it in my stride. That would all change, of course, and before too long that sense of competitiveness and a hunger for winning every trial I entered would start to appear. The problem was that this all happened just as I began losing!

The turning point was when I started competing at the Junior Championship in A class, and the lad responsible for the vast majority of my misery was Graham Jarvis. These days Graham's a very successful extreme enduro rider and he's won the Scott Trial a record nine times. Back then, though, he was doing a right good job of becoming my nemesis and I used to dread seeing him turn up at a trial.

People often assume that I've been a success right the way through, but the truth is I had very little success as a schoolboy and it was only when Graham moved up to the adults that I had a bit of breathing space. It was the same in *Junior Kickstart*, which I'll come on to in a bit.

As I said, it didn't really bother me all that much because I didn't have a hunger. Getting beaten by Graham definitely helped to develop that, though, and by the time he buggered off into the adult class I was starving.

We used to get a lot of snow up in Greenhow. And I mean, a lot of snow! There's a very steep hill that goes from Greenhow down into Pateley Bridge and the moment it started snowing they'd shut it off. This meant only one thing to me – no school! In that respect, Greenhow was quite a popular place to live and back in the mid-1980s when we still had proper winters it could happen anytime between October and April.

The Miners Arms was a great big stone building but in front of it, covering the dining area, there was a slanting felt roof that wasn't too strong. When it snowed we had to clear the roof sharpish so it wouldn't cave in, and during the winter of 1984 this gave us a great idea. It had been snowing like mad the night before and when we woke up we quickly realised that it must have been at least a metre deep. This meant no school, of course, but it also meant that the dining-room roof would be in danger of collapsing.

'Right you two,' said Dad to me and Harry. 'Get up on to that roof and start getting it cleared. And be quick about it.'

After pushing some of the snow off the roof we quickly realised that if we jumped out of Harry's bedroom window we'd be able to slide down the roof and on to the pile we'd made below. Our very own snow slide! Once we'd cleared the roof that was it for the rest of the day, and without even stopping to breathe we went up to Harry's room, threw ourselves out of the window, slid down the roof on to the pile of snow we'd made, ran through the pub and did it all again. Mix in the almost endless supply of pop and crisps and you've got the makings of a perfect day, really.

I used to absolutely love living in a pub, for all kinds of different reasons. Mum and Dad would be downstairs most evenings which meant Harry and I had the upstairs to ourselves. We could go into the pub whenever we liked, so we were never short of company, and Mum and Dad would pop up for a rest every so often to make sure we were okay. The best room in the pub was the taproom, which is where all the fruit machines were, although we were never allowed to play them. This was quite frustrating at first but once I found out how much money Mum and Dad made from them I realised that there was only one winner and I've never played a fruit machine in my entire life. It was actually mine and Harry's job to count all the money from these machines, but in the end it took us too long and so Dad had to buy a machine. I shudder to think how much they made! Luckily for Harry and me we had a pool table and a dartboard to keep us occupied and, because Mum and Dad were okay with us being downstairs, it was like having our own games room. We'd even have our dinner down there. I know what you must be thinking – *You lucky sod, Lampkin!* Aye, that's about right.

In 1985, after we'd been at the Miners Arms about two years, it all got a bit much for Mum and Dad and they decided that it was time to sell up and leave. Mum especially was absolutely exhausted and it had become a case of them living to work, as opposed to working to live. They were victims of their own success, really, as they'd turned the pub into one of the most popular in the area, but I think they'd both enjoyed the majority of our time there. Harry and I certainly had!

The house we moved into was Fishbeck House, which is just outside Silsden. Mum and Dad had bought it about a year before and so when they decided to sell the pub we had somewhere to move into. From a business point of view, Mum and

Dad seemed to enjoy working with the public and so they bought a café in Gargrave called the Singing Kettle. Although busy, it was a lot smaller than the pub and because it was only open during the day they had a lot more time to themselves. During the week we'd live at Fishbeck and during the weekends, when the café was busy, we'd move over to Gargrave. Once again, it was probably a slightly unorthodox existence, really, but Harry and I never wanted for anything. As well as having two tremendous parents who gave us everything and were always there for us, we had an awful lot of freedom. Feeling as secure as we did definitely helped us to enjoy that sense of freedom and the weekends in Gargrave were when it started coming into its own. I was only nine or ten, bear in mind, and Harry just seven or eight.

We did actually work occasionally, so it wasn't all fun, fun, fun. One of Mum's specialities at the Singing Kettle was trout, which she got from the local trout farm, and it was mine and Harry's job to gut them. Although that was the only job I remember doing it was absolutely horrendous and how we didn't throw up I've absolutely no idea.

While Mum and Dad were working in the café Harry and I would have the freedom of the town and the surrounding area and, as well as having loads of school friends nearby, we also had our cousin, Roger. Roger's the son of Dad's eldest sister, Janet, and at the time he was learning to ride a unicycle. There are some very famous stepping stones that cross the River Aire at Gargrave and Harry and I, plus every other kid in the area, used to try to ride over them on our pushbikes. As far as I remember none of us ever managed it, but it wasn't for want of trying. Then, one day, Roger came along on his unicycle and managed to do the lot. I remember being mightily impressed at the time. I still am. Then again, so is Roger. He reckons there should be a plaque somewhere commemorating the feat.

CHAPTER 3

Left Back in the Changing Rooms

In 1986 my cousin John, who's Uncle Arthur's eldest son, was involved in a massive car accident. John had been the Lampkins' sole representative on the trials circuit ever since my dad had retired, and in 1984 he'd finished fifth in the World Championship and had also won one of the rounds. That was the third time John had finished in the top ten of the World Championship so he was certainly no slouch. Despite being just ten at the time I remember the accident well because it rocked our family big time.

John, his brother David and a friend of theirs called James Snowden were driving back from a motocross event one day when a motorbike tried to overtake an oncoming car. Needless to say the rider didn't make it and ended up having a head-on collision with John, Dave and James. The steering wheel almost took John's head off and all three of them were lucky to be alive. Unfortunately, John also broke his femur really badly and after having it pinned he was told that his riding career was over.

As well as being a very, very good rider, John Lampkin is one of the nicest men you could ever wish to meet and fortunately he has the heart of a lion. Instead of letting the accident ruin his life like some might, he got up and started thinking about what he was going to do instead. Then, one day, John saw a motorbike at a trial somewhere called a Beta. Although long established, Beta, who are based in Florence, hadn't been seen in the UK much and, after asking my dad what he thought of the company and getting some positive feedback, he decided he was going to start importing them. Over the next year or so John put his heart and soul into building a relationship with Beta and making the project work, but for a time it was touch and go as to whether it would. Beta were still an unknown quantity in the UK and with so much competition around it was obviously difficult making your voice heard.

I remember at first John was operating out of a small garage that was close to the family engineering firm and one day, just in passing, he mentioned to my dad that he was looking at buying a van. About a week later Dad was at the car auction, as usual, and I was with him. A local parcel company had recently gone bust and consequently there were a load of vans for sale. One in particular, an old Fiat Ducato with a high roof and a long wheelbase, was going for naff all and Dad ended up buying it for John. I think it was about £1,500. Dad didn't tell John, nor did John ask Dad to buy him one. He just did. I remember it had a funny red stripe running across it and had a blue tick on one side. The heating was permanently stuck on cold, which meant you had to keep a rug over your legs, and although it wasn't the tidiest van in the world, at least it went. Once Dad had paid for it we took this van to John and that was it. 'Here's that van you were looking for, John. Now crack on.' I dare say Dad and John sorted the money out somewhere along the way but that would only have been when John was able to pay. It was a very typical Lampkin thing to do, really, and it was how our family operated. Back in the 1960s when Arthur was doing quite well he'd bought my dad his first bike and so it went on. John needed a van, Dad saw one, so he bought it for him.

The only time Dad and John weren't aligned as to what was best for the Lampkin family was in the late 1990s after I'd won the World Championship, when John suggested that I go and see a sports psychologist. Or a head doctor, as my dad used to call them. As they were becoming popular in professional sport, John thought it was the right thing to do. Dad was horrified. 'Bloody hell, John,' he said. 'You only go and see one of them when you're losing. Not when you're winning!' It was never mentioned again.

In 1987, not long after Dad bought him that van, John struck gold when an up-and-coming Spanish rider called Jordi Tarrés won both the Scottish Six Days Trial (SSDT) and then the World Outdoor Championship on a Beta! All of a sudden everybody wanted one and, as Beta's UK importer, all the enquiries were directed to John. Thirty years later John is still importing Betas and despite what he might tell you he's got a very successful business. The crux of his success is the relationship he's built with the Bianchi family who own Beta and it's something he's quite rightly very proud of. As we'll see later on, I almost scuppered all that, unintentionally of course, after winning my third World Outdoor Championship.

The only other sports apart from trials that I ever showed any interest in when I was a young lad were football and golf, and in 1987 I started turning out for Silsden Whitestar once or twice who were my local football team. According to my dad the position I should have played was 'left back in the changing rooms', and to be fair I didn't really know what I was doing. Although I'm not big on footballing positions I think I was a defender of some sort as I seem to remember hoofing the ball up the pitch quite a lot. Not long after I started playing for Silsden Whitestar Dad bought me some awful Gola football boots and I'll never forget him trying to persuade me that they were the best on the market. 'Everyone's wearing them, Dougie,' he said. 'You're bound to win matches in them.'

They weren't the best on the market. They were the cheapest! Everyone else on the team had adidas or Nike. The only reason I ever got a game was because I could score from corners, so that turned me into a bit of a secret weapon. This was always done by luck rather than judgement and only happened because the pitch was on an incline. Dad obviously said that it was because of the football boots. I really was rubbish, though. A proper donkey.

Golf, on the other hand, was a completely different kettle of fish and, as well as being keen on it, I was actually quite good. Since retiring from trials Dad had also taken to golf big time, and once he discovered that I had an aptitude for it he started encouraging me. After getting my handicap down to 13 – I'd only have been about 13 at the time – Dad said that I had to make a choice between golf and trials. He wasn't asking me to ditch one of them completely but in order for me to improve at trials I'd have to play less golf, and vice versa. There was no competition. Trials was in my blood and was something I lived for and looked forward to. Golf, on the other hand, was something I enjoyed playing in my spare time. I was pleased Dad gave me the choice, though. It made me feel grown-up.

It was about this time that Mum and Dad decided they'd had enough of running the café in Gargrave, so they swapped it for a newsagent's in Silsden. With Dad being an early bird this seemed like a right good idea and I think he enjoyed it. It was always busy but best of all it didn't do Sunday papers, which meant him and Mum could actually have a regular day off for a change. Granted, the vast majority of these Sundays were spent carting Harry and me around Yorkshire, Lancashire, Derbyshire and Cumbria riding trials, but at least we could do it as a family.

It was when Mum and Dad bought this newsagent's, which was called Twiggs, that Harry and I finally started doing some work. Well, occasionally. We were standby paperboys, which meant once every couple of weeks we'd get a call at home from whichever parent was down there, saying that a paperboy or papergirl hadn't turned up and that one of us would be needed immediately. 'Get on your pushbike and get down here at the double,' was always the specific order, and whoever's turn it was would have to oblige. There were certain rounds Harry and I dreaded and certain rounds we quite enjoyed, but there were two rounds that I wasn't allowed to do under any circumstances. I promise you I didn't do it on purpose but because I made so many mistakes on these rounds I was banned from them for life. 'You're a liability,' Dad would say. 'It took me two hours to clear up your mess and get the papers to the right homes!' The round including Bolton Road was particularly chaotic, which is ironic really as it's got a funeral director's on it and quite a few nursing homes. I couldn't tell you what went wrong. It just did. Howden Road, on the other hand, was an absolute doddle and I could probably do that now if I got the call – 22 *Daily Mails*, 23 *Suns*, 11 *Mirrors*, 10 *Expresses*, 9 *Telegraphs* and a *Guardian*. There. Doddle.

Sometimes there'd be two or even three people off, in which case it would be all hands on deck followed by a lift to school as we'd have missed the school bus. None of this could happen, of course, until Harry had done his hair, as it was around this time that my brother discovered vanity and did he take it seriously! As well as spending about 15 minutes in front of the mirror each morning he used to go through about 4 gallons of hair gel a week, and with me having dark hair and looking like Stig of the Dump most days and him having fair hair and looking like George Michael, you'd never have known we were brothers. That said, Harry and I were always very, very close when we were kids and we still are today. We don't have to phone each other up every five minutes but I know that if I ever needed anything he'd be here immediately and the same goes for me. We did obviously fight occasionally. I mean, what brothers don't? Harry used to go running to Mum when this happened and I'd always get it in the neck. 'Leave your brother alone,' Mum would snap. 'He's smaller than you.' Then, when I was about 12, the tables started turning and Harry discovered that, as well as being a bit stronger than me, I was ultimately, for want of a better phrase, a bit of a soft arse. After that it was my turn to go running to Mum but she never took any notice. What was she supposed to say? 'Leave him alone, Harry. He's bigger than you.' It doesn't really work, docs it?

When it came to riding trials, Harry was very handy indeed and it was always Dad's opinion that had he stuck with the sport he'd easily have made it into the top ten in the world. What happens after that, you just don't know. When Harry was 16 Dad decided he might have a future in the sport and so started pushing him a bit. Nothing too drastic. He just told him that he'd better start putting in some extra training. Harry, much to everyone's astonishment, told Dad that he wasn't interested in becoming a professional trials rider, and that, as opposed to moving things up a notch, he didn't want to do it any more. Dad was flabbergasted, but it was Harry's decision. He was doing other things by then. He had a little smallholding with a few animals on it, and as well as a good group of friends I think he'd spotted a few girls. Dad in particular was disappointed because he saw a lot of potential in Harry but his sense of disappointment was far outweighed by the fact that Harry was happy. I know for sure that Harry's never, ever regretted that decision and, like he should, he's always done his own thing. He does come out of retirement occasionally and over the last few years he's ridden with me at the SSDT, which has been nice. Because he hasn't done much recently it's fair to say that there isn't a great deal of finesse in his riding. As Cousin James always says (James is Sid's lad, by the way), 'He's the only man we know who can ride a motorbike with his knees.' He can! It's not nice to watch, though. It's like watching an elephant perform ballet.

Because he's so flaming strong Harry would have made a brilliant motocross rider, and Arthur even took him to Hawkstone Park a few times with a view to him doing just that. I think Harry was riding a Honda and Arthur was training him. Apparently there was an accident during one of these races in which Harry was badly winded and after it happened Arthur ran on to the track. You're obviously not supposed to do this as it can be extraordinarily dangerous but Arthur didn't care. He was off and there was no stopping him! Now, you're probably assuming that Arthur ran on to the track at Hawkstone Park to attend to his injured nephew and make sure he was okay. Wrong! Arthur ran straight past Harry, who was still flat on his back, and after picking up his bike and starting it for him Arthur then proceeded to try to drag Harry on to it! I was about to say that only Arthur could do something like that, but that's rubbish. Sid and my dad would have done exactly the same thing.

Now we're about on to my teenage years I suppose I'd better give school another mention. Although I enjoyed school, educationally I was as flat as a pancake and if there was a line for average I was on it for pretty much everything.

Every single report I got at secondary school said something like, 'Does okay, but could try harder', and I remember there were lots of requests from the teachers for me to start applying myself more. I never did, though, and the lessons themselves are a bit of a blur really. I never got into trouble much, and if you asked me to remember something from any one of those times and at any point in time I'm afraid I'd fail miserably. Actually, I did get into trouble. I had a fight once when I was about 14 and this kid hit me right square on the nose. It hurt like bloody mad and after that I retired from fighting altogether. I haven't had one since and I don't intend to. To me, it's like gambling. There's only ever going to be one winner and it won't be me!

Socially, things were slightly different and although I wasn't the most popular kid in school I didn't have many enemies. I know I'm going to get ribbed for this but to be honest I always got on better with girls than I did lads and most of my mates were girls. I'll never live it down, but that's the truth.

Because I was away a lot and because I wasn't into the usual stuff like rugby and football, I never really fitted into either a gang or a clique and so I rubbed along well with most people. The thing that turned me from Mr Innocuous into Mr Popular was being on *Junior Kickstart*. For those of you who are too young to remember it or just weren't all that bothered, *Junior Kickstart* was a television programme that ran on the BBC between 1980 and 1992 and was basically a trials competition for children. The obstacles were generally man-made using things like skips and barrels, so in that respect it was almost like an indoor trial. Appearing on that was a proper game-changer, and because most of the pupils used to watch it I temporarily became king of South Craven School. Back then there were only four channels and with fewer programmes on offer we all ended up watching the same thing. But in addition to that, the sport of trials has always been very popular around our way, so if you didn't watch *Junior Kickstart* there was something wrong with you.

After the World Championship and being Arthur Lampkin's nephew, *Junior Kickstart* is probably what I'm best known for. This is quite ironic really as I never won it, and on my final appearance when I was 16 I had a nightmare and I don't think I cleared a single obstacle. They used a clip of that on the Dougie's Wheelie documentary (2016) and it still hurts watching it. My only excuse is that instead of using my Beta 200cc I asked John to lend me a Beta 240cc instead. It was dead muddy and I thought this would be a good move. It wasn't! For a start the bike was too powerful but it was also too big and so even when I did put my foot down, which was often, I had the bike leaning against me and that almost pushed me over. Worst of all, John was commentating on this episode so he had to try and make excuses for me as I cocked it all up. I'm not sure who I feel the most sorry for, him or me. Another low point for me – one of many, in fact – was when they did a pro-am *Kickstart* in 1988. I was obviously expecting to be paired with John, who was also taking part, but for some reason the producers decided to keep us apart. I forget who I was paired with now but he was absolutely useless and so yet again I'm afraid I failed to make an impression.

The first time I went on *Junior Kickstart* was when I was 11 and the thing I remember most when reading the information sent by the producers was that you got £200 for appearing. TWO HUNDRED POUNDS! To an 11-year-old who was too lazy to find himself a job that was an absolute fortune and, best of all, Dad used to let me keep it. When we first turned up to where it was being filmed I was expecting crowds of people, massive cameras and about ten articulated lorries, but instead there were just a couple of trucks, two or three cameras, four or five people shuffling around and a big tent where all the riders waited. It was all quite underwhelming, really. Like a village fete!

My nemesis on the programme was the aforementioned Graham Jarvis. As well as being a year older than me, which was always my excuse for him beating me, he was a lot smoother than I was and he also had a few more tricks in the bag. I think the rest of us all suffered from nerves quite a bit which Graham never seemed to. He didn't smile much and he didn't talk much either. He just got on his bike and did what he had to. I'm pretty sure Graham won every series he rode in, the sod!

I used to suffer terribly from nerves, especially in those early days. I once entered the YMSA Six Day Trial down in Matlock in Derbyshire when I was about 12 and I had to retire after three days because I was being sick. Happens to the best of us.

Apart from the money, and appearing on national television, the best bit about being on *Junior Kickstart* was meeting the legendary Peter Purves, who had also presented *Blue Peter* and was a household name in the 1970s and 80s. What a lovely bloke. He was obviously very interested in trials, which was great, and he was dead friendly. Before you rode he'd come and have a chat with you and make sure you were okay. He'd also ask you a few questions so he could talk about you while he was commentating, so I was always very careful how I answered those! I read an interview with Peter a few years ago – well after *Junior Kickstart* had finished – and he said that when he gets stopped in the supermarket the majority of people want to talk about *Junior Kickstart* as opposed to *Blue Peter*. Bearing in mind the programme went off air in 1992, which might or might not have had something to do with my final performance, it's obviously still incredibly popular and there have been dozens of attempts to revamp it and bring it back to our screens. I don't think it would work now sadly, for the simple reason that it's no longer such an extreme sport. That's a pity as I'd love to have another crack!

Whenever I meet people who aren't into motorbikes I always use *Junior Kickstart* as an explanation. The conversations go something like this:

'What do you do then?'

'I'm a world champion motorcyclist.'

'What? Like the TT?'

'No. I ride trials.'

Look at me blankly.

'Trials? What's that?'

'Do you remember *Junior Kickstart*?'

'Oh, right! I used to watch that all the time.'

'Well, that's what I do.'

Instant new-found respect.

Apologies for the massive name-drop but Nicola and I went to a Robbie Williams concert once and afterwards we were invited to have dinner with him. We were with Neil Hodgson and his wife Kathryn and eventually the conversation got around to bikes and what I did for a living. I didn't just get a knowing look from Robbie Williams, though, not once I mentioned *Junior Kickstart*. I got a rendition of the bloody theme tune! Not bad, eh? He still didn't have a bloody clue who I was but I think the link stopped him from calling security.

Despite failing in my final attempt to win *Junior Kickstart* I still had my GCSEs to look forward to. All this actually meant was that I had something else to cock up and in that respect I didn't disappoint. After taking eight or nine of the flaming things I came away with one – design and technology – and a final report that wasn't too dissimilar to the one I'd have received from *Junior Kickstart* if anyone had been bothered to write it. Let's just say that expectations were quite low!

The only thing that I had going for me at this time from a career point of view was the fact that my performances in competitive trials had begun to improve and, after a year or so without Graham Jarvis, who'd moved up to the adult class the year before, I'd been able to establish myself, gain some much-needed confidence and develop that hunger I talked about earlier. Now, though, I was at an impasse. In order to take things to the next level and compete in the European Championship I would need a licence and in order to get a licence I had to be 17. This meant I had nine months to wait before I could move on and so the question naturally arose as to what I was going to do with myself.

'You can't just sit around here all day,' Dad said. 'You'll have to make yourself useful.'

Fortunately, just as I was about to leave school and become one of the great unwashed for a few months, an opportunity arose. Dad was working in the shop one morning when a regular customer of his called Alan Airey came in to get his paper and his usual packet of fags. He was always in a rush was Alan and he used to screech up in his white van, burst into the shop, grab his stuff, say 'Now then' to my dad, fly out again and then screech off to wherever he was going. Alan used to have his own construction business and as he flew in to grab his stuff he mentioned to Dad that he'd been let down by one of his lads.

'Our Doug's available,' said Dad immediately. 'He'll come.'

'Right,' said Alan. 'I'll pick him up in't morning at quarter to seven.'

'Hang on,' said Dad. 'He's got one of his last exams tomorrow. I've just remembered. How about the day after?'

'Aye, go on then.'

The morning after the exam I stood in the shop with a packed lunch that my mum had made for me, waiting for Alan to screech up and not knowing what the bloody hell to expect.

'What will I be doing, Dad?' I kept on asking.

'You'll be helping Alan,' was the only answer he could give me, although he did tell me why I was doing it.

'It's about time you learned the value of money,' Dad said to me. 'You'll be earning a wage from Alan so this will be your opportunity to save up and stand on your own two feet a bit.'

To be honest, I don't think I really appreciated what Dad was saying at the time, although it soon started to make sense.

When Alan screeched up to the shop at quarter to seven he grabbed his paper and his fags, told Dad that I'd be back at about seven o'clock that evening, bundled me into the back of his little Astra van and set off like hell for leather. He was working on the Knaresborough bypass at the time, laying concrete shuttering, and so for the next few months that was what I was going to be doing. For those of you who don't know, concrete shuttering is basically the kerbing and the job itself was extremely labour-intensive.

At seven o'clock on that first evening Alan dropped me at the end of our road and, according to Mum who was watching out of the window, I weaved my way down the road to the house.

'How was it, Doug?' asked Dad.

'Eh? Oh, fine,' I said, flopping on to the sofa.

'I'll go and get your tea,' said Mum.

By the time she got back a few seconds later I was fast asleep. Gone to the world! Although I was quite a fit lad I'd never really worked before and the closest I'd come to manual labour was shifting the wheelbarrow for Mum. This had been a very, very rude awakening and that evening before I went to bed Mum was on at my dad to stop me from going again.

'Look at him. He's absolutely broken! You can't make him go again, Mart.'

'Rubbish! It's high time he did some manual work and at the same time he'll be earning a few quid. He'll be up tomorrow and the next day.'

The following morning when Dad gave me a shout I honestly thought I was lying under something dead heavy. I couldn't move! When I did manage to shift myself a few inches I realised that I was in all kinds of agony and if it hadn't been for the fact that Alan was relying on me – and that I was earning £3 an hour, which then was quite a bit of money – I'd quite happily have stayed there for the rest of the week and allowed Mum to wait on me hand and foot. She would have too, just to wind my dad up.

As well as the long days during the week we also used to work a few hours on a Saturday morning, and I remember getting out of the van once at about 11.20am but instead of going indoors and putting my feet up I jumped straight into the back of John's van and set off for a round of the adult British Championship in Wales. Because it was held off-road I was allowed to ride it and we only just got there in time. I came twelfth and John came tenth, which he takes great pleasure in reminding me, so I wish I hadn't bothered!

After nine months of what was hard but enjoyable labour I'd managed to save up a grand total of £2,700. That was quite an achievement for a young lad who'd never lifted a spade before and the whole lot went towards riding the 1993 European Championship. Before that, though, I still had a few months in which to work and so after the job with Alan on the Knaresborough bypass had finished, I tried my hand at being a roofer for a while for a man called Ian McCrink. Ian was from Silsden and tended to work locally, and for the three months I worked for him I really quite enjoyed it. I did have a bit of a scare, though, which I admit took the shine off a little bit. We were doing a big house at Eldwick one day, which is near Bingley, and as I was carrying a big slate on my back down a roof ladder I suddenly slipped. Because it was on a slant I had no choice other than to run down the roof and ended up jumping off into the sandpit below. I honestly thought I was a goner! The slate never made it I'm afraid and I ended up getting a right bollocking for that. I could never really enjoy the job after this and when Dad saw me on a very high flat roof in Ilkley one day carrying a bucket of hot tar he panicked, handed in my notice and got me a job fitting UPVC windows for a man called Russell Clark.

This was to be my last ever normal job and, after realising my potential to inflict damage, Russell put me in charge of braying out the old windows. I thought this was brilliant as I was basically getting paid to make a massive mess, and even though I had to tidy the mess up it was well worth it. Have hammer, will destroy! The only time Russell ever had me fitting windows instead of destroying them was on a job in Ilkley once and it cost him a fortune. The house was massive and the owners had ordered these high-security windows that cost an arm and a leg. I was screwing some of these windows in one day but instead of opening them first and just screwing in the frames like you were supposed to, I left them closed and ended up basically screwing them shut. They all looked fine. You just couldn't open them. I tried explaining that this could be an added security feature with extra ventilation but the boss didn't buy into my vision and I ended up having to knock them out again. As this was what I should have been doing in the first place it all seemed a bit ridiculous. I'm afraid I just wasn't cut out for a normal job. Or a job that required any kind of common sense.

CHAPTER 4

The Scottish Six Days Trial

Before I could compete in the 1993 European Championship, which was due to start in Belgium on 16 May, I had to complete two very difficult but also very different tasks: getting my licence, which I had a feeling was going to be an obligatory nightmare, and competing in the Scottish Six Days Trial (SSDT), which, regardless of how I fared, was going to be an absolute dream come true.

The Scottish Six Days Trial was the first trial I ever went to as a child. Not that I remember any of it. I was only a few weeks old. According to my mum she pushed me around in a Silver Cross pram and the first section she took me to was the infamous Pipeline on the fourth day. Anyone who's been to the SSDT, either as a spectator or a competitor, will know why this wasn't such a good idea. For those of you who aren't aware of it, Pipeline is a pretty tortuous uphill section and not what you'd call pram-friendly. Mum managed, though, and Dad went on to win the trial – the first of three consecutive SSDT wins – on his Bultaco. I must have brought him luck.

First held in July 1909 as a five-day event devised by Campbell McGregor of the Edinburgh Motor Cycle Club, the SSDT is really the pinnacle of motorcycle trials, whether you're a club rider or a professional. That's in the world, by the way. As a stand-alone event nothing comes close and the terrain you have to ride is unforgiving and at times terrifying. Some of it, like Pipeline, is absolutely brutal and each day you can cover anything up to 100 miles. The scenery up there is absolutely stunning, although I try to do the majority of my sightseeing between sections! Put simply, the SSDT is the best in the world and has been the highlight of my year since I was a kid.

The first one I actually remember attending was in 1982. The American Bernie Schreiber won that year, and if me and my cousins weren't watching one of the sections we'd either be playing in the stream on our pushbikes, as my children do now, or cycling around the paddock badgering all the different bike manufacturers and tyre companies for stickers. Collecting stickers was our sport, if you like, and we used to come back with piles of them. We'd also get the odd autograph if we could scrounge a pen and paper, but my abiding memory has always been us bombing around on our bikes. The trial itself was almost secondary in a way. Once again, having that kind of freedom at such a young age and in an environment that we all found dead exciting was an absolute privilege, and I think I've always been aware of that. Even back then. We were lucky kids, that's for sure. To top it all off we got a week off school when we went to the SSDT, so there wasn't much to dislike. Back then you could take your kids out of school without it causing a flap. I'm not saying it's right, though!

The first year I entered the SSDT as a rider was obviously 1993 and the only thing standing in my way was the afore-mentioned obligatory bike test. I obviously couldn't take the test until I'd turned 17 so, with the trial taking place during the first week in May like it always did, that left me with just over a month. A month, I hear you say. Surely that's plenty of time? Normally yes, but to a 17-year-old SSDT fanatic who'd been dreaming about little else since he was a young lad it felt like about five minutes. I'd never felt pressure like it. Not even on *Junior Kickstart*! I didn't tell anyone how I was feeling, though. That's not the Lampkin way. What I did do, however, was work out what I'd do if I failed the test: start blubbing and try to appeal to the examiner's better nature! I was ready to plead and beg if necessary. There's no question about it. That's how much it meant to me. To top it all off I also had the first round of the Europeans coming up which was vital for my career, so that added a nice dollop of extra pressure.

When it came to preparing for the test I couldn't have done any more. All kinds of people had given me advice and I must have practised every manoeuvre under the sun at least a hundred times. I was ready physically then, but was I ready mentally?

The test took place in mid-April at the motorcycle test centre in Keighley and it was an absolutely shocking day. Quite normal for Keighley. Luckily, I'm quite good in the wet and as we set off the examiner began talking to me through the intercom.

'What does that sign in front of you mean?'

'Slippery road ahead?'

'Well done. Okay, indicate . . . now!'

As we turned a corner the examiner said he'd like me to do an emergency stop.

'No problem,' I said. Everything had gone well so far and although I didn't usually enjoy stopping, I definitely knew how to do it.

When the examiner said 'Stop' I yanked on the brakes sharpish and came to an immediate halt. There was no skidding either, so I was sure I'd done a good job.

'Okay, carry on,' said the examiner. I thought he sounded a bit disapproving when he said that but I didn't give it a second thought.

When we got back to the test centre I was expecting nothing less than a pat on the back and a few words of congratulation. Every question had been answered correctly and I hadn't put a foot wrong on the bike.

Or had I?

'Can I have a quick word with you, Mr Lampkin?' said the examiner as we entered the test centre.

This sounded ominous. 'Yes, of course,' I said. I'm pretty sure I actually called him sir.

'Your emergency stop was dangerous,' he said, looking quite stern.

'How do you mean?' I asked. 'I didn't skid.'

I was absolutely bricking it by this point and was all ready to switch on the waterworks.

'You stopped too fast because you were covering your front brake. You do realise you're not supposed to do that?'

I did realise that but to be honest it had completely slipped my mind.

'I'm so sorry,' I said, trying to wobble my bottom lip. 'I ride trials usually and it's a force of habit.'

I couldn't believe it. The only reason I was doing the test was so I could ride in a trial. *The* trial, in fact. And it looked very much like I was about to be denied because of something I do in trials. Hoist by my own petard, is the appropriate saying.

'Anyway, that's the only groan I've got,' said the examiner, suddenly holding out his hand. 'Congratulations. You've passed.'

I've said right from the off that I never had much to whinge about as a child. Even so, I'd never felt as happy as this. It was like a hundred Christmases all rolled into one.

'Thank you very much indeed,' I said, taking his hand and shaking the living hell out of it. He looked at me quite strangely after that, so before he could change his mind or call for help I did one.

Before the test I hadn't really ridden a motorbike on the roads before and so, instead of turning up wearing all my sponsored trials gear, I was advised by my dad to go and see Colin Appleyard. Colin was a friend of Dad's who owned a couple of bike dealerships and after explaining my predicament to him he very kindly lent me a bike, a helmet and some nice unassuming and unsponsored clothing. It was definitely a case of all the gear, no idea.

Actually, I'm telling a lie. I had ridden on the roads before and on something with two wheels. It certainly wasn't a motorbike, though. It was a 50cc Honda Camino, also known as a pedal and pop. I'd been an absolute laughing stock when I first got it and rightly so. It was, after all, a proper little virgin chariot and it sounded like a baby crying. On a flat surface it could reach speeds of anything up to 25 miles per hour, and if I'd been given a pound every time I was overtaken by something like a dog or a fat jogger I'd have been able to buy a fully restored Douglas. Take it on a hill, however, and the moment it went above 7 or 8 degrees you had to pedal. I didn't actually mind the ribbing. It became a running joke, really. Or in this case a standing one. Then, after a while, my cousin Dave offered to tune it for me and once he'd worked his magic it was an absolute monster. Okay, that's probably a slight exaggeration. It could definitely tickle 40, though, and for a while I was the fastest virgin charioteer around the school bus park. I'd arrived! The only problem was that if you held it flat out for anything more than 30 seconds it would blow the front light bulb.

'Keep rolling the power off and let it have a little moment to itself,' was my personal tuner's advice.

Believe it or not, I've still got the Camino but I'm afraid she's a non-runner. I blew her to smithereens.

After leaving the test centre I went back to Colin's dealership, returned everything, said thanks very much and asked if I could phone my dad. There weren't many mobile phones back then and even if there had been you wouldn't have been able to get a signal. Not in North Yorkshire circa 1993. You can barely get one now!

'How did you get on?' he asked.

'Not bad. I passed. I almost didn't, though.'

'What do you mean?'

'Because I was covering my front brake my emergency stop was a bit lively.'

'You prat. I told you about that!'

'Did you? Anyway, will you come and pick us up?'

Because of what had been riding on the test I don't think I'd actually listened to anybody for weeks and that was pretty much how it remained until we got to Scotland. My head was always elsewhere. Then, shortly after the weigh-in, which always takes place on the Sunday, everything changed. One of Dad's rivals from his riding career was competing that year and when Dad clocked him he instructed this poor man that I'd be following him for the full week. There was no 'Would you mind?' by the way. It was an order. The man in question was Nigel Birkett, who these days is the UK importer for Scorpa motorcycles. The look on his face when he realised what he'd been forced to take on was a picture. Horror first, followed by resignation. Translated into words, it would have said, 'Aw, bloody hell!'

Nigel had been competing at the SSDT since 1971 when he rode a home-built 128cc Suzuki, and in 1975, which was the year my dad won the inaugural World Outdoor Trials Championship, he'd finished second in one of the rounds and according to Dad he knew a thing or two.

'Ask Nigel as many questions as you want,' Dad said after introducing me to the condemned man. 'You're bloody lucky he's agreed to this, isn't he Nigel?'

Again, the look on Nigel's face was a picture. 'I didn't agree to anything!' is what it said.

In all seriousness, I'd have struggled massively had it not been for Nigel and I stuck to him like glue the entire week. I was like his shadow. When he went back to his bike, so did I, and he advised me both before and after every single section.

'You were a bit fast there, Dougie lad,' he'd say. 'Just be careful on that rough stuff.'

After one section on the moor he gave me a right dressing-down.

'For God's sake stop riding through all the bogs,' he said. 'You're covering everything and it's not good on your bike. You need to keep your bike good and you need to keep yourself good. Remember that. Ride *around* everything and keep a nice pace. Look and ride, Dougie, and don't get stuck in the queues.'

This time I was like a sponge. In fact, I don't think I'd ever been as attentive with anyone in my entire life. It was a proper masterclass and I knew it. Nothing went to waste. Not a single word. I also must have asked him at least one question for every mile we covered and, because I was riding well, Nigel responded to all of them.

Thanks in no small part to his patience and constant stream of advice I ended up finishing sixth that year, out of 275 riders. I also won best newcomer, so all in all I had a pretty decent week in Fort William. I remember it had been snowing on the first day so I'd have been happy just not finishing last. Sixth though – and on my first attempt? This was just madness.

Nigel Birkett still competes today and is SSDT's most experienced rider. Forty-six years and counting, by all accounts. That's an unbelievable feat. He must be as fit as a butcher's dog.

About four days after my maiden SSDT had come to an end we were packing up the van again for the first round of the European Championship, which was taking place in Bertrix in the south of Belgium. Because this was a career-led excursion and was what I'd been saving up for, it was to be funded out of my own pocket. This is when I got my first real lesson in the value of money because when we went to fill the van up for the first time it was me who had to pay for it, not my dad. Fuel was obviously a lot cheaper back then but it was still a fair whack, and when I was walking back to the van having paid I was already trying to work out how much it was going to cost me to go to Belgium and back. *Hang on*, I thought to myself. *After Belgium we've got Italy, Spain and then Switzerland, followed by Germany and then France. I was going to have to take out some shares in Shell! Either that or start digging for oil in the hills above Silsden. Bloody hell!* It was going to be a dear job, that's for sure. I knew that I didn't want to go back to having a proper job, so despite the shock of me having had open-wallet surgery with a lot more to come, it was actually just the incentive I needed. If I wanted to carry on doing this I'd have to make a success of it, end of. The thing is, I hadn't beaten Graham Jarvis yet, let alone the lads at the top like Jordi Tarrés and Marc Colomer. I was an unknown quantity, really. Not just to the public, but to myself.

Unfortunately, nerves got the better of me in Belgium and I got the same result as I did at the SSDT – sixth. This would be the last time in a while, though, and by the time I left Italy after finishing fourth I was not brimming with confidence exactly, but I was definitely starting to find my feet. Next up was Spain and, as well as registering my first ever win abroad, I went into it believing and thinking that I was going to win. Previously to this I think I'd always approached each trial with a certain amount of humility, both inwardly and when being interviewed. Outwardly that stayed the same, really, and if anybody ever asked me what I thought my chances were prior to a trial I'd play them down and start extolling the talents and virtues of my competitors. Inwardly, though, I was completely and utterly focused and I barely even noticed anyone else. It wasn't an especially convincing win – I finished on 56 points and Antonio Benítez finished on 58 – but I'd backed up what I believed was going to happen and mentally that was a massive step forward.

As good as that first major win felt, it was unfortunately marred later that day by a freak accident. While celebrating in a bar, Blackie Holden, the friend I mentioned earlier who is restoring my Bultaco, dived into a swimming pool and from the moment he entered the water he knew he was in trouble. Blackie Holden has been a friend of mine all my life and his dad, who was also known as Blackie, used to be best mates with Arthur. We'd ridden together since we were kids and, despite him being there to mind for another rider, he was as pleased with the maiden win as Dad and me. The bar we were in was inside a sports centre and because there was a pool nearby Blackie decided to go for a celebratory dip. We all had to drive back first thing in the morning, so everyone was taking it easy. We were still on a high, though. I can still picture him now jumping into the pool. Actually, it was more of a belly flop really, but the moment he hit the water he started shouting something. We all thought he was messing around at first but when we realised what he was shouting and that he was having trouble staying afloat that started to change.

'I can't feel my legs,' he shouted.

A friend of Dad's called Arthur Scott was the person who called us to action. 'I've seen somebody drowning in a swimming pool before but we managed to get them out,' he said. 'That lad's in trouble.'

As soon as Arthur said that we all piled out to the swimming pool and the two people who were nearest to it dived in and pulled Blackie out. He was still shouting the same thing, 'I can't feel my legs.' Blackie later told me that he knew there and then that he'd been paralysed and, to be honest, I think we all did. He was taken to hospital in next to no time but there was nothing they could really do for him. It was just awful.

Twenty-five years on, Blackie's now spent more time in a wheelchair than he has done out of one, but that hasn't stopped him living life. As well as continuing to be one of the best friends I've ever had, if not the best, and taking care of my ever-growing bike collection, Blackie's also played an integral part in some of my biggest projects, including the Isle of Man wheelie (more on this later!).

Going into the sixth and final round of the 1993 European Championship, which was taking place in France, there were three riders in contention: me, a Spanish lad called Cèsar Panicot and an Italian lad from Como called Dario Re Delle Gandine. The week previously I'd had all my bikes stolen from home, which was a right bugger. Fortunately, the British round of the World Championship had recently taken place in Pateley Bridge and Beta's factory rider, Takumi Narita, had left his bike at John's. The season was over now and so John made a call to the Beta factory to see if they'd mind me using it. I wasn't expecting them to say yes for one moment but for some reason they did! This bike had just been ridden to seventh place in the 1993 World Outdoor Championship, so although it wasn't set up for me (I changed the handlebars to Renthals which is what I'd always used) it had a lot more going for it than against it. Even so, it still wasn't good enough.

You see, while all this was going on, Beta had given Dario Re Delle Gandine a new prototype they'd been working on that would eventually come out the following year. I was as sick as a parrot when I saw this bike and all of a sudden Takumi's top-tenner seemed obsolete. I honestly can't remember why I thought the prototype was so special. It just was! Dad thought it was an absolutely shocking bike and did his best to convince me that, as opposed to being badly done to, which I hadn't been, I'd actually dodged a bullet. I didn't believe him, though. You know what it's like when you're that age. You always want the newest bike on the market.

The trial, which took place in Caille in south-eastern France, was challenging but doable and without wanting to sound like an arrogant big-head I rode a blinder on the first lap. In fact, if memory serves me correctly I think

I was the only rider to finish on single figures. On the second lap things went from good to excellent, and while everyone else was again in double figures I posted a one. Not bad for a lanky Yorkshire prat who until a few hours ago was still whinging about that flaming prototype! That was it, though. I was European champion. Incidentally, the European Championship had been reintroduced the year before, in 1992. Now though, instead of it featuring the best of the best like it had done previously, it was seen as a kind of showcase for all the best young riders and could be won only once. Those who do well in the championship are often approached by manufacturers about becoming factory riders or even full factory riders (there's a difference which I'll explain soon), so it's a stepping stone really.

One rather bittersweet moment towards the end of that European Championship was being joined by a friend of ours called Ernie Page. Ernie and his family had been very close friends of ours since I was tiny and his son David, who was an absolutely phenomenal trials rider, had been one of my best friends. He'd always been the envy of the paddock when we were riding together and not just because he was talented. As well as having a spare bike, which was almost unheard of for a junior, he also had more helmets and boots than the rest of us put together. He was the full package.

Ernie used to have a motorbike shop in Edinburgh and while David and I were competing against each other as schoolboys our families would get together. Unfortunately, David had leukaemia in his teens and had tragically passed away about two years previously, aged just 19. Since then, Ernie had gone to ground and for the last two years no one had seen hide nor hair of him. He'd been missed, but we could all understand why he'd stayed away. As I said, David had been a prodigious talent on a motorbike and so travelling to trials as normal would have been torturous.

Ernie had actually first turned up at the penultimate round in Thalheim, Germany, and when we saw him pulling in we were all absolutely overjoyed. If there was one person who wasn't there who I'd like to have shared that win with it was David. Ernie was a close second, though, and it made that last round in particular very special indeed.

When we returned home from France on 18 October 1993 we allowed ourselves to celebrate a little bit. My nickname among friends and family had always been The Scooter Man. Cousin John had given me the name while I was a junior on account of me footing on one side as I was riding a kid's scooter. There was a sheet draped over the front door saying: 'I USED TO BE A FAN OF THE SCOOTER MAN. BUT NOW I'M A FAN OF THE EUROPEAN CHAMPION.' To be honest, I never even knew that our Harry could write, so as well as it being a big compliment, it was also a surprise. The following day we met up with the rest of the family and although I was too young to imbibe the adult Lampkins and Hemingways got well stuck in.

The following week a present arrived from the Beta factory. At first I thought it might have been a motorbike but instead it was a mountain bike. Dad was absolutely mortified. 'You've just won the European Trials Championship and they've given you a bloody pushbike? What's going on?' I was chuffed to bits. In fact, I've still got that bike somewhere.

Pushbikes notwithstanding, the best thing to come out of me winning the 1993 European Championship, apart from seeing Ernie again, was that John was now able to speak to Beta on my behalf about a contract. Then and only then would I be able to have a proper crack at the World Championship.

CHAPTER 5

Coming of Age

Because of what I'd learned in 1993 I went into the following year's Scottish Six Days Trial (SSDT) brimming with confidence. Not arrogance or a belief that I was going to win like I'd had in Spain, just confidence. Mark my words, foregone conclusions do not exist at the SSDT, so if you go in cocky the chances are you'll come a cropper. You just have to do your best.

Fortunately for Nigel the number he was given for the trial (each rider has their own number) was nowhere near mine this year so he was left to ride in peace. I was quite close to my cousins Ben, Dan and John, which was good, as well as a very good friend of mine called Paul Dixon. These days you can request to ride close to people if you like but back then it was pot luck.

My ambition that year was to improve on sixth. Simple as that. The pressure was obviously immense after having such a good result 12 months before but it was offset by the fact that I was just desperate to ride. Nothing had changed in that respect and it was still my favourite trial. I'd also made quite a few mistakes in 1993, let's be clear, and despite winning the European Championship I was nowhere near the finished article. With that in mind I figured that any kind of improvement had to be my immediate goal. Trials is such an unpredictable sport and regardless of how confident you are in your own abilities you can't let that, or your overall ambitions, get the better of you. I was desperate to win the SSDT but if I didn't take it section by section I knew I'd be on a hiding to nothing.

I remember setting off really well and although I wasn't leading after the first day I was in touch. What I remember most about the entire trial is how good it felt riding alongside members of my family. That represented the enjoyment aspect and I think it also helped keep me relaxed.

The SSDT always finishes on Ben Nevis on the Saturday and by the time we got there I had a good advantage. Again, it wasn't a foregone conclusion, but as long as I didn't make any major cock-ups I'd be home and dry. The cock-ups didn't happen, fortunately, and so I won. There's a photo of me, Harry and Mum on Ben Nevis that was taken just after the final section and it's one of my favourite photographs ever. Because it's my all-time favourite trial I get a very different feeling winning the Scottish. Even winning a World Championship's not the same. That's work-related and, as much as I love doing it, that's the day job. Despite entering the SSDT as a factory rider and a professional, I'm actually there as an enthusiast first and foremost. That trial is in our family's blood – the Lampkins and the Hemingways – and the fact that I'm the fourth member of my family to win it after Arthur, Sid and Dad is pretty special.

People often ask me what you get for winning the SSDT and my answer is always a source of some regret. You actually get handed a huge trophy but because it's so valuable you have to hand it back after five minutes and off it goes to a safety-deposit box. It's such a shame as melted down it would be worth a fortune. Joke! It's happened a lot to me over the years, handing valuable trophies back, but the Scottish is actually one of the only ones I'd like to take home with me. It's an amazing piece of work.

Shortly after winning the SSDT I was awarded the Sunbeam MCC Pinhard Prize, which is given for the best performance by an under-21-year-old in all areas of competitive motorcycling. Uncle Arthur had won it when he was 18 and the award itself is a rose bowl. I was actually allowed to keep that one but these days it too gets taken straight back and locked away.

The best part of winning the SSDT – apart from getting my hands on that coveted trophy for a few minutes – was receiving a bonus from John. I can't remember how much it was exactly but knowing John it would have been a good whack. At least enough to pay for my spare parts! I was also sponsored by Dunlop at the time and the SSDT was a big, big deal for them. So much so that when I won they gave me a fresh set of van tyres. I was delighted with that! I remember getting quite a few new sponsors after winning the Scottish, the highlight being 12 pairs of gloves from a contact of John's. Being a Lampkin certainly made a difference with regard to how much interest there was in my career, but when it came to things like sponsorship you were judged on your results. A name means nothing to sponsors if you're not performing. These days I think sponsorship can bring a lot of added pressure, especially with the amount of money involved. You're effectively an ambassador for that company, so however you're performing is a reflection on them. That's the reality. The only person or company I've ever felt pressure from is myself. That said, I'm a pretty difficult taskmaster and if I lose I'm the most miserable man on earth. That'll never change.

A few months after winning the SSDT I became a bona fide factory rider for the first time. I'd been riding Betas ever since I was 11 or 12 and because John was the importer the relationship had always worked well. Dad had bought the bikes from John and because of John's position we got a certain amount of leeway and support.

Once I became a factory rider I began getting bikes that were semi-prepared. To me, this was like having your own mechanic and the night before the first one arrived I didn't sleep a wink. For those who don't know, semi-prepared bikes are made in a competition shop as opposed to on a production line, and as well as having factory forks and suspension they'll have various other modifications. In my case the mechanics at Beta had done a little bit of work on the cylinder to make sure it had more power and they'd also had a look at the clutch. Best of all, though, my name had been written in marker pen on the engine. For me that was the game-changer. It really was *my* bike. They spelt it 'Dugy Lampkeen', but that's beside the point. It was the thought that counts and I was grateful. I certainly never rubbed it

off. Full factory riders, by the way, are the full-time professionals who travel with the team. As well as having fully
prepared bikes, they also have mechanics! That was obviously the ultimate dream, but for now I was as happy as a
pig in you-know-what.

Even before becoming a factory rider, the people at Beta
had been helping me wherever they could and by the beginning of 1994 I'd started to develop my own relationship with
them. By the time I won the SSDT in May the only thing
that had been separating me from being a full factory rider
was having a semi-prepared bike as opposed to a fully prepared one. Everything else was there. They obviously saw
some potential and because I'd already been riding Betas for
six or seven years I felt a certain amount of loyalty towards
them. More importantly, though, they made damn good
bikes. I was surprised they could understand me, but after
dealing with John for so many years they'd obviously got
used to the Yorkshire accent. That must take some doing.
Italian to Yorkshire. Blimey!

What finally pushed me towards becoming a full factory
rider happened at Hoghton Tower near Preston. It was the
UK round of the 1994 World Championship and it was one
of those days when I could have walked on water. I was on
perfect line and perfect balance all day long and everything
just clicked. Although my performances had been improving I'd never really come close to winning a round before,
so it was a big surprise to everyone. Even me. Funnily
enough, during the press conference somebody had actually
suggested I might win, and although it had been laughed off
it did plant a little seed. It was going to happen one day, so I

hoped. Why not now? Dunlop, who were already a sponsor of mine, were the ones who'd organised the press conference and, because the British round of the World Championship was such a big deal to them, I think they were the ones who suggested it. 'What about our boy Dougie? He could win.'

'Naa, don't be daft. He's not ready.'

Winning a round of the World Outdoor Championship was and is a big deal in our sport and for the rest of that year Beta began treating me more and more like a full factory rider. The mechanics looking after the existing full factory riders began checking my bike over before and after races and I started spending a lot of time in the factory truck. This was a real thrill for me but more importantly it helped with my performances. I remember once they changed the rear shock for me because it was shot. I didn't realise at the time and when the mechanic pointed it out I couldn't believe it. The difference afterwards was amazing and that's what I mean about it helping my performances. You can't put a price on that kind of expertise and the more involved I became and the more help I got, the more I wanted in. Until then my 'team', if you like, had always been my dad, John and myself, and to be fair we'd done very well. We'd won the European Championship, for heaven's sake! Then, when I started doing well in the World Championship I'd see people like Jordi Tarrés around the place. As well as having a mechanic or three, he seemed to have somebody to do everything and I remember looking at him one day and thinking, *I want a bit of that!* Then, when the Beta relationship started to blossom it all became a possibility. All I had to do was perform.

The third highlight for me in 1994 was winning my first British Championship. I'd finished seventh in 1993, one place behind Graham Jarvis, and although it wasn't as important as winning the European Championship, not with regard to getting a factory contract, it was obviously my home championship and one that I was keen to win. The list of former winners is mightily impressive, and to be mentioned in the same breath as the likes of Johnny Brittain, Gordon Jackson, Jeff Smith, Sammy Miller, Malcolm Rathmell and Steve Saunders was something worth fighting for. My dad had won the British three times – 1973, 1978 and 1980 – so that made it even more desirable. It wasn't that I wanted to surpass my dad's total – actually, that's rubbish, of course I did!

Dad was absolutely chuffed to bits when I won it and in terms of my long-term championship ambitions I'd ticked the second of three boxes. First the European and the British. Now for the Worlds.

The fourth and final high point of 1994 (this year's going to take some beating) was winning the coveted Scott Trial, which I've recently won again for the sixth time. I think we're very lucky in the UK because we've got the best two events in the world in the Scott Trial and the SSDT, although the two are completely different. I dare say the majority of you reading this will know all about both, but for those of you who've heard of the Scott but have never been, let me give you a quick heads-up.

The Scott Trial is run over an off-road course of 84 miles divided into 76 sections. It takes place near Richmond in North Yorkshire and is a time and observation trial. This means that whoever goes around the fastest sets the standard time and for every minute you're behind the leader you get one penalty point – plus the points you've lost in observation in the sections. There are about six fuel stops in all and, as well as finishing with no skin on your hands, you'll be a broken man, both physically and mentally. Like the SSDT this is a real high point in any club rider's career and finishing it, which you have to do within two and a half hours of the eventual winner (who generally takes around five hours), is a big old achievement. Imagine that, though, having to ride seven or seven and a half hours. It's ridiculously punishing and a real test of character. The people at Richmond Motor Club who run the event obviously know if riders are going to make it or not, and they'll start pulling them out at the third, fourth, fifth or sixth fuel check. It's limited to two hundred riders, by the way. They put the flag out and say, 'Sorry, but you've got to come in. You're not going to make it in time so you have to stop.' That must be absolutely demoralising but they have to do it because of safety.

The first time I rode in the Scott Trial was 1993. It's only an hour away from home so it was our local big event. Arthur, Sid and my dad have won it eight times between them so there is also a little bit of family history there. Unlike the SSDT, at which we used to just bomb around on our bikes, we actually used to watch the Scott Trial quite intently and, like the Scottish, it was something I was champing at the bit to take part in. Because it was so taxing, the main piece of advice people gave me was to pace myself, but my dad refuted that when he heard. 'Mark my words,' he said. 'You'll be too knackered to pace yourself. Just don't set off like an idiot.' Due to the amount of adrenalin pumping around my body and the fact that I hadn't listened to him, I'm afraid I did just that. I was just too excited.

Within half an hour of setting off I got a front puncture and within about three hours I'd also had two backs. I forget how far back I was in the end but it was just something I put down to experience. I did finish, though, and obviously within two and a half hours of the winner. I don't remember it being that punishing to tell the truth, probably because of the adrenalin. The three punctures also gave me a nice breather. I'd got the bug, though, and October 1994 couldn't come around soon enough.

In 1994, as well as winning the Scottish, the World Championship round at Hoghton Tower and the British Championship, I'd also been lucky enough to be asked to make one or two television appearances and had ended up appearing on *Top Gear* a couple of times. We recorded these bits sometime in the summer and afterwards the producers had asked if they could film me riding the Scott. I didn't have a problem with that. In fact, I was well up for it.

Instead of setting off like a bull in a china shop I took my dad's advice this time and set off sensibly. I had a bit of experience now, which counts for a lot, and knew first and foremost that I had to keep my feet up. I remember it was an atrocious day, really foggy, and the visibility was rubbish. All two hundred riders were in the same boat though, so I wasn't complaining. Once again, I don't remember feeling that tired afterwards, but as opposed to it just being the adrenalin I think I was actually quite fit. These days I'm a broken man after I've ridden the Scott and I always clear my diary for about a week afterwards. In fact, after winning the one just gone I collapsed in the back of my van and could barely move. I went to my cousin's house in Richmond after that and they had to literally carry me to the presentation ceremony. I just wanted to sleep. In fact, I still do! It was about a month and a half ago now and I'm still feeling the effects. People keep asking me if I'll ride it in 2018 but I haven't made up my mind yet. I probably will.

I remember my dad saying to me that to win the Scott and the Scottish in the same year was one of the biggest things you could achieve in trials. 'A monumental achievement,' is what he said. 'The holy grail!' This might have had something to do with the fact that he'd done it twice, in 1977 and 1978, but I gave him the benefit of the doubt. My Uncle Sid had also done it in 1966 but as opposed to their heroics piling any additional pressure on me it actually galvanised me. Sometimes a little nugget like that is exactly what you need to focus the mind and when I ended up winning I think even Dad was impressed. 'Well done, Doug,' he said afterwards. 'Do it once more and you'll have matched me.' I knew he was going to say something like that. I felt like I'd found a quid and lost a fiver! In all seriousness, although we never used to show our emotions in situations like these – that's just not the way we do things – I knew that my dad was immensely proud when I won the Scott and Scottish in the same year, just as I was proud of him.

By the end of 1994 I'd won my first SSDT, my first Scott Trial, my first British Championship and my first round of the World Championship. And I'd appeared on *Top Gear*, although I can't remember what I did. A good haul, even though I do say so myself. From then on I was appreciated in my own right and was no longer described as Martin Lampkin's son. I'm not saying there's anything wrong with that and nobody's prouder of my dad than I am. What I mean is that until then I'd been clinging on to his coat-tails – and Arthur's, Sid's and John's, to be fair – and I think there were some people out there who thought I was only mentioned in the press because I was a Lampkin. This quartet of wins definitely helped separate me from that and from then on, although proud of being a Lampkin, I began being treated as an individual. An individual with a very recognisable surname! I still get people coming up to me and saying, 'Aren't you Arthur Lampkin's nephew?' That will never change.

After 1994 my relationship with all my sponsors changed and entirely at their behest. Renthal were one of the first ones to get in touch. I'd been using their handlebars since I was 12 years old and the relationship, although mutually beneficial, had until then been based around some handlebars and a bit of bonus money. Now everything was different. Renthal wanted to formalise things and instead of getting equipment and a bonus I was paid to endorse their products professionally. I actually enjoyed this change and not just because it made me money. It made me feel like a professional. Like Jordi Tarrés! More importantly, though, it also gave me a much closer relationship with Renthal and from a performance point of view that was only going to be an advantage.

Saying that, the bonuses I'd earned from sponsors over the

past couple of years had started to add up and by the time
we got to the beginning of 1995 I had enough to buy my
own car. I set my sights on buying myself a Ford Fiesta RS
Turbo. That was my absolute dream car and although it was
probably going to cost me an arm and a leg to insure, I didn't
care. After telling my Uncle Arthur about my intentions he
said something I will never, ever forget. 'Spend everything
you've got lad,' said Arthur. 'You always ride better when
you're skint.' I've thought about those words a lot since then
and, although I'm not sure if he's right, it was a cracking line.

Because of Dad's history in buying and selling motors I
allowed him to take charge and after emptying my piggy
bank we took a trip down to the auctions. I had about three
and a half grand to my name and, as I said, I wasn't going to
be happy unless I left the auction with a Fiesta RS Turbo. A
man's car if ever there was one.

As it was, I'm afraid they didn't have any Fiesta RS Turbos
so I ended up buying a red 2-litre Toyota Celica on a J plate
instead. A man's car if ever there was one. I had to borrow a
few grand to get it. Four grand to be exact. But I didn't care.
If what Arthur had said was true I was about to improve my
riding skills more than somewhat – *and* I was mobile.

The first person I noticed who also drove a Toyota Celica
was the Spanish rider – and soon to be my rival – Marc
Colomer. I was out training in Spain one week in early
1995 and noticed he was driving a GT4 model. Much better
than mine.

'He's obviously doing a bit better than you, Dougie lad,'
said Dad. 'And I bet he didn't have to borrow four grand
from his old man to buy it.'

'Thanks for pointing that out, Dad.'

'No problem.'

Marc Colomer may have had a better model than me but he didn't get to cruise around Silsden in his. I did. What's more, it made me feel like a king. King Doug of Silsden! That was a great time, though. I used to drive the Celica to the gym in the morning and then go practising in the afternoon. Car in the morning, van and bike in the afternoon. I had it all back then.

There were several reasons why I started training in Spain, apart from the climate. With so many of my competitors being Spanish it made sense to train in the same environment as them, which is when I noticed Marc's GT4. Or rather, Dad did. Trials is also a much bigger sport in Spain and the facilities are a bit more professional. Something else that made a difference was the fact that Beta had a factory near Barcelona where they did a lot of pre-assembly. It was called Beta Trueba and was in a town called Esparreguera. It's still there today. Practising close to your manufacturer is never a bad thing and it definitely paid dividends.

Dad used to borrow an apartment from Antonio Trueba, who owned the factory, and if ever it wasn't available we'd stay in this tiny little hotel in the centre of Esparreguera. I remember it was about a tenner a night for both of us, including breakfast, but because it was so cold my dad used to call it Hotel Antarctica. You had to sleep in your clothes it was that cold but the price tag made it just about bearable. I know what you're thinking, *Tight as a duck's bum, these Lampkins.* You're not far off.

Antonio Trueba was very good to me in those early years.

He's since been instrumental in launching several high-profile careers, including a young Spanish upstart named Toni Bou. Antonio's never really had the credit he deserves in our sport but in my opinion, and in the opinion of many other people he's helped over the years, he's a complete legend. I wish he'd unleashed Toni a couple of years later though! I might have won another World Championship. Then again . . .

When I first started training in Spain I was a bit of a novelty I suppose and the Spanish lads were all very friendly. Then when I started beating some of them I became slightly less popular. Nobody was nasty to me. They just gave me a wide berth. Story of my life, really.

The journeys over to Spain, which I obviously made with my dad, are something I'll treasure for the rest of my life. Dad always had to drive because if I did I obviously wasn't doing it right. I was either too fast or too slow and that was the way it always remained with Dad. He was the designated driver, no arguments, and it was best to let him get on with it. He wouldn't fly, by the way. Not unless he had to. He wasn't in control if he was flying and on the few occasions when he did get on an aeroplane he was a nightmare. 'I don't like it, Doug,' he'd say. 'It's not safe!' Said the man who used to ride trials for a living.

We always had to drive through the night when we went to Spain and as soon as we left Silsden it was next stop Barcelona. There was no taking it easy. Once we were off, that was it. 'Come on Doug, let's crack on.' He never needed a map, either. Dad had been around Europe that many times in the past that he knew every road backward. It was ingrained in his brain. The only time he came unstuck is when they built a new road, but even then he never had to stop and ask anyone. It was instinctive with him. The only downside to this internal European navigation system of Dad's was that he also knew exactly where all the transport cafés were. Not the nice ones with things like menus translated into English or a cook who didn't have dandruff and a fag hanging out of his mouth, these were grotty ones where instead of trying to ask for something you just pointed or made a noise. If you asked me to name one thing we ate at these places I couldn't tell you. We used to have some right unlucky dips. Dad was in his element, though. Not because the food was good. It wasn't! I think they just reminded him of his days competing around Europe with the likes of Uncle Sid and Malcolm Rathmell.

As well as training in Spain I eventually started competing in some indoor trial events there. We still only had outdoor trials in Britain so it seemed to make sense. Like the training facilities, everything was very professional and the crowds they attracted were absolutely massive. Every event had 6,000–10,000 and, despite me being about as Spanish as a Yorkshire pudding, the crowds were quite kind to me. Again, I think I was a novelty and as long as I didn't win everything, which I didn't, they let me live.

Apart from winning the SSDT again, which was obviously a big thrill, the rest of 1995 was, in hindsight, ever so slightly disappointing. In 1994 I'd finished sixth in the World Championship because that's where I deserved to be. Jordi Tarrés, Marc Colomer and the Finnish rider Tommi

Ahvala were the three to beat and, despite them being quite far ahead of me in 1994, I should have been nipping at their heels in 1995. To be brutally honest, though, I don't think I gave it 100 per cent that year. It's a strange thing to admit really, but it's true. Because my rise to the top had been quite meteoric, I think I thought the rest would happen naturally; that talent alone would see me through. It didn't, though, and when I ended up finishing fourth in the 1995 World Championship I was a bit shocked. At the time I thought last year's win at the World Championship, and everything else come to think of it, might have come a year too soon. It hadn't, though. I just didn't knuckle down and work as hard as I should have.

CHAPTER 6

Nice Forks!

Fortunately for me, the people at Beta seemed more than happy with my progress and in 1996 I was offered a new two-year contract as a full factory team rider. This was now the real deal but there was no way I was going to rest on my laurels. Not this time. Last year I'd had better bikes and a lot more practice, yet I hadn't really improved. Now, for the first time ever, I had parity with Tarrés, Colomer and Ahvala and I had to make it count. There were no excuses now. No hiding places.

The biggest difference in immediate terms was having my own mechanic. I thought having your name spelled incorrectly on the engine had been impressive, but this was in a different league. The lucky man assigned to me was Riccardo Bosi. He'd been Jordi Tarrés's mechanic for a number of years and according to those who knew him, he was one of the best in the business. Fortunately, this proved to be correct and between 1996 and 1999 he and a chap called Donato Miglio, who was head of riding development at Beta, produced some absolutely bionic bikes for me. Until then I didn't really understand how testing worked and was of the opinion that something different was always better, hence my fascination with the prototype. I was like a kid in a big sweet shop, I suppose. Everything looked great and I wanted to try the lot. One day, after I'd been working with Donato and Riccardo for a few weeks, some fancy new front forks arrived from a company called Paioli. We had some, Honda had some, Montesa had some and so did Gas Gas. They were all billet aluminium and they looked absolutely fantastic. *I'll have some of that*, I thought. And while Donato and Riccardo were out of the garage I fitted them. Donato was the first to notice and he wasn't impressed.

'What have you done, Dougie?' he said. 'Why have you changed your forks?'

'Well, look at them,' I said, pointing at the front wheel. 'They look fantastic. They're billet aluminium. All the big outfits are using them.'

'Take them off now.'

'What?' I couldn't believe it. 'But Honda are using them. So are Gas Gas and Montesa.'

'I don't care. They're not as good as the ones you've got.'

'Really?'

'Yes, really. Get them out.'

When we got to the first trial and everyone realised I wasn't using these forks the mechanics at Honda, Gas Gas and Montesa got into a right flap. Come the next race they'd disappeared altogether. The forks, not the mechanics! That's how respected Donato and Riccardo were.

Donato could jump on my bike and knew within 100 metres if it was right or not, especially when it came to setting up for altitude. Because the air's a bit thinner bikes always run a bit strangely at altitude and in that situation they're often difficult to set up. Very difficult, in fact. Donato had no problem with this and I learned more about developing and setting up bikes in that first year than I had in the previous 20. I became a bit of an anorak, really. In fact, I still am.

Before that I'd always had an interest in developing and setting up bikes, but I was very much an amateur. If something didn't work I'd just hit it a bit harder or go a bit faster. That was the way I'd been taught and sometimes it worked. Not much, but sometimes. A lot of the time it didn't, though. Learning about all the different aspects, permutations and possibilities that are involved in setting up or developing bikes professionally was like a minefield at first. Once I started getting the hang of it I became hooked and, as opposed to just getting in the way or sneakily fitting fancy-looking spokes to my front wheel, I might even have been of some use. I think before that my interest in testing and development had been born out of necessity as opposed to interest. After all, if I didn't set the bike up who else was going to do it? Now it was still necessary, but for Donato, not for me. I was just an interested bystander, so all I had to do was watch and learn. It was yet another masterclass and, just like Nigel at the Scottish Six Days Trial, it's paid dividends over the years. Especially now I'm a team manager with Vertigo. In fact, before too long I could be in danger of knowing what I'm talking about.

*

I needed a big year in 1996. Certainly with regard to the World Outdoor Championship, which was held over ten rounds: eight in Europe, and two in the rest of the world which are known as flyaways. The off-season had been productive and with Donato and Riccardo behind me, not to mention all the other advantages that went with having a full factory contract, I was in a good position. The bike Donato and Riccardo had built for me was in a different class to anything I'd had before so when I ended up finishing fourth in the opening round in Spain I was a bit red-faced. I think it was nerves more than anything so after I won the following two rounds in Hawkstone Park and Redhall in Ireland I felt a hell of a lot better. Three rounds in and for the first time in my life I was actually winning the World Outdoor Championship. Being honest once again, I think I knew that Marc Colomer was still the better rider. I'd definitely made progress, though, and felt confident about giving him a run for his money.

Despite having already won the World Indoor Trials Championship twice, Marc hadn't yet been able to clinch the World Outdoor Championship and that was undoubtedly the more coveted of the two. The World Indoor Championship had only been going since 1993 and, regardless of how many people were watching each event, without that history it just didn't have the attraction of the Outdoor.

Marc's nemesis with regard to winning that all-important World Outdoor Championship – and mine and everyone else's, come to think of it – was the formidable Jordi Tarrés, a quiet and incredibly focused man who had raised the profile of trials to a completely different level, especially in Spain.

He'd already won the World Outdoor Championship five times and on a global scale he was the biggest star the sport had ever seen. Everybody looked up to him, riders and fans alike, and he seemed to have more sponsors than the rest of us put together. His riding suit alone was like a patchwork quilt! I remember counting them once and he must have had at least 20. There was Diesel jeans, Ducados, Coca-Cola, Quaker State oil, Larios gin. Isn't it amazing what extreme envy can do to your memory? I remember all of them. He also used to have a minder driving him around and even flew his own private mechanic in for each Grand Prix. He was living the dream, all right! That man was the benchmark. The fact that he was so quiet – aloof, even – just made him seem even more impressive. He was walking, or should I say riding, on a different plane to the rest of us.

As the reigning World Outdoor champion Jordi was still the man to beat, but by the time I was leading the championship after round three he was back in fourth place. He'd finished down in eighth in Hawkstone Park so something wasn't right.

By the time we left America, which was round four, I still led the championship, with Marc in second, but by the time we arrived in France for round six we'd swapped places. Damn! To be fair to Marc he'd ridden an absolute blinder in round five and ended up winning three of the last five rounds. Jordi Tarrés had been having a nightmare by his very high standards and after seeing an opportunity I think Marc had upped his game. Don't get me wrong. Jordi Tarrés was still a world-class rider and he ended up winning three rounds that year. Not bad for an old man!

The final round, which was round ten, of 1996 was a two-day event in Belgium in a place called Bilstain. There used to be a lot of two-dayers back then, with 20 points up for grabs on the Saturday and 20 on the Sunday. By this point Marc had one hand on the trophy but it wasn't over by any means. I'm pretty sure he had to come, at worst, third in Belgium to clinch the title but with me and Jordi nipping at his heels it was going to be close. I bet he was terrified. I would have been.

On the first day in Belgium I ended up having a massive crash and although I didn't realise it at the time I'd actually broken my scaphoid. That's the one when your thumb goes back and hits your arm. By the following morning I knew full well what I'd done because I was in agony, but after getting it strapped up I carried on. In hindsight that was a pretty daft thing to do, not least because the pain was excruciating. I think Marc had all but won by this point and all I could think about was clinching second place from Jordi Tarrés. If I hadn't had him breathing down my neck I'd have gone to bed and taken some painkillers! The previous year I'd suffered a shoulder injury towards the end of the British Championship and, as well as putting me out of that tournament, it had prevented me from entering a few others. That had been my first bad injury as a professional, but it certainly wasn't my worst.

In the end the 1996 World Outdoor Championship finished with Marc in first place, me in second and Jordi third. Although I was a bit peeved at not beating Marc all I could think about was the fact that I'd beaten Jordi. That's the thing I was going to tell people back home. Guess what? I beat Jordi Tarrés!

All in all, I think I was ever so slightly disappointed by my performance in the World Outdoor Championship but the progress I'd made far outweighed any discontent. An awful lot had changed since 1995 and it had been a period of transition. For a start, I no longer had to take my own bike to trials or events. That was now Beta's job. This had probably saved me hundreds of hours over the year but it had all been eaten up by things like testing or working with sponsors. Not that I'm complaining. It had just taken some getting used to.

What I had to do for 1997 was concentrate on the positives. For a start, I'd led the World Championship for the first time ever. That had been an amazing feeling and the encouragement I'd received from Beta had been outstanding. Nothing had been too much trouble for them and they'd made me feel so welcome. My family, too, had been absolutely spot-on, as per usual. Especially Dad. Unless he thought I was about to get into trouble or make a fool of myself, he only ever gave me advice when I asked for it. I appreciated that. It was fantastic having him there but he never once tried to tell me what to do outside riding a section. I was left to make my own decisions and stand on my own two feet. That's exactly what I'll do with my kids.

Another positive to take into 1997 was the fact that, despite finishing third, King Jordi was perhaps nearing the end of his reign. He was 30 now and had achieved so much. Was there anything left? Perhaps he was about to call time? I hoped so! If that was the case and he wasn't planning a big comeback, that left Marc Colomer. I'm not saying it was going to be a two-horse race, but providing I performed to the best of my ability I was sure that he was the only rider capable of beating me. He'd been good this year and had been a worthy champion. The question was, could he carry it through?

CHAPTER 7

Fourth Time Lucky?

Testing and development was minimal in 1997 for the simple reason I was happy with my bike. Donato made one or two minor alterations, but they were upgrades as opposed to actual changes. 'If it isn't broke, don't mend it,' is what Dad used to say, and ever since I'd been told off for changing those forks I'd thought exactly the same.

If I'd been a betting man (I'm not, by the way) I'd have put a quid or two on Marc Colomer pushing forward in 1997 and consolidating his position as the best in the world. I was going to give him a damn good run for his money, but after toppling Jordi Tarrés after years of coming second I thought it was going to be his time.

As it worked out, that's exactly why Marc *didn't* push on. Or at least I think that's why he didn't. These days he's one of my best friends but I've always stopped short of asking him. He won't mind me giving my opinion, though. I think Marc was so relieved at beating Jordi that he almost lost interest after that. He certainly wasn't the same rider. Something was missing. Everything was in place, though. Well, almost everything. Marc's fitness regime was like nothing I'd ever seen before and he was the fittest on the circuit by a mile. That in itself is a big box to tick in our sport and nobody worked harder than him. Just because we don't ride at speed doesn't mean we don't have to be in shape. How else do you think we manage to ride six or seven hours in one stretch? Marc Colomer also had the talent, obviously. That was never in any doubt. Then you've got the bike and the team. Well, he was with Montesa. They were by far the wealthiest team, and as far as I know he was happy and had a great relationship with them. Marc also had a World Championship now, so was no longer seen as being a nearly man.

One thing you need above all of this, however – certainly when it comes to winning a World Championship – is desire. That is an essential ingredient. You can have all the gear, support, money and practice time in the world, but if you don't want that championship more than anything else, you'll be on a hiding to nowt. I've seen it lots of times with riders and it's frustrating. The thing is, you can't teach somebody desire, the same as you can't teach them to be talented. You've either got it, or you haven't.

If that was how Marc *was* feeling going into 1997 (I could be wrong, of course), it's fair to say that I was the absolute polar opposite. I'd now had a taste of what it was like to be at the top of my sport. Not a sniff, like I'd had in 1994. Winning a round had been excellent but it didn't guarantee your place on the leader board. Time-wise, I think I'd only led for about a month all told, but I'll tell you this much, it had been the best month of my life. Being the best in the world is massively addictive. Dangerously so.

The first three months of 1997 were spent competing in the World Indoor Championship, in which I'd finished third the year before. Unlike the World Outdoor Championship, which then had ten rounds, the World Indoor Championship was held over nine, with the final round this year taking place in Monaco. If I said I was as keen on winning the Indoor Championship as I was the Outdoor I'd be telling a fib, but that's only because indoor trials aren't as popular here as they are elsewhere. At the end of the day, though, it was a world championship, and by the time we arrived in Monaco I had a lead of just three points over Marc Colomer.

I don't remember being that nervous at the start of the final round – anything but, in fact – and that feeling of self-assuredness must have stayed with me as I ended up getting the maximum 20 points and pipping Marc at the post. At last, I was a world champion. I didn't feel like one, though. Not completely. That would only happen once I'd won the Outdoor. That was the holy grail.

The first round of the 1997 World Outdoor Championship took place in San Frutos in Spain. Funnily enough, the same place that Marc Colomer did all his training. It was another two-dayer (they were all two-dayers from 1997 until the end of 2005) and because everybody knew that this was Marc's backyard we were all expecting him to come out flying. Yes, there was going to be a bit more pressure, but as the reigning world champion that should have been soaked up, no problem.

In the end Marc did come out flying but right from the

off he was wobbling a bit. He still came second on both days but his performance had been far from convincing. He seemed a bit subdued.

My weekend was a little bit more eventful and, after finishing first on day one, I went into day two brimming with confidence. In fact, I was having problems telling the difference between confidence and invincibility, much to my ultimate misfortune.

The only big difference for me in 1997 was having my cousin James minding for me full-time. James is Sid's son and like most of my cousins, Lampkins and Hemingways, he was a damn good rider in his day. In fact, he finished third once at the Scottish Six Days and also won the British Expert Championship. That's basically the second tier and so the standards are extremely high. As a minder, though, James was, and still is, one of the best in the business and so having him there was the icing on the cake.

On day two at San Frutos, and with about three sections to go, we came across a rather nasty-looking hill climb. I was a fair way in front by this point and because nobody was really having a go at this section I thought I'd show them how it's done. It was a bit dangerous to be honest, but at that moment I thought I could do anything. I was back walking on water again, except this time I'd forgotten my flippers.

After winding myself right up I had a go at this hill and after flying through the first bit okay I came to a massive boulder that must have been at least 25 feet high. I could see James hanging off by a rope at the top but the moment I started to climb I could feel myself veering away from him. There was nothing I could do about it and I knew it was going to end in trouble. Just out of the corner of my eye I could see James running across the top of the boulder, hanging on to the rope. I could tell he was panicking and to this day I can still hear his voice as clear as anything.

'I haven't got you!' he shouted at the top of his voice. 'I HAVE NOT GOT YOU!'

Suffice to say I decided to jump off when I heard James shout and as the bike began cartwheeling down the hill bits started flying off it. It was a right mess! God knows how, but we actually managed to piece the bike together again (the rules state that you're not allowed to change the engine, the silencer or the frame during a trial, but everything else is fair game) and although it was a very different machine to the one I'd started with, I ended up managing to complete the sections and win the event. James and I have spoken about this a lot since then and I still have to question how he failed to catch me. He says I went the wrong way but in my opinion his arms weren't long enough! To be fair, James and I always talked things through professionally when something went wrong. Then, after we'd both had our say, we'd decide I was right. With Dad it was the other way around!

Back then the rules were a lot more flexible with regard to minders and assistants, so I was very lucky to have James and Dad. Dad would always be at the bottom of a section lining everything up and James would be at the top doing all the catching. If he could reach me, that is! They were a dream team, really, and head and shoulders above everyone else. This went beyond riding the sections, though; they also always had this habit of knowing exactly what to say to me and when. They could be quite harsh sometimes, but it was necessary. That's an art in my opinion and having now been a team manager, first for Gas Gas and now Vertigo, I appreciate how important it is. It's like being a caddy, I suppose, and if you threw James into the World Outdoor Championship even now I bet any one of the top riders would take him as a minder. Nowadays you're only allowed one and to be fair I agree with the rule.

As the season went on Marc began to falter and, with Jordi Tarrés dropping off a bit more like I'd hoped he would, the World Championship was basically mine to lose. The only other rider who gave me anything to think about was my teammate at Beta, Kenichi Kuroyama. On his day, Kenichi was absolute dynamite and when he won it was always by a big margin. The rest of us used to scratch our heads and say, 'How the hell did he do that?' The thing is, if Kenichi won a round you knew full well that he'd cock up the next one, so although he was always interesting and entertaining to watch, he just didn't have that consistency.

Incidentally, I decided not to ride the Scottish Six Days Trial (SSDT) or the Scott in 1997, for the simple reason that I wanted to concentrate on the Worlds. I'd already won both and didn't want to risk injury. Saying that, I did compete in the British Championship and I'd already won that. I can't for the life of me remember why I entered. Too many knocks on the head!

The climax of the 1997 World Championship – for me, at least – happened at the penultimate round in a place called Nepomuk in the Czech Republic. Again, it was a two-day event and I knew that, providing I finished in the top three on both days, I'd be taking the trophy back home with me to Yorkshire – the second Lampkin to do so. My nerves were comfortably at bay, and with Dad and James already in situ and Mum and John now present I felt more confident than ever. Some people can get a bit spooked when their families are in the crowd, but I've always been the opposite. Providing they don't start any trouble or get rowdy or try to talk to me when I'm losing (that's never a good idea) they're always welcome. Having my mum around always made me feel quite secure, and as a young lad on the brink of winning his first World Outdoor Championship she was just what the doctor ordered.

Funnily enough, being 'a young lad' was probably the final weapon in my arsenal that year. I was about twenty-one and a half by the time we reached Nepomuk and because I was still quite naive it meant I had very few external distractions. I knew that in order to be able to behave like an adult outside the sport – i.e. going out and having a drink – I first had to learn how to win, and I refused to allow myself to become distracted until I'd won the big one. Like so many sports, the World Championship is the pinnacle of motorcycle trials and, as far as I was concerned, I hadn't achieved a thing until I'd won it.

The first day of that penultimate event was, as usual, held on a Saturday and from the moment I let out the clutch I felt absolutely spot-on. There were a few butterflies in my stomach, but given what I was on the brink of achieving that was only to be expected. I'd led this year's World Championship from the very first event and so if I was feeling a little bit nervous the riders chasing me must have been terrified. Sure enough, that seemed to be the case and apart from the Japanese rider Takahisa Fujinami putting in a good shift, who was way back in fourth, the rest of the chasing pack had absolute stinkers, and so, even after making one or two mistakes, I still ended up finishing the day second. It was the first time that season I'd been affected by nerves, but it was only the fourth round out of sixteen that I hadn't won. There were still far more positives than negatives, and as we went into the final day the only person who could prevent me from becoming the 1997 World Outdoor champion was me.

A few days ago, I watched a TV report from that first day on YouTube and, as well as looking very young and a bit nervous, I sounded like I'd been given media training by Steve McClaren. I was interviewed twice for the report and each time I answer a question I do so in a kind of cod English–European accent. My only excuse is that the person interviewing me must have been Czech and, like the former England manager, I was merely adapting to my audience. I shan't be watching that again.

When I woke on that final day I was, for want of a better word, knackered. I've never been what you'd call a brilliant sleeper but so far that season I'd managed pretty well and even the dark rings under my eyes had started to fade. Now, the sleep problems were back with a vengeance and, as well as only managing to scrape two hours' sleep, I looked like a stretched panda.

In truth, not getting much sleep was probably an advantage as it kept me on my toes and heightened my senses somewhat. Come to think of it, I was wired! Not on caffeine or anything stronger. Just good old-fashioned adrenalin and anticipation. That wouldn't last all day, but with the trial starting mid-morning I was confident that it would see me through. Confident and hopeful.

The first four sections of that last day went brilliantly and although I didn't dare look at the leader board I knew that I was up there. The crowds had swelled to at least double what they had been the previous day and the anticipation I'd been experiencing had obviously become infectious. I'd never really taken much notice of the atmosphere at events before, either indoor or outdoor, but this was just impossible to ignore. My family and friends who'd travelled over were all carrying T-shirts with 'DOUGIE LAMPKIN – WORLD CHAMPION' on the front and when I first saw them I remember thinking, *Flipping heck, what if I fall off?*

'Don't worry,' said Dad. 'I'll not let them put them on until you're standing on that podium. Let's get it in black and white first.'

It didn't matter where I looked, though, all eyes were on me and about halfway through the round I started to allow myself to become just a little bit excited. That's not like me at all. In fact, if I ever did decide to start punching the air after a win, I'd have to take lessons.

The final section of that day was held in the town square and so shortly before it started all the spectators from the other four sections gradually made their way there. I'd never, ever seen anything like it before. There must have been at least two or three thousand people there, and because the atmosphere had moved up a notch it was now more like a music festival than a motorsport event. It was the first time I ever remember experiencing the hair standing up on the back of my neck. Until then I thought it was just something you said.

By the time I got to the last section the crowd had become so loud that I could no longer block them out, and as some of the voices started to register I remember being amazed by how many languages were being spoken. It's funny the things you remember when you're about to become a world champion. I could hear Japanese, French, Spanish and obviously Czech, but no English. Just for a second that alarmed me a bit and then out of the blue I heard Malcolm Rathmell shout to Dad who was running behind me as usual. Malcolm had been one of Dad's biggest rivals in the 1970s and, as well as winning the SSDT twice and the Scott six times, he'd also won the European Championship in 1974, which was the year before, in its previous incarnation, it became the World Championship. Malcolm had been minding for Graham Jarvis. Malcolm and Dad may have been rivals but they were also very good friends.

'How's he doing, Mart?' Malcolm asked.

'I think we're there now, Malc,' shouted Dad. 'He's done it.'

'Congratulations, Mart. We'll have a drink in a bit.'

'Aye, we will that.'

The moment I heard the words 'He's done it' everything seemed to stop for a few seconds, like somebody had pressed a giant pause button. I hadn't really thought about the championship during the day so it was a bit of a shock. *Bloody hell*, I thought. *This must be it!* I could still hear everything okay – the sound of my Beta engine and the crowd – but everything else was motionless. It was very bizarre. Like an out-of-body experience. The only way I can explain it is that my brain must have gone into shock for a few seconds.

Fortunately, I came around just in time to negotiate the final few rocks and as I rode off the last one I remember seeing my mum and John in the crowd. A second or so later I crossed the finish line and when I came to a halt I was immediately engulfed by a barrage of officials, family, friends and well-wishers – not to mention a huge wave of relief. That's the emotion I remember experiencing most. Not excitement or joy, but relief – with just a tinge of mental exhaustion! I'd done it, though, and with a round to spare.

The podium that day was obviously very special, despite it being for the event as opposed to the championship. I'd finished second, ironically, behind Marc Colomer. That was only his second victory of the year, although he did finish second overall. That's the thing – despite there being some-thing missing he was still a quality rider.

As I took to the podium I remember spotting Lapo Bianchi in the crowd. As the owner of Beta Motorcycles he was effectively my boss and he had one hell of a grin on his face. I was so glad he came.

In addition to receiving a trophy for coming second I was also given a fish, of all things. Don't ask me what kind it was but it was handed to me in a bag and was very much alive. I remember looking at Mum, as if to say, 'What the hell do I do with this?' She's a big animal lover and so whatever I did with it had to be humane. In the end I spotted the fountain in the middle of the square and so darted off and put it in there. The thing is, just as I did that all the locals jumped in after the bloody thing so as far as I know it was straight back out again. I suppose it must have been either valuable or lucky. Either way, Mum was not happy!

Because there was still one more event to go, which would be taking place in Germany just a week later, I decided not to get too involved in the immediate celebrations. Dad, John and the rest of the travelling contingent more than made up for my absence and, as far as I know, we left the Czech Republic with beer sales being at an all-time high.

As it was I may as well have joined them because that last round still ranks as one of the worst performances of my entire career. I was shocking! Nothing went right from beginning to end and by the last section on the second day it was beginning to remind me of one of the nightmares I'd had on *Junior Kickstart*.

By that time I think I'd been away from home for about a month solid, and because I'd now won the World Championship my entire body had just gone on strike and was refusing to start work again until we were back home in Silsden.

Within about an hour of me finishing the last section we were packed up and on our way back home. Dad drove through the night – obviously – and when we eventually arrived home I was absolutely gone, fit for nothing. The day after, a big get-together had been arranged at the Robin Hood pub in Silsden and by the time it came around I was still exhausted.

'You'll be fine once you've got a couple of drinks inside you,' Dad reassured me. And he was right.

I've never been what you'd call a big drinker and hadn't touched a drop all season. I never did when I was competing in the World Championships. I certainly sank a few that night, though.

It had never really occurred to me that the reason we were going to the pub was to celebrate my win and it was only when I walked through the front door that it began to dawn on me. There must have been about a hundred people in all, all friends and family, and everybody there was sporting one of the T-shirts Mum and John had been wearing at the podium in Nepomuk. Even my two grandads were wearing them! This time, though, they weren't being at all presumptuous – I was the World Outdoor champion. That in itself was a revelation as it hadn't really sunk in yet. There just hadn't been time. Now, I had about a hundred reminders in front of me and, despite talking to almost everybody throughout the course of the evening, I only had eyes for what was written on their T-shirts: 'DOUGIE LAMPKIN – WORLD CHAMPION'.

Now it felt real.

CHAPTER 8

You've Been Passed
by Jake Miller!

The first three months of 1998 were spent defending my World Indoor Championship title which I managed to do, successfully winning five of the seven rounds. Although I still preferred competing in outdoor trials, I fully appreciated the advantages of the indoor alternative, not least because the fans could actually come and see us en masse for a change. Outdoor trials are obviously not the most accessible events on God's earth and, unless you're good at map reading and are comfortable with the prospect of standing around in the rain for several hours, there won't be much to draw you in. Plus, what indoor trials lack in authenticity and spontaneity they more than make up for in atmosphere. Somebody (a towny, probably) once described outdoor trials as being 'a hundred farmers in a field with a few motorbikes' and that's not far from the truth. Even farmers have to come indoors sometimes.

While I was defending my title, Dad was talking to Beta about a new contract. He was working full-time with me now and had become part of the equation. He wasn't after cash, though. His demands were far more straightforward.

'Stick on four bikes,' he said. 'That's all I want.'

'That's *all* you want? Blimey Dad. Are you sure four's enough?'

Just before I signed the contract Dad came up with the idea of sticking on a bonus if I won the next two World Outdoor Championships. Only three people had won three in a row before: Yrjö Vesterinen, Eddy Lejeune and Jordi Tarrés (twice), so it was going to be big for Beta if I managed to pull it off. And for me, of course. In the end they agreed and although it wasn't the be-all and end-all, it was a nice little carrot to have dangling in front of me. A man's got to live, after all!

About ten days after clinching the Indoor Championship, which I did in Madrid on 8 March, I made my way to Spain for the first round of the World Outdoor Championship. I got off to a flyer and by the end of the season I'd only lost three individual days: one in the Czech Republic, one in Germany and one in Norway. I also ended up winning the British Championship, so things couldn't have gone any better, really.

The only thing I was actually missing now was a manager to deal with things like sponsorship and appearances. Until then, Dad had always sorted this out, but to be honest with you it wasn't really his forte. He was fine with manufacturers. After all, he'd had a lot of experience. Sponsorship, though, just wasn't his thing and the only reason he'd sorted it so far was to allow me to concentrate on riding.

The thing is, as everything became more professional things like sponsorship required more of Dad's time and in the end we decided that help was needed. Easier said than done. For a start, it had to be somebody we could trust. But also, somebody who knew about trials. Then in 1998 we found the very man. Or rather he found us.

When John had started importing Beta motorbikes in 1987 he had two young lads riding for him called Steve Hole – or Woody Hole, as he's better known – and Jason Miller, who's more commonly known as Jake. They were both on the outer fringes of the World Championship at the time but acted like they were Jordi Tarrés. They were playboys, for want of a better word, and despite their lowly position in the world rankings they had a fancy van each, more stickers than you could wave a stick at and a never-ending supply of hair gel. Jake even had a sticker on the back of his van that read: 'YOU HAVE JUST BEEN PASSED BY JAKE MILLER'. As if anyone would know who they were! Apart from Jake Miller or Steve Hole, of course!

When he wasn't being an international playboy or failing at winning the World Championship, Jake had worked for an awning company called G. H. Awnings. Around the same time a printing company called Screenart used to sponsor the Beta UK team, and because Jake and Woody were such great self-publicists they'd persuaded Screenart to have thousands of stickers made with – naturally – their names plastered on them. Apparently, anyone who attended a trial they were riding got at least five each whether they wanted them or not.

Joking aside, Jake was obviously a lot more adept at

promoting people than he was at riding a trials bike, and so he ended up starting a company called Gone Too Far Promotions, which eventually became G2F Media. This would have been in the mid–1990s and because of all his contacts he'd started to make a success of things. Building a profile and attracting new sponsors seemed to be two of Jake's specialities and sometime during 1998 he approached John about the possibility of doing this for me. Timing-wise, it couldn't have been better. I was already a two-time World Indoor champion and was well on my way to matching that in the Outdoor. The sponsorships I already had in place were all spot-on, but I didn't have nearly as many as my competitors. In fact, I probably had the fewest sponsors of anyone in the top ten. That's ridiculous when you think about it, and when we met with Jake for the first time I was impressed, not only by his enthusiasm, but by his ideas.

'It's not just about attracting new sponsors,' said Jake. 'You've got to look after the ones you've got.'

'How do you mean?' I said. 'I do everything I'm contracted to do.'

'Yes, but do you entertain them?'

'Eh?' I was out of my comfort zone now. 'You mean take them for a pint?'

'Not exactly,' said Jake. 'Take the indoor trial at Sheffield. Your dad runs it, doesn't he?'

'That's right.'

'Well, why don't you have a hospitality area for guests, sponsors and any potential new sponsors?'

'You mean like food and that?'

'Yes, food and that!'

Jake's from Essex by the way and persuading a tight-arsed Yorkshireman like me to spend money on vols-au-vent must have been a hell of a task. We also needed an interpreter each.

'I'll tell you what,' he said. 'It's the Milan Motorcycle Show in a couple of weeks. How about we go over there and show you off?'

'How do you mean, show me off? I'm not a dog.'

'I mean build your profile!'

This was the first time I'd ever worked with anyone on the commercial side of things and although I didn't know Jake from Adam, I felt I could trust him. So much so that I even allowed him to parade me around the 1998 Milan Motorcycle Show like he suggested. By that time, which was November, I'd managed to retain the World Outdoor Championship and Jake exploited this big time. Over the five days we must have visited every single stand and, yes, I did feel like a dog! A dog dressed in a suit, though. Dad had been pestering me to buy myself a suit for years and I'd always resisted. Now I had no choice and, when Jake and I entered the halls for the first time in the huge exhibition centre, I felt like a schoolboy on his way to see the careers adviser.

To be fair, I actually enjoyed myself at the show and because I was riding an Italian bike I got a really nice reception. We also came away with a couple of new sponsors, which was good. More importantly, though, the show allowed me to present myself in a very positive and professional light for a change and there's no way that would have happened without Jake.

*

Despite his immediate influence, meeting Jake Miller was actually only the second most important encounter I had in 1998, as in the autumn of that year I met Nicola. When I realised I'd have to include a bit in this book about meeting my lovely wife I panicked a little. I'm absolutely rubbish with dates and I know for a fact that if I don't get everything absolutely spot-on – to the day, in fact – there'll be an inquest and probably a bit of blood. *Was it in the autumn of 1998 or 1999 that I first met her?* I wondered. *No, it was definitely 1998. September, to be exact.* I'm going to have to come clean and admit that I can't remember the date, but I do remember the venue. It was a pub in Skipton called the Red Lion. Nicola had been at school with James and Mark Buckley. Mark's one of my best friends, so although I didn't know her personally I'd definitely seen her around before. She was local, very good-looking – obviously – and when I saw her standing in the Red Lion I thought, *I'm going to buy you a drink!* There was no Facebook back then. If you wanted to ask a girl out, you had to go and make a fool of yourself.

Until a few months before I'd been going out with a girl called Tina for four or five years and after we split up I'd decided to take some time off. Since then, I think I'd lost a bit of confidence (not that there was much to start with) so as opposed to gliding over there and telling her a few gags, I asked a couple of mates to come with me. 'Wingmen' is what I think they're called. Anyway, when Nicola saw these three goons walking towards her she must have thought she owed some money or something, but fortunately she didn't run. I must have fixed her with my legendary gaze. Come on! There's no point having looks like these if you're not going to use them.

After engaging her in some witty conversation for a few minutes I threw caution to the wind and asked her if she'd like to come for a drink with me. I was just about to run out of patter, so it was now or never. I'm not sure what I was expecting her to say, really, but when Nicola turned around and said, 'Yes, that would be nice' I was slightly wrong-footed. I suppose I was expecting her to say she'd think about it, so I had to think quickly.

'How about next Saturday?' I blurted out.

You see, no messing.

'Yeah, okay,' said my beautiful wife-to-be.

'Right then.'

With that, I gave her a friendly nod and guided my wing-men back to base. I was shaking like a leaf by this point and needed a drink.

Cousin James must have got a sniff of what had gone on so came over.

'Have you just asked Nicola out?' he said.

'Aye, I have.'

'And?'

'And what?'

'What did she say?'

'She said yes.'

'Good for you. Where are you taking her?'

'Just to a local pub.'

'Ooh, lucky her!'

The date itself started off as quite a nervous affair, not surprisingly, and after rocking up to the boozer in my van I ordered myself an orange juice, parked myself at a table and tried not to look too conspicuous. That was impossible I'm afraid and I must have screamed – FIRST DATE!

When Nicola arrived and saw my orange juice she must have thought, *Hello, I'm in for a proper wild night here.* Once I'd fetched her a small red wine I sat down and let nature take its course. Nicola, who was studying to be a primary-school teacher at the time at St Martin's University in Lancaster, talked about what she did and I talked about what I did. A lot! Fortunately, we both seemed to be interested in what each other did and we ended up having a really good chat. The next day, I woke up and decided that I was going to buy Nicola some flowers. Don't ask me why. It's not something I'd normally do. I suppose it was just an impulse. When it came to actually buying the flowers and getting them to Nicola I realised that I didn't have a clue what I was doing, and so in the end I asked a mate of mine to do it for me. I wrote the message, though, which was the important bit and made sure he stayed within budget. It was amazing what you could get for £4.50 back then.

The flowers went down an absolute storm and it was arguably the best 90 shillings I'd ever spent. Inspired by my new-found sense of romance I decided it was time to take things to the next level. I was obviously terrified, but felt it was the right time.

'Nicola. Would you like to go to the last round of the British Championship?' I cooed seductively.

There, I'd said it. There was no turning back now. I'd put all my cards on the table and had shown her my hand. All I had to do was wait for her reply.

'Erm, I suppose so,' she said, very unenthusiastically.

I don't know what Nicola thought I was going to ask her, but I could tell by her voice that it definitely wasn't that. Anyway, it was good enough for me.

The following weekend Nicola accompanied me to the final round of the 1998 British Championship, and after a pretty tough day I ended up winning the round and subsequently the championship itself (my fourth, which meant I'd beaten Dad!). When I asked Nicola if she'd enjoyed herself she just looked at me blankly and didn't say a word. She was obviously overawed by all the excitement *and* by the fact that her new boyfriend had just won the British Championship. She knew she was on to a good thing.

From then on, Nicola and I started seeing each other regularly and, without wanting to sound soft or anything, it was all quite agreeable. In fact, a few months later I suggested we go on holiday together.

'Where to?' asked Nicola.

'How about the south of France?' I suggested. 'We can get some flights to Nice, hire a car and then play it by ear.'

Nicola seemed well up for this and so the following day I booked two nice cheap economy return tickets to Nice. The night before we flew we went out for a meal with some family members and sitting on the table next to us were two friends of mine, Neil and Kathryn Hodgson. About a year previously I'd bought a place on the Isle of Man, which is where Neil and Kathryn lived, and we'd become friends. I still spent a lot of time on the mainland, of course – even more so when I started seeing Nicola. Neil, who I'm afraid is from Lancashire, would later become the world superbike champion.

Once I'd introduced Nicola to Neil and Kathryn, I asked if there was any occasion for the meal.

'Yes, we're off on holiday tomorrow,' said Neil. 'We're off to the south of France.'

'Really?' I said. 'So are we.'

To cut a long story short, Neil and Kathryn were actually travelling on the same plane as us, but instead of leaving it to chance accommodation-wise, they were staying with Neil's manager.

'We should meet up for a meal while we're over there,' suggested Kathryn.

'Okay, why not?'

The following day we caught our flight to Nice and after landing at about 6pm we went to collect the hire car. That took an absolute flipping age and by the time we left the airport in search of a hotel it was almost 8pm. Unfortunately, the day we arrived happened to be a French holiday and so every single hotel in the area was full. Every one! We drove into the hills and along the coast but nothing. We were like Mary and Joseph, but instead of a donkey we had a Renault Clio. I dread to think how many miles we covered. It must have been at least a hundred.

By the time the clock struck midnight we'd knocked on the doors of at least forty different hotels and bed and breakfasts and, in the absence of any benevolent innkeepers with stables at the rear of their establishments, I made an executive decision.

'Look. We're going to have to park up and sleep in the car,' I said finally.

'What?' cried Nicola. 'But it's a Renault Clio!'

'I know it's a Renault Clio. I hired it.'

'So why didn't you get something bigger?' she asked.

'Because I wasn't planning on sleeping in the bloody thing when I hired it!'

What an outrageous question.

In the end we found some services and after using our towels as curtains we settled down and tried to get some sleep. I actually didn't sleep too badly in the end, which probably had something to do with the fact that I'd saved myself about a hundred quid. It may have been a bit cramped, but it was definitely cosy. Before I could suggest to Nicola that we might spend a second night in Dougie's Mobile Motel she issued an ultimatum.

'If we haven't found a hotel by midday, I'm flying home. That was the worst night's sleep I've ever had!'

I could tell by her bloodshot eyes and by the smoke coming out of her ears that she meant business, and so once we'd had a coffee and a quick breakfast we set off in search of somewhere with a bed that was longer than 3 feet and not bent in the middle. The only place we could find that had any vacancies was a Hotel Mercure, which was situated on a massive golf course.

'How much is the room?' I asked the receptionist.

'It's seven hundred francs, sir.'

Despite wanting to politely decline the room and run like bloody hell, I knew it would be more than my life was worth, so I coughed up and went to tell Nicola the good news. Seven hundred francs, though! That was about 180 quid back then, which in the Bank of Lampkin is worth at least a grand. To be fair, the hotel was absolutely beautiful and Nicola and I went back there just a few months ago to refresh our memories and reminisce. We even passed the service station where we'd hauled up for the night. That was nice.

Fortunately for both of us the rest of the holiday went without a hitch and we even managed to meet up with Neil and Kathryn a couple of times as planned. We also did some paragliding on the beach one day, which I absolutely loved, and by the time we arrived home we'd had a really good time. Believe it or not, that had been my first proper holiday since leaving home and I hadn't even been away with the lads before. It was just time constraints really, but my contracts with manufacturers were also very specific about me not taking part in any dangerous sports. It's a good job I kept quiet about the paragliding!

In 1999 I started pulling away from the competition a bit. That's not a brag, by the way. It's just the way it was. As well as winning the British Championship, I won four of the eight events at the World Indoor Championship and when it came to the Outdoor I only dropped two days. That was quite frustrating actually, as the year before I'd only dropped three days in total and had convinced myself that I had it in me to get a clean sweep. Marc Colomer and Steve Colley were the only people to beat me that year, and so were the ones who spoiled the party. Fair do's.

People sometimes ask me if anything changed while I was dominant in the sport and what I think they mean by that is, did the other riders treat me differently? Well, the answer to that is, no, they didn't. At least not in the World

Championships. It got a bit tasty in Spain once, but I'll come on to that in a bit.

Although I get on well with them all now, I never used to talk to my competitors that much back then, and if any of them were getting fed up with me winning everything, they didn't say it to my face. Maybe they had a Dougie Lampkin doll that they used to stick pins into? Now there's an idea. Dougie Lampkin dolls. That'd scare a few children.

Life on the road wasn't that different to life at home in a way. Apart from Nicola, who came to the odd round, I spent most of my time with the same people I hung around with at home: Dad, John and James. The only difference was that we were driving a lot of the time and staying in hotels. We still talked about bikes, though. That wouldn't change regardless of the situation.

What I did notice while all this was going on was how I was being treated by the press. As opposed to asking me what I thought might happen at a trial, they started asking me how many points I'd win by and I didn't like that one little bit. Not just because it was disrespectful to my competitors. It meant that they thought it was a fore-gone conclusion and, as I've said before, that's not good for sport. The thing is, that's what everybody was thinking and so they were the questions that had to be asked. That said, however much I disliked it, I wasn't about to start losing on purpose. It wasn't up to me to start losing the championships, it was up to my competitors to start taking championships from me. I remember being completely focused then and the only thing that unsettled me at all was that line of questioning. I was like a machine, really, and had a very straightforward and systematic approach: do section one, do section two, do section three, win at the end of the day, go home, practise and then do it all again. There was no worrying about the future, and because I wasn't losing much I wasn't really affected by any recent mistakes. I was 'in the zone' as they say and pretty much lived in the moment.

It actually sounds like quite an isolated existence when I read it back, but that's the nature of trials. With racing you're sometimes at the mercy of other drivers, whereas with trials it's just you against each section. You take the blame if it goes wrong and you take the glory when it goes right. Sometimes in order to either create or maintain a decent run in trials you have to isolate yourself from the rest of the world. Although I'm no longer world champion, it's fair to say that in certain aspects of my life not much has changed, and if you asked me what I had on next week there's no way I'd be able to tell you. I leave that to Nicola and Jake mainly and just do as I'm told!

I can still get into that zone by the way, where I have to isolate myself. I'm not sure I could do it for the duration of a World Championship any more, but for something like the Scottish Six Days Trial or the Scott Trial it comes naturally and is still an essential part of my preparation. How else do you think I've managed to win 11 SSDTs? I can't think of many other sports, apart from, say, gymnastics and ice skating, that are as isolated as trials. Even then a lot of what they do is marked by judges so to a certain extent it's subjective. Trials on the other hand is conclusive. There really is no hiding place. I remember 1995 at Hawkstone

Park. I was lying 14th at the time in the second round of the World Outdoor Championship and was having a nightmare. Everything went wrong and it's no exaggeration to say that by the end of the day I hardly knew how to turn left or right. I was buried. I came away wanting to give it all up and I think that's when I realised that, ultimately, I was on my own. Dad tried giving me a few pep talks, but they didn't touch the sides. I had one week in which to pull myself together and effectively save my career. That's how close I was to becoming an average rider. I knew that the only person who could pull me out of this was me and, when I managed to come second the following week and third the week after, I knew what I had to do. It wasn't something I perfected immediately, but from then on, I suppose I became a work in progress.

The only downside to my domination in the late 1990s and early 2000s was the effect it had on Marc Colomer. I suppose I'm almost contradicting myself in a way, but he went from being number two to Jordi Tarrés for heaven knows how long, to winning a World Championship and then coming second again to me. A lot of people might be happy with that, but not if you're a champion. Marc was a champion, but he wanted to be a multiple champion as he had been in the Indoor, and with me and Jordi either side of him it was going to be tough. One World Outdoor Championship was never, ever going to be enough for Marc. Not in a million years. He was still a factory rider at Montesa and was the bee's knees on a world scale. He just couldn't get past me.

Would I have done things any differently if I had my time

again? Well, of course I wouldn't. As I just said, it was up to the likes of Marc to come and take the World Championship from me, not for me to give it to them. In any case, that's not what Marc would have wanted. He wanted to beat the best riders in the world. That's all. It doesn't stop me feeling bad for him, though, and if that makes me less of a champion in some people's eyes, so be it. Trials is without doubt one of the friendliest, most inclusive sports there is and if a competitor's feeling the pinch, even at your expense you'd rather he or she wasn't suffering. That's not what it's about. It's just not that kind of sport.

I think the fact that I'm such good friends with Marc, and with Jordi Tarrés, to be fair, tells you everything you need to know about the culture that runs through trials. Take my Uncle Arthur. He spent the whole of his career battling against the likes of Dave Bickers and Jeff Smith. Week after week they tried getting one over on each other. Not just with a few hundred or a few thousand people watching them, like us. This was on *Grandstand* and in front of millions. At the end of the day, one of them was going to win. And at the end of their careers one of them was going to be deemed the most successful. Dave's now passed away, unfortunately, but Arthur and Jeff, who now lives in America, are as thick as thieves. They have nothing but admiration and respect for each other, despite being two of the most competitive people you could ever meet. That's not only the mark of the men, it's the mark of the sport. The fact that Marc, Jordi and I are almost mirroring what Dave, Jeff and Arthur had makes me happy and very grateful. I bet there were times when Marc would have liked to kick my arse, though, had I given him a free hit! And me him, probably. We're only human, after all.

Because we hadn't killed each other in Nice, and because we actually seemed to rub along together quite well, I suggested to Nicola during the summer of 1999 that she might like to move to the Isle of Man and rent a room from me. Joke! Nicola had fallen in love with the place while visiting me and so as soon as she'd qualified as a primary-school teacher she set about looking for a job over there. She ended up landing a role at a new school called Ballacottier, which was about 500 metres from where I lived and, just like the island itself, Nicola loved it. The only downside, for Nicola at least, was that I was away an awful lot which must have been very hard for her. When I was in town, though, we always had a cracking time and it was great getting to know each other. That bit's serious, by the way. It was!

I don't remember this but according to Nicola the only thing I wasn't keen on sharing with her back then were details of my finances, and whenever we went to the bank together I used to make her wait outside. In hindsight, I really shouldn't have done that. I should have asked her to wait in a café or something! It was instinctive, though, and the need to prevent Nicola, or anyone else for that matter, from seeing my bank balance was overpowering. Nicola always says it made her feel like a dog, but I never tied her to a lamp post or anything. She's exaggerating.

Our best friends on the Isle of Man were obviously Neil and Kathryn Hodgson and, as well as going training together at the gym, Neil and I also did a lot of motocross.

As somebody who's always disliked the gym, I sometimes used to suggest mountain biking as an alternative and we used to go all over the island. Motocross, though, was our big passion and whenever we had time we'd ride up to the motocross track, which is in the north of the island, and have a quick blast around.

Neil Hodgson's mechanical know-how goes about as far as putting new stickers on his bike, if and when he can be bothered. One afternoon just before we started a session, his rear spindle fell off his bike.

'Just how has that happened?' he asked, looking completely amazed.

'You obviously didn't tighten it up, Neil,' I replied.

'I did! I did tighten it up.'

'You won't have, Neil. You know what you're like.'

'Actually, you're right,' he said after a pause. 'I remember now. I didn't have a spanner, so I was waiting for you to do it.'

'You were what?'

'I was waiting for you to do it.'

'Did you tell me it needed doing?'

'No.'

'Then how would I know?'

'I don't know. I just thought you would.'

Racers are funny beggars. Some of them, like John McGuinness, like tinkering with bikes and are dead good mechanically, but a lot of them, like Neil Hodgson, haven't a flaming clue. We off-roaders are generally quite competent when it comes to this side of things and I think that has a lot to do with the fact that we're often just left to get on with it. When my Uncle Arthur became a factory rider

Mum and me in the early days. For some reason I always had a bib on.

Dad with the world's best sideburns, and me with a bib, again!

Dad, Harry and I holding Scott Trial trophies after the presentation. He was our hero and we were incredibly proud of him.

Cruising around a paddock on my little SWM. It's one of my favourite memories.

Dad and me at Flappit as I attack the 'big one'. I love this photo.

Competing for the B Class Schoolboys. Only 12 years old but I was already riding a Beta.

My wonderful wife Nicola and I all dressed up. I don't like to admit it, but I'm a lucky lad.

I've always loved classic bikes and have built up quite a collection over the years. This Ariel HT500 is perfect for the school run.

Always a fun day out riding with my boys.

The 2004 World Trial in Japan. Cousin James was my number one minder here and boy was he good!

1999: Ile La Reunion. My manager Jake (far left) had to be drafted in to help the team as my mechanic, Riccardo (far right), had broken his hand.

The 2001 Barcelona Indoor Trial. As my team's home race this
was always the one to win.

It always rained in Japan, but I loved riding in front of these great fans!

The only time all my World Championship bikes have been together in the same place at the same time which was an amazing occasion. The photo was taken by a great family friend, Eric Kitchen.

2004 Italy World round on my way to losing the title for the first time in seven years.

The second round of the 2005 World Championship. Who'd have thought a few splashes of salt water could cause so much flaming trouble!

Back on a Beta in 2008. Things were never quite the same, but it was still good to be back.

for BSA back in the early 1960s, you'd have thought he'd have had a mechanic. He didn't, though. Even as a factory rider you were given a bike and that was it. No mechanics. No support. Nothing. It was a case of, 'Here's a bike. Go and ride it!' Arthur wasn't especially bothered about this, for the simple reason that he was always happier doing it himself. He'd been building and mending motorbikes since he was a young lad, so a mechanic would probably have got in the way. I wouldn't like to be in the way when my Uncle Arthur's working on a bike. No chance! I don't think these speed merchants get the same grounding we do and subsequently they're often surrounded by mechanics. Says the man who used to have two at Montesa! Neil was very good at cleaning his bike, though, I'll give him that. He's a dab hand with a sponge.

After a while I think we got a bit carried away with our motocross 'training' and we ended up having a few crashes. From the moment we got into Neil's Ducato van, which was frightening on the TT course, it was foot down and from then until the end of the afternoon it was all a question of how fast we could go, whether it be on the road in the van or on the track with the bikes. It was fantastic fun but after the fourth or fifth accident I looked at Neil and said, 'We've got to reel this in a bit, Hodgey. Otherwise, one of us is going to get badly hurt.'

What finally put paid to our motocross madness was a misunderstanding that quickly turned into a bit of a nightmare. One day, after pulling up to the main gates at the track we realised they were locked so we left the van where it was, got on our bikes and set off to find the other entrance, which was round the other side. This took us up a lane that ran alongside the track, but we had to go on to the beach for a bit to get back on to it. Anyway, in the end we managed to get to the other entrance, which was unlocked, and ended up having a fantastic afternoon as always. I wiped the floor with him, obviously, but Neil put in a good effort and he should have been proud of himself.

After making our way back to the van we arrived to find a couple of policemen waiting for us.

'What's up officers?' I asked.

'You've been seen riding illegally on the beach,' said one of them.

'We were only on there for a hundred yards or so,' said Neil. 'We were on and off in seconds.'

'Makes no difference,' said the officer. 'You're not supposed to ride on the beach. Therefore, in the eyes of the law, you were riding illegally.'

Unfortunately he had us bang to rights and for two professional motorcyclists who had recently been invited to help promote an Isle of Man road-safety campaign it didn't look good. To be fair to us, we thought the rule was that you weren't allowed to tear up and down the beach like madmen. And, as I said, we hadn't done that. We'd been very respectful and the fact that the authorities went for us so vigorously was a bit disappointing. There'd been another lad with us at the time who was Manx born and bred and for some reason they didn't go for him. Neil and I, on the other hand, were hauled over the coals and ended up being summonsed to appear before a magistrate. The papers were all over this like a rash but little of what they printed was true.

The story they wanted was that Neil and I had been tearing up and down the beach and even though that wasn't the case that's what they wrote. What should have been a quick rap on the knuckles got turned into a drama and blown out of proportion. It's the first and only time I've been in trouble with the police and I'm hoping it stays that way.

Neil and Kathryn and Nicola and I became so close that we ended up buying apartments next door to each other. So, when Neil and I were away, which was often, Nicola and Kathryn could keep each other company. Neil even bought himself a trials bike at one point, but he was absolutely useless. It was as though he'd never ridden a motorbike before! I couldn't believe it. I'd go off riding a few sections and he'd just wobble about a bit. I think he had the bike about a month before he got rid of it. That was about three and a half weeks too long in my opinion!

One day, Neil and I decided we were going to buy a sports car each and so set about trying to arrange a few test drives. A friend of Neil's was a Ferrari dealer and he let us have a Modena for a couple of hours.

'Let's take it on to the mountain,' suggested Neil.

'Why?' I asked.

'There's no speed limit up there.'

I should have known this would end in tears.

Once we were on the mountain we parked up and started looking at all the buttons in front of us.

'What do all these do?' I asked, thinking Neil would know.

'Absolutely no idea,' he replied.

'That's not good,' I said.

'Never mind that,' said Neil. 'Watch this!'

With that he turned on the engine, gave it a massive handful and after lurching forward a few yards we suddenly started spinning around in circles. Not on purpose, by the way. These weren't donuts like you see on *Top Gear*. It was just a lack of control!

'What the hell are you doing?' I shouted.

'I don't know,' replied Neil.

All this was happening in the middle of the flaming road, by the way, and as well as bringing the traffic to a standstill there were horns being blown all over the shop. Finally, the out-of-control Modena came to a stop and, as Neil and I caught our breath, the traffic jam we'd caused gradually began moving. Every single car that passed us had at least one person inside shaking their head and, as well as making a few fairly unwholesome gestures in our direction, they were mouthing some even more unwholesome words.

'What the hell happened there?' I said finally. 'I thought you knew what you were doing?'

'So did I,' replied Neil. 'Shall we take this bloody thing back?'

'I think we better had.'

Needless to say, neither of us ended up buying a Ferrari and I decided to put it on hold for a while. I ended up resurrecting the idea in 2003 after I'd won the World Championship, and this time I had my heart set on getting a Porsche. Me and my dad went to our nearest Porsche dealership in Yorkshire one day with a view to actually buying one. When we arrived we started kicking a few tyres, as you do, and after finding one that I was interested in test driving we looked around to see if anyone could be arsed to come and help us. We must have been there at least 40 minutes but not one of the salespeople had even acknowledged us yet. It's not as if we were easy to miss, for heaven's sake.

After waiting another five minutes, Dad finally gave in and so Muhammad went off to find the mountain.

'Excuse me,' he said to some lad in a sharp suit. 'We're looking at a car over here. It's eighty-two thousand pounds and you haven't even come out to see us.'

'I'm busy,' said the salesman.

'Well, so are we,' said Dad, and we walked out. The salesman ran after us but Dad wasn't having any of it.

I was happy the dealership was doing so well that it could afford to turn down eighty-two grand.

'Bloody idiot,' said Dad. 'We'll take your money to somebody who appreciates it!'

Talking of my dad, which I often do, in 1999 he told me the story of when he broke his sternum during a trial in Watkins Glen in America. We were on our way there at the time for the American rounds of the World Outdoor Championship and, by the time he'd finished telling us, James and I were ready to jump out and make a run for it. My dad was a great storyteller and once he got going there was no stopping him.

'I fell off this bloody cliff,' he said. 'Massive it was. Massive! I tried grabbing hold of a tree on the way down but it hit me on the bottom of my chin instead and I ended up losing six teeth. Then, when I landed, I broke my bloody sternum. That cliff, though. Massive it was!'

'How big was the cliff, Dad?'

'Massive. Eh, are you taking the mick?'

When we got to Watkins Glen we asked the organisers of the trial to show us this massive cliff, but it was just a bit of a bank and there was no tree.

'Where's this massive cliff, Dad?' I said sarcastically. 'And where's the tree? I'm surprised you broke anything falling off that.'

Dad was horrified.

'That's not how it was. You tell 'em,' he said, addressing the organisers. 'Didn't there used to be a cliff there?'

Luckily for Dad, one of the organisers confirmed that there'd been some subsidence there a few years ago and that the banking had shrunk somewhat. I could tell Dad was relieved!

'We'll just have to imagine it, Dad,' I said, still ribbing him. 'I'm sure it used to look massive. At some point.'

'It did!'

I was later told by somebody who'd been at that trial that if Dad hadn't had oxygen at the section he'd probably have passed away. Funnily enough, I've never seen oxygen at a trial before so he was obviously lucky they had it. Very lucky!

Apparently, at the hospital Dad had one of his hands clutched dead tight and when the nurses peeled his fingers away it had his teeth in it. He'd obviously spat them out and clung on to them! He was in intensive care for a day or two but ended up signing himself out because it was costing him too much money. Only a Yorkshireman could do that.

'But you might die, Mr Lampkin.'

'I'll take my chances, thanks very much. It's costing me an arm and a leg.'

And a sternum.

In the end, Malcom Rathmell collected him from the

hospital and put him on the plane home. As soon as he landed he went straight to an NHS hospital, one that wasn't going to cost him anything bar his national insurance, and he remained there for about two weeks. Who on earth travels from New York to London and then London to Yorkshire with a broken sternum and several teeth missing? A Yorkshireman who's in serious danger of losing a few quid, that's who.

CHAPTER 9

Montesa Man

In August 1999, I received a fax from Montesa Honda. Montesa was founded in 1944 by Francesc Xavier Bultó (who later formed Bultaco). Honda had begun investing in Montesa way back in the 1980s during a period of Spanish economic unrest. The main reason for this was that Honda had been unable to export bikes to Spain due to ridiculous tariffs, so it gave them a much-needed foot in the door into what was a massive market. (The Montesa name would later be dropped, which was a shame, and these days they're just Honda.)

The fax, which I still have somewhere, said something like:

Dear Dougie, [At least they spelled my name right!]
We're sorry for contacting you out of the blue like this but we wanted to know if you might be interested in signing for us? We understand that your contract

with Beta comes to an end soon so would like to talk to you as soon as possible.

Yours sincerely,

There was no messing about. It was very direct. This resulted in two conflicting emotions for me. Obviously, I was excited. After all, Montesa Honda were the biggest team in the paddock, certainly in terms of resources. They always had the most trucks and the set-up Marc Colomer had was just ridiculous. In that sense, it would be a dream job.

On the flip side, I'd been riding Beta motorcycles since about 1989 and, as well as the link with my cousin John, I'd also become an honorary member of the Bianchi family. The owner, Lapo Bianchi, had been to every single Grand Prix in 1999 and he couldn't have been more supportive. I was even known as the 'Bambino' at the Beta factory, so I was almost ingrained within the company. We didn't have the biggest set-up in the paddock, but we were definitely the most successful. The bikes were fantastic and working with the likes of Riccardo and Donato had been a dream come true for me.

The first person I told about the fax was John. He and I have always been very, very close and we're more like brothers than cousins. Together with Dad, and later James, he's been one of my biggest supporters and his reaction to this was typical. 'I just want whatever's best for you, Doug,' he said. 'And whatever you decide, I'll back you all the way.' Bearing in mind John was, and still is, Beta's official UK importer, that was a pretty selfless thing to do. That's John, though.

Because the whole of Spain basically closes down in

August, the World Outdoor Championship gets put on hold for a month. This meant that me and the people from Montesa had some time to negotiate and first of all they suggested bringing a bike over for a test. Although the World Outdoor Championship still had two rounds to go, I'd already done enough to secure the title, so I thought it would be okay. Even so, I still spoke to John and Beta first, just to make sure. John was obviously fine about it and, to be fair, so were Beta. At the end of the day, because of the size of the team – and because of pressure from Japan – Montesa Honda needed to start winning World Championships and, as much as Beta would have liked me to stay, I think they knew it was a foregone conclusion. I only learned this later on but there'd been rumours going around for ages about me going to Montesa, but fortunately they hadn't got as far as me. I could well do without those kinds of distractions and had I not had more than one hand on the trophy, I'd have rebuffed Montesa's initial approach without question. I was still employed by Beta and I respected that, which is why I asked their permission to test.

A couple of years prior to this, before I'd signed a new contract with Beta, I'd actually been to Spain to test a Gas Gas. It was a pre-production bike and to be honest the test was a bit of a nightmare. For a start, the frame hadn't been painted so it had a kind of rusty finish to it. The forks, too, were absolutely appalling and were ones they'd made themselves. There's no two ways about it, the bike was an absolute pig.

We were riding in Sant Feliu, which is near Barcelona, and shortly before the end of the test, just as I was going over a triple step, I fell off. As the bike cartwheeled down everything fell off it – and I mean everything. It was like it had been stuck together with tape. In fact, some of it had. The fuel tank was actually a 1-litre oil bottle that had been taped on. That was the first thing to fly off, followed closely by all the plastics. I remember a man called Andrew Cordina was the export manager at the time and he was holding his head in his hands.

The only thing that test did was make me sign again for Beta all the quicker, but I think they also realised that it might well happen again. Especially if I kept on winning World Championships. I'm not saying it was inevitable I was going to leave, but providing the test with Montesa wasn't a disaster and providing we could agree terms, there was a very good chance I would.

To be honest, I wasn't really sure what to expect when they arrived for the test. I knew it was going to be different to the Gas Gas fiasco (which was not a fair representation of how that company usually works, by the way) but that's about it. First to arrive was the kit, which had been sent to Jim Sandiford Motorcycles in Bury, their importer. I'd requested to do the test at one of my favourite practice grounds near home, partly because I liked it there, but also because it was well out of the way. Nobody, apart from John and the bosses at Beta, knew about the test and the last thing I wanted was somebody spotting the Montesa juggernaut rolling into town. No. It had to be as private as was humanly possible.

In the end, I think I played a blinder by keeping them out of the way because the amount of people and vehicles that turned up was just astonishing. It was like the Spanish Armada! Although I said I didn't know what to expect, I certainly didn't think it would be anything like this. The team manager and a couple of mechanics, perhaps? With maybe somebody from development? As it was, I got the team principal, the team manager, four mechanics, the export manager, a test rider and a couple of chaps from development. It was a delegation, for heaven's sake! Then you had the bike and the parts, of course, which arrived separately in one of Jim Sandiford's vans. I don't know what they were expecting me to do to the bike but I'd never seen as many parts in my entire life. I remember looking at John's face when all this arrived and I could tell what he was thinking. *Good night Vienna!* Or in this case, Silsden. *Our Dougie's off.* I think the people from Montesa had been surprised when John stepped out of the van with me and my dad, but he was the first to walk over and welcome them all.

On the first day of the test I rode what I thought was quite average, but the people from Montesa were absolutely bouncing. 'Okay Dougie,' they said. 'Let's make some changes. What would you like to do?'

To be honest, up until that moment I hadn't really done much of this. I'd always start the test, but before too long Donato would jump on and finish it. That's not a criticism, by the way. You do whatever works.

In the end, I asked the test rider to help me out. What's more, I'm very glad I did, as not only did he become my mentor and an invaluable member of my team, but he also became the only friend I've ever known who my dad ever referred to as being one of the family. His name is Amos Bilbao, and when it comes to the admiration stakes he's right up there with John, James and Dad.

Amos's influence on me was immediate and as we stood there in that field surrounded by bikes, parts and people, he started throwing some ideas around. At the end of the day, he knew the bike a lot better than I did so I was Gary Lineker. All ears.

'Why don't we lift the back a bit?' was Amos's first suggestion. 'We'll put a couple more plates on the linkage.'

'Fair enough,' I said.

That worked an absolute treat, so even after five minutes Amos already had my trust and attention.

As soon as I got off the bike he made another suggestion.

'Would you mind if we changed the forks?' he said. 'It'll take about twenty minutes.'

I thought, *As long as they're not billet aluminium!*

'Be my guest,' I replied.

'How was that?' said Amos after I'd had ten minutes.

'It's a bit close on the front with the handlebars,' I told him.

'No problem,' he said. 'We've got another top yoke for the front.'

I couldn't believe it. They really had brought everything. In fact, the only thing they hadn't brought was another bike.

After switching the yoke over they moved the handlebar position and it was perfect.

When the bike had first arrived, it had had different handlebars on to the ones that I was used to and I was expecting to have an awkward conversation about that. After all, whoever manufactured the Montesa handlebars was obviously a sponsor and so they'd be expecting to be part of the package.

'I've never used anything other than Renthal,' I'd said to Amos.

'No problem,' he said. 'We'll take a pair off one of your bikes, if that's okay?'

It most certainly was okay!

I think if I'd have asked them to paint it pink with green spots and tie a couple of balloons to the back they'd have done exactly that. I didn't feel like they were going over the top, either. They weren't trying to please me. They were just being professional and accommodating.

At the end of the first day the Montesa team went back to Bury with Jim Sandiford's people, probably to talk business. As far as I was concerned it had all gone quite well and I'd really enjoyed working with Amos. He was exactly the same as Donato with regard to the confidence he instilled in me. The difference was that he wanted me to do the testing, which was a big bonus.

The following morning, we all met in exactly the same place. It was Addingham Moor, by the way, which is above the family home. Just as I arrived Amos came racing up to me. 'I've been thinking about the footrest position,' he said. 'I reckon we should just drop back a little bit. You look like you're over the front.'

'Fair enough,' I said.

'Trust me,' said Amos. 'You'll get more traction.'

He was right.

'By heck,' I remember saying to Dad. 'This lad knows what he's talking about!'

After riding for a couple of hours, without making any more drastic changes, Mum decided that she was going to make lunch for everyone. My mother is one heck of a cook and when she makes lunch, she makes lunch! You couldn't see the table for food and I don't think the people from Montesa and Sandiford's knew where to start. I did. Start in the middle and work your way out.

Once Mum was satisfied that everyone present was going to leave the house at least half a stone heavier, the Montesa team manager suddenly piped up.

'We need you to come and ride for us, Dougie,' he said. 'You do know that?'

I looked over at Dad. I could tell he was putting his negotiating cap on. Sponsorship might not have been his thing, but he knew his way around a manufacturer all right.

'Ooh, hang on,' he said.

When Yorkshiremen negotiate they usually start off with a kind of pained expression on their face, as if to say, 'This is going to hurt you more than it will me.'

'Well,' said Dad, sitting forward. 'You do realise he's only ever ridden a Beta before?'

'Yes, we realise that,' said the team manager. 'He's done well for them.'

'Very well!' was Dad's immediate response. 'He also loves the bike, and the people.'

Regardless of Dad's negotiation tactics, he was absolutely right. I did love the people at Beta and they'd always given me fantastic bikes, even before I became a factory rider. I wasn't going to just walk away.

'Cards on the table,' said the team manager. 'Dougie rides

our bike better than anyone we've got at the moment and he's only had it a day and a bit.'

Well, I wasn't going to argue with him.

As Dad and the team principal and team manager carried on chatting I sat back and asked myself a few questions. First and foremost, did I think I could win the World Championship on the bike I'd just ridden? Well, yes, I did. It wasn't anywhere near as good as the bike I was riding for Beta but John and Dad had reminded me that that was to be expected. 'You could win on it, though,' said Dad. John had echoed that.

What had convinced me that I could actually win on the Montesa was the progress I'd made having spent a day or so with Amos, and with the chief mechanic, to be fair. He was called Jordi Granell and he's still a legend at Honda. He became my chief mechanic for two or three years and, like Riccardo, I trusted him implicitly.

Every concern I'd mentioned to Amos and Jordi, and there'd been a fair few, especially on the first day, had been answered honestly – I thought – and they'd managed to reassure me on just about everything.

When Amos had suggested the back might need lifting, it had taken me completely by surprise and to be brutally honest I thought he might have been saying it for effect. At least at first. Better to say something than say nothing at all. He'd only been watching me for a few minutes so how could he know that?

When it turned out to be correct I was more than impressed and from that moment on I'd hung on his every word. More importantly, though, I'd really, really enjoyed myself and as much as I wanted to win the World Championship – and everything else, for that matter – I also wanted to do it with a smile on my face. So much had changed, though, and in such a short space of time. Just a few years ago, if I couldn't get up an obstacle my dad would be there saying, 'Go a bit faster, Doug. Go on, lad. Faster!' Now it was a bit more complicated. Every part of every section was mulled over well in advance and the bike would be set up accordingly. A lot of that development had happened in the last five years or so and luckily for me I'd been witness to much of it. It was a work in progress, though (it still is), and as I looked around the table at Amos, Jordi and the rest of the Montesa team, I was sure that they would be at the forefront of that.

Once Mum had finished clearing away, the team manager took out some paper and placed it on the table.

'What's this?' I said. I honestly had no idea.

'We'd like to offer you a contract, Dougie,' said the team principal.

'Really?' I said. 'Now? Don't you have to go and report back? Talk to Japan or what have you?'

'We've already done that,' he said, pushing the contract forward. 'And this is the result.'

'Dougie won't be signing anything today,' said Dad quickly. 'It's only right that he speaks to Beta first. Out of respect, more than anything.'

'Well, we'd like you to speak to them now, if you would,' replied the team manager. 'We'll still be here tonight. Why don't we all have dinner? John too.'

I don't think Dad was expecting that response. I most certainly wasn't!

'Aye, okay then,' said Dad. 'Although we've still got an afternoon's testing to do first. You go on and Dougie and I will try and speak to Beta. We'll see you up there.'

Later that night after everyone had packed up we met for dinner in a local restaurant. I seemed to get on really well with everyone around the table, but especially Amos and Jordi. We were like old mates and I'd only known them a couple of days. I think the Spanish contingent got the shock of their lives at the end of the meal because instead of getting a nice little espresso like they'd been expecting, they all got dirty great cups of weak filter coffee. Welcome to Yorkshire! I told them they should have stuck to tea.

Once everyone had finished spitting out their coffee, the team principal pulled out the contract once again.

'We'd like you to have a good look at this,' he said. 'I take it you've spoken to Beta?'

'We have,' said Dad. 'And they've told us what they can go up to.'

'Well then,' said the team manager. 'Let's see what you think.'

Before I could even put my hand out to take the contract, Dad was turning to the back page. He was like lightning! Straight for the headline.

Before Dad could react to what he'd seen, the team manager spoke again. 'We don't want to leave this table until we've signed you, Dougie,' he said.

As a point of negotiation that was a massive own goal for Montesa, because if Dad had been suitably impressed by the numbers he'd have said so there and then. He wasn't greedy. Then again, he wasn't daft either. As the team manager spoke, Dad tried to look cool. The atmosphere was electric. Like a high-stakes poker game.

As Dad went back to looking at the contract he suddenly took out a pen from his inside pocket. *Blimey*, I thought. *He's going to sign it for me!*

Instead of signing the contract, Dad turned to the back page again, which listed the salary and all the possible bonuses, and began adding everything up. I couldn't believe it. He was writing all over the flipping contract!

After totting everything up he wrote a figure at the bottom and slid it over towards the team manager.

'That's what it'll cost you,' he said.

I'd actually caught a glimpse of this figure he'd written and all I remember thinking was that it was over double what I was on with Beta. Well over!

Although I didn't sign before we left that night (I couldn't after Dad had vandalised the contract!) we shook on it and said we'd get everything finalised as soon as possible. The following morning, I called Lapo Bianchi at the Beta factory and told him what had happened.

'Those numbers are amazing, Dougie,' he said. 'You know we can't match that.'

It was a very short conversation and although I never fell out with Lapo, or anybody else at Beta, I don't think I quite went with his blessing. One thing he did say was that it had to remain a secret until the end of the season and I completely respected that.

'I don't want my season ruined, Dougie,' he said. 'The World Championship isn't even over.'

I should point out here that Lapo wasn't obliged to let me

sign for Montesa. Not while I was contracted to him. He did it out of the goodness of his heart. And because he knew it was what I wanted. It really did have to remain a secret, though, otherwise there'd be financial implications, as outlined in my Beta contract. I called Montesa later on and told them about this and they said they'd make sure it didn't get out. I have to admit it was a horrible few months, though. Trials is such a small sport and it's hard keeping anything a secret, least of all the news that one of its main riders is switching teams.

What didn't help matters was that Montesa had informed Marc Colomer that he was free to look for a new team. Once that got out the rumour mill went into overdrive and it did nothing to smooth the transition. In fact, it made things a lot worse.

What also hurt was the number of people I had to lie to; friends and family alike. I held a dinner towards the end of the season to thank sponsors and friends, etc. and after making a speech somebody piped up and asked me who I'd be riding for next season. I forget what I said exactly but it wasn't the truth. That room was full of my favourite people and I had to lie to them en masse. That was without doubt one of the most awful evenings of my life.

The final nail in the coffin with regard to my relationship with Beta happened at the final round of the World Championship, in Italy. After the event Beta announced their new bike for the following season and I had to say how wonderful it was: a) having never ridden it; and b) having already signed for somebody else. That was just a farce, really, and it certainly tarnished my relationship with the Bianchi family. Temporarily, at least. How could it not?

The big irony here is that from the moment that fax had arrived back in August nobody had put a foot wrong. I'd been transparent and so had Beta. They'd also gone out of their way to make this happen for me and I'd repaid that by keeping my mouth shut and by rounding off the championship with two resounding wins. It was the circumstances that messed things up and they were out of our hands.

The thing is, as unfortunate as all this undoubtedly was, and as much as I loved the people at Beta, I had to think about my own future. There was never going to be an easy way of doing it but I certainly don't regret the decision. Careers are short in motorsport and you have to make hay while the sun shines. It wasn't just about the money, though, although I won't pretend that wasn't a big factor. It was, as I said before, about enjoying what you do. Everything about Montesa – the people, the set-up and their vision for the future – had excited me big time and I wanted to be part of it. End of story. The desire they showed in signing me was also very flattering and, when that huge Montesa armada had turned up to Addingham Moor, I'd felt like a flaming king.

But what was even more difficult than severing my ties with Beta was severing my ties with John. Although Lapo and I had always enjoyed a very, very good relationship – and the rest of the Bianchi family, to be fair – it had been based around a professional agreement. He was my boss and I'd always done my best for him. And him, me. With John it was obviously different. We were family, first and foremost, and unlike Lapo, whose priority was clearly Beta, John's was a lot closer to home.

After I'd spoken to Lapo I told John what had happened

and suggested we all went out for a meal to celebrate. Despite him working with Beta I wanted him to be part of it, although perhaps that was a bit much to ask. In the end John shook me by the hand and said, 'Good luck, Dougie. We'll always be a partnership, you know that. I can't come tonight, though. It's not where I should be. I hope you understand.'

Of course I understood. I can't say I wasn't upset, though. Not just because I wanted him at the dinner. It was the end of an era. John had been by my side from when I was a kid, taking me practising and helping me fix my bike. He even used to lend me a bike for my minder when I couldn't afford one. And then there was the whole Beta relationship. That had all come about because of John. All of it. I can't think of anybody, even my dad, who was as instrumental in making me a world champion as John Lampkin. What I think hurt us both is that the partnership came to such an abrupt halt. Had we been given time to talk about it, it might have felt easier. Who knows? That's the nature of the beast, though. If an offer comes along that you think's right for you, you have to grab it with both hands. I just hoped I'd done the right thing.

CHAPTER 10

What's Wrong with Your Van and Your Caravan?

Jake's next idea for commercialising Dougie Lampkin, which happened at the end of 1999, was to have some clothing made with the words 'THE SCOOTER MAN' printed on it, which was my old nickname. The idea was to ask friends and family to wear the clothing to trials, so it seemed like I had a fan club. I should probably apologise to them, really. It wasn't what you'd call high fashion and some of the colours were definitely a bit suspect. Looking back, it was an awful idea really.

Despite the fashion faux pas and him treating me like a show poodle, Jake and I are still working together today and we've never had so much as a cross word. The basic rule of thumb has always been, if it's got handlebars I deal with it and if it hasn't, he does. It was only after working with him for a while that I realised how much I'd needed a manager, and not just because of the commercial side of things. Dealing with the press, for instance, is something that has to be taken seriously when you're doing well and, left unguarded, you can get yourself into all kinds of problems. That never happened, fortunately, but with the advent of social media you have to be so, so careful. Thank God Twitter wasn't around when I was leaving Beta!

I think my relationship with Jake really came into its own when we were first approached by Red Bull, which I'll come on to, and later with Dougie's Wheelie. I don't want to big him up too much but if it hadn't been for him none of that would have happened. At the end of the day, though, he was absolutely shocking on a motorbike, so somebody had to help him find alternative employment. There's a fabulous video on YouTube of Jake making a right pig's ear of things at the Scottish Six Days Trial (SSDT) in 2008. Worse still, he's riding a Beta. John's going to be mortified when he sees it. It's well worth a look, though, if you've got time. Just search 'Jake Miller, SSDT'.

You're welcome.

The reason I'm going out of my way to embarrass my esteemed manager is because not long after he started looking after me, he persuaded me to spend an unbelievable amount of cash on a new truck. To be fair, the only reason I needed a truck was because I was doing more and more events, which Jake had been instrumental in arranging. Even so, it was going to take me a long time to get over this, and how I never needed counselling I've no idea. It all started when he rang me up one morning.

'I know this bloke called Whittaker who makes

horseboxes,' said Jake. 'He's desperate to get into motorsport and he's willing to do you a deal.'

'How much?' was my immediate and instinctive response.

'Don't know yet. We'll have to go and see him.'

With a truck becoming more and more necessary, me, my dad and Jake all made our way down to Retford to see this Whittaker bloke and hear what he had to say. Yan Whittaker was his name and as he started reeling off all these ideas as to what he could do for us, all I could think was, *This bloke's trying to take all my money!* I could tell Jake was being taken in and as that happened I could almost feel my wallet shrinking. It was inevitable, though, and I crawled away from Whittaker's Horseboxes about 70 grand poorer. I was a broken man. Destroyed. Necessity may well be the mother of invention, but mark my words, it's also on speaking terms with bankruptcy and despair.

'What have I just done?' I said to Dad as we got in the car.

'Lost your mind by the looks of things,' he said. 'What's wrong with your van and your caravan?'

'He's beyond that now,' said Jake. 'Dougie can't turn up to a sponsor's event or an appearance driving a van and pulling a caravan.'

I hate to admit it, but Jake was right. I didn't have to spend that money, but as much as I go on about it, I knew it was the right thing to do. Jake sold me well in 2000. In addition to becoming an athlete with Red Bull, I was also working with Radson (radiator manufacturers, who were a main sponsor of the World Motocross Championship), as well as the likes of Alpinestars (boots) and Airoh Helmet. At the time Airoh didn't make a trials helmet but, because they were keen on getting involved with the sport, Jake had persuaded them to use my big old head. He was a bit like Del Boy in that respect; he could sell a black cat to a witch. Or, in this case, a slightly awkward-looking Yorkshireman to an array of unsuspecting commercial organisations. Jake once said that he'd been sent up north to educate us northerners. My word. Where would we be without him?

In 2001 Jake and Dad set up a company together called L&M Events, specifically to organise rounds for the World Championship. Jake did all the paperwork and Dad concentrated on the manual side. In the end they ran three World Outdoor Championship rounds at Hawkstone Park, two rounds at Fort William and various additional one-off events with Red Bull. These included an outdoor event called the City Trial and an indoor one called the Moonwalker Trial. Both took place in Manchester and the pièce de résistance of Dad and Jake's efforts was managing to get Deansgate closed off so the City Trial could take place. Bearing in mind that's probably one of the busiest roads in the north of England, it was an astonishing achievement and we got a hell of a crowd.

Red Bull had just staged two similar events in Northern Ireland, where they had an office, and because they'd been a success they set their sights on the mainland. Jake had done the commentary for one of the events in Northern Ireland and afterwards somebody from Red Bull had asked him if he could recommend a venue. Jake, who was quite refreshed at the time, suggested the centre of Manchester and about a week later, after he'd sobered up, the woman he'd mentioned it to called him up.

'I want to come and look at this venue,' she said.

'Eh? What venue? Oh God, you mean Manchester?'

'Yes, Manchester.'

'Erm, okay. Let me speak to the council.'

I bet he was squeaking a bit when he got that call.

The woman in question from Red Bull was a 21-year-old graduate intern and when she turned up for the meeting with Jake and the council she was wearing ripped jeans and carrying a skateboard! After the meeting, which went very well, surprisingly, the skateboarding intern asked Jake how much he thought the event would cost to stage. Jake then told her the amount, thinking she'd need to speak to a few people, but instead she gave him the go-ahead there and then and actually signed it off.

A few weeks later there was a second meeting with some of the council bigwigs and once again the intern on wheels turned up wearing ripped jeans and carrying a skateboard. According to Jake the people from Manchester Council were gobsmacked, but they couldn't say anything, as she was effectively the event boss, so she could wear what she wanted.

Soon after that, Red Bull hired a guerrilla-marketing team to fly-post the whole of Manchester and the council went up the wall! Apparently, they rang Jake up and said, 'You know we said we were behind your event coming to town? Well, we're starting to go off it a bit!' Fortunately, things had gone too far for it to make a difference, so it went ahead. The trial was an actual competition, so Jake and I had to invite some riders to take part and to be fair we got a really good crowd in, people like Adam Raga, Robert Crawford and Shaun Morris. We even got Takahisa Fujinami, or Fuji as he's better known, there, which was good. The thing I remember most about that event was reversing my van into a bollard and not being able to open the flipping thing. I was mortified. We had to jump the Manchester Ship Canal as part of the trial and in case somebody had an accident we needed to have a diver. The way he charged us was hilarious. He was £250 dry or £500 wet! He stayed dry, much to Dad and Jake's relief.

The only time Dad and Jake clashed at all was when it came to spending money, surprise, surprise. Jake wanted the best of everything – i.e. the trucks of this world – and Dad wanted the vans and caravans. Nine times out of ten Jake got his own way, but Dad definitely kept him in check. He was an international playboy, after all, and international playboys have very expensive tastes. What exemplifies their relationship best is when they first put on a round at Fort William. In the two weeks leading up to the event Dad lived in a caravan with some of his workers, whereas Jake stayed in a hotel. Jake spent a week trying to persuade Dad to move into the hotel, but he was having none of it. It was an unlikely partnership, but it definitely worked.

When news finally got out in early 2000 that I'd signed for Montesa I think the vast majority of people assumed it was just because of the money. That was the feeling I got and I suppose it was the easiest assumption for them to make. After all, the press and the public didn't know what was going on inside my head. Or what was going on with Beta. How could they?

I'd started riding the Montesa again in December 1999 and once again I'd decided to do it out of the public gaze. As well as using Addingham, I also went over to Spain a few times and, although it was the same bike as I'd ridden during the test, I was riding terribly. The Montesa just didn't feel like my bike and although I didn't regret my decision it actually made me appreciate just how good those Beta bikes had been. Especially the bike I had in 1999. Looking back, that's definitely the best bike I ever had while I was competing in the World Championship, and I don't mind admitting that there were times just prior to the 2000 campaign when I wished I could have it back. Just once or twice. I suppose I wanted to have my cake and eat it!

The first time the general public saw me riding a Montesa was at the first round of the World Indoor Championship at Sheffield in 2000. My dad used to put on this event with his business partner, Neil Crosswaite, and in those days it used to sell out within hours. Dad and Neil used to begin work on the Sheffield round about five months before it took place and the work that went into it was astonishing. Dad, in particular, used to work night and day and, as well as designing and building the majority of the sections, he'd set them all up a few days before. In fact, the only things Dad didn't make that year were the giant cigarette packets and giant oil bottles that we riders had to negotiate. One of his other responsibilities when designing these sections was making sure they were clearable on the night. This is probably one of the most difficult jobs when designing a section for trials, as you obviously want it to be as difficult as possible, but possible all the same. If everyone fived the first step of a section you'd be handing out refunds all over the place and that would never do. Indoor trials are all about entertainment and to be fair to Dad and Neil they did one heck of a job. We also had some great British riders at the time such as Graham Jarvis and Steve Colley, and it was an event that everybody looked forward to. It still is, come to think of it.

There was one person who wasn't looking forward to appearing at Sheffield Arena – me. In fact, I was crapping myself. Sorry about the language, Mum, but I was. We still hadn't gone public yet about the move to Montesa and by the time Sheffield came along things had reached fever pitch. It may well have been one of the worst-kept secrets in motorsport, but without any announcements or proof it was, to all intents and purposes, still just a rumour. People wanted confirmation and, to be honest, I wanted them to have it. I was fed up with having to ride in secret and just wanted to get on with my job and concentrate on the forth-coming season.

A few days before Sheffield took place, either my dad or Neil, I forget which, decided it would be a great idea to bring me into the arena in a giant transport box. Then, once I'd been introduced, the sides of the box would collapse and I'd be there punching the air on my new bike, revving the engine and probably looking like a right wally. After that, I'd ride on to the arena floor, do a few donuts and then wave to the crowd.

However . . .

After riding into the box backstage the sides went up.

'Are you all right in there, Doug?' said Dad.

'I am at the moment.'

'Good lad. A forklift is going to lift you up and take you into the arena.'

'Eh? A forklift?'

Not exactly Cirque du Soleil, was it?

'Stop moaning! Once you're in position you'll be announced to the crowd. Then, the sides of the box will collapse and all the fireworks will go off.'

'What fireworks!?'

'Did I not tell you about the fireworks?'

'No, you didn't!'

'Well, be careful. They're a bit lively by all accounts and there's a lot of them. There may be smoke.'

By this time, I was sweating like a pig locked in a sauna wearing a duffel coat and there were three very good reasons why. First, it was absolutely sweltering in that box. It may have been Sheffield in January but you could have fried an egg on my forehead. Secondly, my dad had just informed me that I was about to be lifted by a forklift truck about 20 feet in the air before being driven into Sheffield Indoor Arena and then annihilated by about five hundred quid's worth of pyrotechnics. No wonder he didn't want to do a rehearsal! Thirdly – and this was the most daunting of the three – I would then have to face my home crowd on my new bike for the very first time. Oh yes, and I was the last rider to go out. That's four.

I could hear this forklift coming a mile away and the closer it got, the more fearful I became of what was to come. It sounded older than my dad! Bearing in mind I could hardly see a thing inside this box I wasn't exactly looking forward to the journey ahead. Sure enough, the box started wobbling around from the moment it left the ground and by the time it was in position I felt as sick as a dog. I thought, *What if I puke up?* That'd look good, wouldn't it? Imagine:

'Ladies and gentlemen, please welcome the reigning World Indoor Trials champion, from Silsden, Dougie Lampkin!'

BLUUUUGH . . .

It could've happened, though. I felt flipping awful.

About two minutes later the compere, Steve Berry, started his preamble. Fortunately, my stomach had settled down by this point but my nerves certainly hadn't. They were worse than ever.

I think the worst bit was not being able to see anything. The noise was unbelievable but in the dark it was terrifying. Eventually, Steve got to the end of his warm-up and when I heard him say 'Ladies and gentlemen' I started up my bike. The crowd heard this and a cheer went up. I felt better now. Well, a bit.

'Please welcome the reigning World Indoor Trials champion, from Silsden, Dougie Lampkin!'

As all four sides of this box collapsed the fireworks started. BOOM! Dad was right, they were a bit lively and for the first few seconds all I could see was smoke. They did the trick, though, and by the sound of things the crowd were loving it. After punching the air a few times, as you do – or usually don't, in my case – I drove down the ramp on to the arena floor. After almost mowing down a couple of promotion girls I started doing a few donuts and at that point I realised that the arena had gone quiet. The crowd had seen my bike by now, not to mention my liveried kit, and it was like, *Oh my God, he has actually done it. He's signed for Montesa!* It felt bizarre riding around an arena with ten thousand silent people in it. Very, very unsettling. Fortunately, they seemed to pipe up a bit once the shock had worn off and I don't mind admitting that I felt quite relieved after that.

What had actually compounded my nervousness, and I forgot to mention this earlier, was the fact that I'd never actually ridden the Montesa indoors before. It was definitely a day of firsts! All I'd had so far were a few dry days in Spain and a few wet ones in Addingham. My knees had been absolutely clanging in the warm-up beforehand and because I don't normally suffer from things like nerves, it almost floored me. I remember saying to myself, *What the hell's going on? Pull yourself together!* It was no use, though, and when the crowd fell silent I'm surprised I wasn't carted off in a straitjacket.

I remember one of the first sections included the giant cigarette packets and as I approached the first box my knees started going again. I know I joke about it but this really was unknown territory for me. I've watched it since on the playback and how I managed to get up the first two boxes I'll never know. I was far, far too low and I scraped the hell out of them! I remember thinking, *I reckon I need a longer shock absorber!*

Sorry, but there's yet another reason why I was crapping myself. Because it was my first event for Montesa Honda, half the flipping team were there. It was like the test all over again. Naturally, I was flattered that they'd all come to show their support, but they must have taken up half a stand. There were at least 20 of them.

149

God only knows how, but I actually managed to win the event. After riding a clean in round two I only had to come second in the two-man race between me and Steve Colley and even I could work out that I wasn't going to lose. The relief I felt when I took off my helmet and handed my bike to Jordi was unbelievable. Because of the suspension issue I honestly thought I was going to have problems, but somehow I managed to compensate. What a start, though! The crowd had been amazing and I don't think I'd ever enjoyed an indoor trial as much. Even the transport box and the fireworks had added to the occasion and for the third year running Dad and Neil had played a blinder.

As soon as I left the podium I had a quick word with the press then it was backstage for a debrief with Amos and Jordi. They'd obviously noticed the suspension problem and that was the first thing on the agenda. 'It's just not going up,' I said. 'And I feel like I'm a bit low on the back.' The following week they modified the frame and made a longer shock. All this was done in Japan, by the way, and in addition to all this they also changed the linkage. The bike was back with me by the following weekend. I couldn't believe it! It also felt miles better now so although I couldn't improve on my position in Sheffield, I was confident that I could start building a lead.

By the end of January, I was absolutely flying and at the risk of sounding like a broken record I had another absolutely cracking season. In all, I only lost six rounds in both World Championships – three in each – and won a total of 24. Obviously, I was as happy as Larry, but so were Montesa. Apart from Marc's win in 1996 they'd only won the Outdoor Championship once since my dad won it in 1975 and, bearing in mind they'd had the mighty Honda behind them since the mid-1980s, it wasn't where they wanted to be. Success had been imperative, especially after moving heaven and earth to sign me, and the fact that I'd been able to deliver straight off and repay some of their faith and enthusiasm gave me an awful lot of satisfaction. Big moves are always scrutinised in sport, and rightly so. The added pressure had been good for me, though, and together with Montesa's professionalism and support it was a perfect combination. To top it all off, because of all the success we had they'd also managed to bring in a few new sponsors, Repsol oil being the biggest name on the list. Montesa had been trying to work with Repsol for years and when I heard they'd signed a contract I was chuffed to bits.

By the time I arrived at Montesa they already had in place a young Japanese rider called Takahisa Fujinami. He'd finished second to me in the World Outdoor Championship in 1999 after beating Marc Colomer into third and was tipped as being a star of the future. Unfortunately for him, but luckily for me, he hadn't been able to improve on that position in 2000 and I had no intention of letting that change. To be honest, it felt strange being the senior rider in a team at just 24 years of age. Especially such a big established team. I suppose I had been the senior rider at Beta, really, but I hadn't noticed it as much. My teammate there, Kenichi Kuroyama, wasn't as good a rider as Takahisa and I never really got to know him. I'd always been the upstart in the paddock, though; the young lad who'd been out to take the crown from King Jordi Tarrés of Spain and prevent his countryman Marc Colomer from succeeding him, and to become the first Briton to win the World Outdoor Championship since my old man. Now, the roles had been reversed. I was King Doug of Silsden – tall, determined, humble and remarkably good-looking. Takahisa was the young pretender – the Crown Prince of Japan – and, with parity at the team with regard to resources and no team orders in place, the only thing he needed to beat me was to become a better rider. He'd certainly give me a good fight.

Like Jordi Tarrés and Marc Colomer, Takahisa has become a very good friend of mine, despite the fact that his nickname for me is Seven Times Lucky, which is a reference to the number of Outdoor Championships I ended up winning. Or should I say the number of championships he didn't win! Cheeky beggar.

The last highlight of my first year with Montesa was winning the British Championship, which made it five in a row. That was a strange one, to be honest, as John and I had always looked forward to doing the British Championship together. He was the first person to congratulate me, though, and I'm happy to say that once the dust had settled with Beta we were back to how we were before. There was no elephant in the room. No awkward moments or animosity. It was like nothing had happened really and that's a testament to how strong we are as a family. He wants me to win, I want him to sell bikes, and whatever happens we'll always be there for each other.

My first team meeting with Montesa in January 2001 was quite a happy occasion if I remember correctly. Everyone had had a good Christmas and I'd just won the first round of the World Indoor Championship in Sheffield. About halfway through the meeting the team manager said he'd like to try something different this year.

'How do you mean?' I asked.

'We'd like you to enter the Spanish Championship,' he said.

'Really? Wouldn't that be a bit controversial?'

'Possibly. It's top of our agenda this year, after the World Championships.'

The Spanish Championship was obviously massive to Montesa. For a start, they were a Spanish manufacturer, despite Honda's involvement, and they were keen on chasing down Bultaco's record 11 Spanish Championships. Montesa were on eight at the time, but having won the last four on the bounce with Marc Colomer they were keen to continue their success. On top of that they were courting all kinds of new Spanish sponsors, so in that respect it was probably as important as the Worlds.

As this was above and beyond what I was contracted to do with Montesa we came to an arrangement whereby if I won the Spanish Championship for them I'd get a nice bonus. They'd also recently done a deal with a very swanky hotel company called Paradores. All their hotels are in castles and chateaux and my dad was a big fan. With six out of the eight rounds of the Spanish Championship being close to one of these places they said they'd put us up. I didn't have to agree to any of this, by the way, because Dad did it for me. He was made up!

I don't remember a great deal about riding the actual rounds, but one thing I do remember is that each one was centred around a town. This gave each event a real sense of occasion, as if the circus was coming to town, and consequently there were a lot more spectators than I was used to. In the UK, trials are often pretty difficult to get to and sometimes even the start venue can be in the middle of nowhere. You don't usually see a lot of folk about.

The only downside to me riding the Spanish Championship was that it generated an awful lot of moaning from the other riders. This was the first time I'd ever experienced something like this in trials and it obviously made life a bit awkward. The reason they were all upset was because they were on big bonuses for winning the Spanish Championship and if I tipped up and won that as well it would be adding insult to injury. A non-Spanish rider had never won it before but there was nothing in the rules to say they couldn't compete. An old Finnish rival of my dad's, Yrjö Vesterinen, had won the British Championship back in 1982, so I wouldn't be the first rider to win a national championship that wasn't my own. I suppose the only difference is that this was a lot more lucrative than the British Championship of 1982 and a lot more professional. The fact remained, however, that it was well within the rules for me to compete so, once we'd got the accommodation and the bonus sorted out, we just cracked on. I remember getting a bit of stick off some of the lads, especially because I was winning, but it was water off a duck's back to me. I was just doing my job, so as far as I was concerned if they wanted to have a whinge, they should whinge to Montesa.

To make matters worse, I ended up winning the Spanish Championship at a canter, so although the crowds had been happy to see me, and me them, the riders were left fuming. Hey ho! One thing I do remember about that championship, apart from the argy-bargy, was staying in those Paradores. They were absolutely tremendous and me and my dad felt like a couple of kings. It was a far cry from the days when we'd try to grab an hour or so in the bunks in the back of the van in a lay-by somewhere, but I'm glad I experienced both. In fact, because I was with my dad, and because we were on an adventure, I think I'd take the bunks.

World Championships-wise, 2001 was another cracker for me, although I did tail off towards the end of the Outdoor Championship. I forget why. The Indoor had been a complete triumph and the only round I lost was Italy. Ten out of eleven wasn't bad. The absolute highlight of the year with regard to the two World Championships was my dad claiming that he'd been shot. It happened in Goldendale, which was the venue for the two American rounds of the Outdoor, and it's one of my favourite stories about Dad.

Goldendale is situated on the west coast of America in Washington State and is an agricultural town. It's an absolutely great trial and by the time we were halfway around the second leg of the first day I was running second to Adam Raga. Goldendale was a big old lap and I seem to remember us being a bit late on time that day. We always seemed to push the limits timewise and by the looks of things it was going to turn into a bit of a race.

After getting to a new section I had a quick look around and then met with my mechanic. He always went ahead once I'd started so that when I arrived at the next section he could take the bike off me and give me a drink. In certain places he'd also give me something to eat, so actually he was more than just a mechanic. After having a glance at this section, I went back to the bike and noticed that Dad, James and Amos hadn't turned up yet. Dad was number one minder, James number two and Amos was like a full-time mentor. They seemed to have disappeared, though.

'Where the hell are they?' I asked my mechanic.

'No idea. They should have been here ten minutes ago.'

All of a sudden, I heard bikes coming and out of the trees flew James and Amos. They looked quite serious for some reason and because Dad wasn't with them I was a bit worried.

'Where's Dad?' I said, as soon as they stopped.

'It's all right,' said James as he got off. 'He's with the medical team.'

'Oh God, has he fallen off?'

It was quite a way in between the sections and because we were pushing on I thought he must have fallen.

'No,' said James. 'He's all right. Honestly. He'll be fine.'

'So, what the heck's wrong with him?'

'Erm. He's been shot in the back of his leg,' said Amos.

The only thing that stopped me from getting on my bike and charging off was the fact that Amos was clearly trying not to laugh.

'It's all right,' he said eventually. 'It's nothing serious. He says he's been shot in the back of the leg but reckons he'll be fine. He's back there with the medical team now.'

I obviously had no idea what to make of this. James and Amos were doing their level best to remain serious, though.

After all, we were in the middle of a round of the World Outdoor Championship and we were on the cusp of victory. In the end we had to get going because time was against us, but as soon as we got to the end we saw Dad sitting by a lorry so rushed over to him.

'What happened to you then?' I asked. 'James and Amos said you'd been shot!'

I'd never seen my dad looking embarrassed before.

'You lot are just going to take the piss out of me now,' he said eventually.

'How do you mean?' I asked. 'You were shot, weren't you?'

I knew full well by this time that he hadn't been.

'Well it *felt* like I'd been shot,' said Dad. 'Something twanged in the back of my knee.'

'Something twanged in the back of your knee? Seriously? And you told the medical team you'd been shot?'

'Well it bloody well hurt!'

This was like gold dust! I thought, *We'll have some fun with this.*

Poor Dad was crumbling before our very eyes.

'What did the medical team say?' I asked.

I could tell this was the killer question.

'Cramp!' he said after a long silence. 'All right? Happy now? It was bloody cramp!'

The following morning he was absolutely brand new and ready to go again. Well, physically. Mentally, he'd obviously suffered quite a bit of damage, but that was nothing to what he'd got on the way home. We hadn't even started yet!

What made me put all this on hold and become serious for a bit was Adam Raga's performance the previous day.

We'd both finished the day on 20 points, but I'd had a last lap of eight and he'd had a last lap of one. *One!* That was absolutely unbelievable, as the next best laps, which were both mine, were the aforementioned eight, and twelve. That was only the second time I'd been beaten in the Outdoor that year and it certainly made me sit up a bit. To be fair to Adam, it was undoubtedly one of the best performances of the entire season and, although I won the second day in Goldendale and the next two rounds in Italy, I lost five out of the following six. I'm not saying the wheels were coming off, but by the time the season finished there was absolutely no doubt that the competition were closing in.

With regard to my dad's assassination attempt – sorry, cramp! – it became a bit of a Christmas joke, really, in that it would be dragged out once a year and given a good airing. A very good airing! To be fair, he took it all very well.

A few weeks before the end of 2001 I received a letter that had something like 'HER MAJESTY'S SERVICE' printed on the front of the envelope. For some reason the letter had been sent to my parents' address, and when Dad rang me up in the Isle of Man to tell me it had arrived he was in a right panic.

'Can you think of anything you've done wrong, Dougie?' he asked me.

'No Dad. Not that I can think of.'

'Are you sure?'

'Yes Dad. I'm sure!'

After a few more minutes speculating about what the contents were I eventually said to Dad, 'Just open it, will you! If it's a summons, I'll deal with it! I'm pretty sure it's not, though.'

Well, I hoped it wasn't!

Anyway, I told my dad to call me back once he'd had a look and a few minutes later the phone went again. This time it wasn't just Dad, though. It was Mum and Dad! This wasn't a good sign.

'We're just ringing to notify you, Dougie,' began Dad, 'that you've been awarded an MBE.'

Talk about a bizarre conversation. There am I in the Isle of Man, just about to have my tea, and suddenly I've got not one but two parents on the line from Yorkshire telling me I've been honoured by Her Majesty the Queen. I think it was the formality of the call that made it feel strange. We Lampkins are not normally that formal and the only kind of ceremony we stand on is when we wash our hands before tea.

'I also have to inform you,' Dad continued, 'that you have thirty days in which to refuse the honour.'

He'd obviously been moonlighting as either a solicitor or a debt collector. He was good, though.

'That's good news,' I said eventually, although probably not that enthusiastically.

'I don't think you realise what this means, Doug,' said Dad.

He was right, I didn't. Him and Mum had both been quite emotional on the phone so far and to be honest I couldn't really understand why. I'd obviously heard of things like MBEs, OBEs and knighthoods, but they didn't mean anything to me. Why would they? I was into bikes, not gongs.

'Dougie, this is as good as a World Championship,' stressed Dad. 'It's recognition from your Queen and country.'

I'm afraid it still didn't register that much and I think

Mum and Dad must have been quite deflated when they put the phone down. I was just a bit nonplussed.

Over the coming weeks it started dawning on me what the MBE actually meant, but the thing that really brought it home was when Dad sat me down and told me that I was going to be the first British trials rider ever to be honoured by the Queen. Equating it to my sport, as opposed to just me, threw a completely different light on the situation and from that moment onward I started warming to the idea. Trials is obviously a niche sport, so to have it recognised in this way via what I'd achieved was fantastic.

You're obviously not supposed to tell anybody once you receive the letter and I think Mum and Dad had a bit of a problem with this. I say, 'I think' because I don't know for sure. I can't imagine my mum being able to keep quiet, though. Not for so many weeks. It's impossible.

You watch. I'll get a slap for that.

Once the 2001 New Year's Honours List was made public I had the world and his wife calling me up and I was surprised by the reaction. Surprised and happy. Despite having nine World Championships under my belt I'd never even been invited to the BBC Sports Personality of the Year awards, and I just assumed that nobody outside the trials world would really give two hoots. I was wrong! I didn't realise this at the time, but I was about to be entered into an exclusive biking hall of fame that included the likes of Jeff Smith, Joey Dunlop, Mike Hailwood, Barry Sheene and Carl Fogarty. How the heck Fogarty got in there I have no idea, but it won't have involved a bribe. He's too tight. In all seriousness, there weren't that many bikers who'd been honoured by Queen and country before so to be flying the flag not just for trials but for bikers in general was a massive honour in itself.

It was officially announced to the trials world at the opening indoor trial at Sheffield and, despite it already being public knowledge, the reception I got was fantastic. I may even have shed a tear or two. There I was, Douglas Martin Lampkin, the only person in Silsden who was named after a motorbike, about to become an MBE. Who'd have thought it?

Apparently, you need to be nominated for these kinds of honours and my dad was always convinced it was Colin Appleyard who put me forward. I've already explained that Colin was a family friend and he'd always been a big, big supporter of mine. He was also a Silsden man so there's a good chance Dad was right. Colin always kept quiet when Dad asked him and would never confirm or deny it. To be honest, I'm really glad Colin didn't say anything, as with both of them no longer being with us it's something I'd like to remain a mystery.

I guess I should have really given this next bit its own chapter as it involves me, my dad, my mum and Nicola all going to London to collect the medal. That might not seem too significant to some people, but Lampkins and London were never really what you'd call the best of friends and right from the word go I knew it was going to be eventful. We were all looking forward to going to Buckingham Palace, but me and Dad would quite happily have driven there and back in a day. Nicola absolutely loves London, as does my mum, so instead of us doing a quick smash and grab, which is what me and Dad suggested, she and Mum decided we'd make a weekend of it. Oh, brilliant!

'I think we'll go and see a show while we're there,' suggested Nicola. 'And maybe do a bit of shopping?'

'Good idea,' said Mum.

'I'll book the tickets,' said Nicola. 'I think we'll go for *Les Misérables*.'

To Dad and me, *Les Misérables* may as well have been a grumpy French mechanic and to be honest I think we'd far sooner have spent the night talking to one than going to see that rubbish.

We piled into Dad's Jaguar and made our way to London and, after arriving at the hotel, Dad asked the man on the door where the car park was.

'We don't have a car park, sir,' said the man.

'WHAT?' said Dad, quickly turning red.

'We don't have a car park.'

'I cannot believe that a hotel this size and charging this sort of money does not have a car park!'

The old man was furious and rightly so. I was too. Nicola and Mum were just embarrassed, I think.

After taking the car to the nearest car park, which was about a mile away, Dad walked back and by the time he got to the hotel he was still chomping on it.

'It's an absolute disgrace, Doug.'

'Aye, it is that, Dad. Anyway, let's go and have some lunch.'

After having lunch in a nearby restaurant we went shopping, much to mine and Dad's delight. Nicola had been saving up for a Louis Vuitton handbag for ages and so that was what we were shopping for. Eventually we found the Louis Vuitton shop and as Nicola charged in there brandishing her piggy bank, Mum, Dad and me followed her in.

Ten minutes later Nicola emerged from the shop looking triumphant. The handbag had been purchased and she was chuffed to bits. Dad, on the other hand, was crestfallen. He was in mourning. A broken man.

'Four hundred pounds for a handbag?' he kept saying. 'Did she just pay four hundred pounds for a handbag?'

'She did Dad. It's her money, though.'

'Yes, but four hundred pounds? It's a bloody handbag!'

'I know it's a handbag, Dad.'

He really was completely taken aback by this, so before he saw the prices in the Gucci shop over the road we bundled him into a taxi and took him back to the hotel for a rest. First the car park and now this. There was only so much he could take.

A couple of hours later Mum gave us a knock and told us it was time to go to the theatre, and when I saw Dad's face on leaving our room it was clear he wasn't looking forward to it. Neither was I, though. It won't surprise you to learn that Dad's idea of culture was making a trumpet sound through a rolled-up copy of *Motorcycle News* after he'd had a few, and to be fair mine was on a similar level. It just wasn't our thing. This didn't stop Nicola trying to sell it to us both but the more she talked, the less we understood.

'Let's just go and get it over with,' said Dad enthusiastically.

To stave off the impending boredom Dad bought a stack of sweets and crisps once he got to the theatre, although he wished he hadn't.

'Do you know how much this lot cost me?' he said to us.

I could see Nicola and my mum thinking, *No, but we have a feeling you're going to tell us.*

'Ten quid!'

I admit, it was rather a lot for what he had in his hands, but that's London.

After another quick moan we took our seats for *Les Misérables*. I don't know if you've ever seen the episode of *Only Fools and Horses* where Del Boy goes to the opera and ends up making a racket by eating crisps and sweets, well, Dad was like a larger, northern version of that, really. He made a right commotion. Nobody dare say anything to him, though, as he was there under protest, and so while Mum and Nicola carried on enjoying themselves, Dad gave himself type 2 diabetes and I had a nice kip. The dig in the ribs I received about an hour later notified me that it was time to clap and, once the curtain had come down and the lights had gone up, Dad breathed a huge sigh of relief.

'Thank God for that,' he said, standing up.

'Where do you think you're going?' asked Mum.

'Where do you think? Back to the hotel.'

'No you are not,' said Mum. 'There's the second half to come first. Sit yourself back down.'

Things like panic and desperation weren't expressions I'd normally associate with my dad, but the moment he heard Mum say the words, 'There's the second half to come first,' that's exactly what his face said. 'Oh my God. Please, *no more!*' To be honest, I was also pretty devastated, so to get us through the second half we went out, pawned our watches and bought a couple of boxes of Maltesers. We couldn't find any tranquillisers! Once the curtain eventually came down at the end Dad was out of that theatre like a shot.

'Never again!' he said as we emerged on to the pavement.

'We enjoyed it, didn't we Isobel?' said Nicola.

'Yes, we did,' confirmed Mum.

Poor Dad needed his bed.

The following day we were all up bright and early for the trip to Buckingham Palace. Because of the number of people involved it can get quite busy, so we were told to arrive about 11am, which was two hours before the ceremony was due to start. About an hour after breakfast Dad went off to fetch the car from the car park and this time there was no moaning. In fact, as the rest of us piled into the car I could have sworn I saw him grinning. 'Come on,' he said, hurrying us along. 'We've got to get going.' As he drove down the Mall towards the palace gates and saw the flag flying and all the people milling about he actually started smiling.

As we pulled up to the palace gates some tourists started looking inside Dad's Jag to see if there were any celebrities inside. 'Na, nobody,' I heard one of them say. That was about right! Just then a policeman appeared and Dad handed him the paperwork. While he went off to check it, some other officers came out with mirrors and that to have a look at the car. They certainly gave it a thorough inspection. When the first officer came back he pointed Dad in the right direction and waved us through. This was the bit Dad had been looking forward to: driving through the gates of Buckingham Palace in his Jaguar XJ. He'd finally arrived!

Once Dad had parked up we all got out and milled around for a bit. We were all wearing our best bib and tucker, of course, and for a bunch of northerners we scrubbed up quite well. We certainly gave those southerners a run for their money. Once we were inside, Dad, Mum and Nicola all went off to the viewing gallery, which is where the family and friends sit, and I was shown to the seating area in front of where the gongs are given out. At just 25 years old I was the youngest person there by quite some considerable margin, and the only person I recognised who was receiving an honour was Gary McAllister. I was quite impressed with that.

Apparently, the Queen had become overawed at the prospect of meeting me and so Prince Charles had offered to step in to distribute the honours instead, which was good of him. As the person calling the names out got closer and closer to the letter L, I became more and more nervous. I'd never met a future king before and I was bound to say something stupid. That's if he could understand me, of course. I couldn't see any translators. As it was, I needn't have bothered worrying, really, as I was up and out like a shot. It's all done with military precision and, as your name's being called, whoever's dishing the medals out, be it the Queen or Prince Charles, will have a quick chat with somebody in the know. Once they've imparted a few nuggets of information to them as to who you are and what you do – 'Dougie Lampkin, Your Majesty. Northerner, I'm afraid. Rides motorbikes over large objects' – they're ready to receive you and pin on your medal. It obviously doesn't take long to pin a medal on to somebody's lapel, so the chat is short-lived. In my case, he asked me something about the Isle of Man. I'd done a demonstration over there that Prince William and Prince Harry had seen and after referring to that he made a joke about trials being a more sensible choice than racing. I forget what I said back to him, but it was bound to have been sharp. Witty too, most probably. The whole thing can't have lasted more than about 20 seconds and before I knew it I was being ushered outside like a drunk in a nightclub. Soon after that Mum, Dad and Nicola appeared and, after having a quick chat and admiring the medal, we were all lined up to have our photos taken by the official photographer. Once that had been done, me and Dad realised our opportunity and, after bundling Mum and Nicola into the back of the car, we left the palace, waved London a fond farewell and made our escape back to Yorkshire. I forget how long it took us exactly (about three hours I think!), but I definitely saw Dad kiss the ground after he pulled up. He must have thought he was the Pope.

CHAPTER 11

Whatever You Do, Don't Take Your Helmet Off!

I'm not entirely sure why, but for some reason Montesa decided not to enter me for the Spanish Championship in 2002. I think it had something to do with all the hoo-ha that had gone on the previous year and they were probably embroiled in some political row. Since winning it in 2001, Montesa had secured a massive sponsorship deal with a Spanish company called Santiveri, who make diet food, so to be honest, I was a bit surprised by the decision. As I've already said, the Spanish fans seemed to like me so it must have been political. Montesa were all over me riding in the British Championship, though, so at least I'd get some time at home for a change. Funnily enough, Spaniard Adam Raga had ridden in the 2000 British Championship, so perhaps they'd all forgotten about that? I suppose the difference was that Adam was doing it for experience, first and foremost. As opposed to being instructed to compete by his team he was probably there of his own volition. I've always said that there's no better experience for a young rider than riding in between flags in sections at trials. Certainly, when it comes to handling pressure. Adam struggled, if I remember rightly, and ended up finishing seventh. He was only 19, though, and it was brave of him to try. Since then we've had various riders come and take part in certain rounds of the British Championship, but as far as I know Adam's the only well-known foreign rider who's completed it. Certainly, in recent times.

Although I won the first five rounds of the World Outdoor Championship and a total of five more afterwards, the World Indoor Championship was a very different proposition, and for the first time ever in the Worlds I actually realised that, as well as getting on a bit in years (I was still only 26, mind you), the younger lads were now catching me up. There's nothing concentrates the mind like a clever bugger who wins everything and I'd now been winning everything for the best part of six years. In that time the likes of Adam Raga, Marc Freixa, Albert Cabestany and Fuji had all emerged as front runners and, as much as that made me twitch a bit, it was obviously good for the sport. Anyway, I needed to twitch a bit because there's nothing concentrates a clever bugger's mind than having four or five would-be clever buggers breathing down your neck. So, if I wanted to retain my position as the best trials rider in the world, I was going to have to work hard and keep my wits about me. Getting to the top's often the easy bit. It's staying there that's the problem. I was obviously well aware that my reign was going to come to an end one day, but I wanted it to be on my terms, as much as it possibly could be. Anyway, at the time I thought we'd just have to see.

Something else that had changed in 2002 was the number of crashes I had, especially earlier on in the season. Sometimes your body doesn't react to what your brain says as quickly as it needs to and I think that was my problem. The worst of these accidents happened during one of the American rounds of the championship in a place called Duluth. There was a ginormous rock step there that they called 'The Wall' and they'd built a ramp at this thing that was about 45 degrees. Basically, you just had to hit the ramp in fourth gear and hope for the best. If you were lucky, your back wheel would land on the back of the face and you'd be up on to the top. As I said, that's if you were lucky. I wouldn't say it was particularly hard, but you did have to be brave to hit it at the right speed and there was no middle ground with this. You'd either done it and were okay or you were in a whole heap of trouble.

I remember it had started raining that day, which was perfect for me, but when I set off on the run-up to this step I ended up spinning a bit. I was committed by this point and after hitting the ramp full-on I just nosedived into the front of the wall. There was a hell of a crash and, after falling God knows how far, I ended up in a heap on the ground. The only bonus was that the bike didn't land on top of me, and the next thing I remember after the crash is James running over and somebody shouting for the medical team. Dad then shouted something about the doctor and because of the urgency in his voice I assumed he was hurrying him up. I was wrong. In fact, it was the absolute opposite. Dad always used to panic a bit whenever the medical team got hold of you because it usually spelled the end of your day, and when he shouted to James a second time I heard him perfectly.

'The doctor's coming. Quick, get him up!'

James, who was kneeling beside me at this point, said, 'He may as well stay there for a bit, Mart. His bike's snapped in two.'

'Yes, but if the doctor gets hold of him he'll be finished. Can you get up, Doug? Whatever you do, don't take your helmet off.'

As well as hitting my head on the wall, I think I'd winded myself. I was also having problems getting my words out and I was definitely seeing double.

'How many fingers am I holding up?' asked James.

''Av nooo idea,' I slurred.

Shortly before the doctor arrived I managed to get up and walk around a bit, and within just a few steps I began to feel better.

'Thank God for that,' said Dad. 'I'll go on to the next section.'

Once I'd been given the all-clear by Dad's doctor of doom, I made my way over to the mechanics to see what the damage was. The steering head and axle had broken in the frame but the frame itself was still intact. 'We need to take the complete front end out of the spare bike,' said one of the mechanics. 'Including the yokes and the front wheel.' Within about ten or fifteen minutes the lads had created this hybrid for me and once I could see properly I set off again.

My abiding memory of that accident is my dad telling James not to let the doctor get his hands on me!

In hindsight, I don't think I was the only person suffering more injuries at the time. In fact, I'm pretty sure it was endemic throughout the professional end of the sport. The sections were definitely getting bigger, which obviously made a difference, and with the bikes coming on leaps and bounds and some younger, braver riders coming through, it was probably inevitable.

But the sections weren't the only things in trials that were becoming too big. So were some of the teams. Especially mine. You see this a lot in sport, where teams start flashing the cash and before you know it they've pulled away from the rest and some of the smaller teams have even gone to the wall. It's not good for competition, which means it's no good for sport. The rules, too, often benefit the larger outfits and that's not healthy.

To a certain extent this is exactly what was happening in trials. When I first started competing in the World Championship I'd still turn up to rounds with my dad in a van, but that didn't happen any more. Every rider had a wagon, at least one mechanic and a couple of minders. They had entourages. Now, because of the amount of money involved, a lot of people weren't bothering any more. I've always taken a lot of pride in the fact that motorcycle trials is one of the cheapest forms of participation motorsport in the world, but this was going against that ethos.

The thing is, I was part of the problem. It had first occurred to me while we were in America. Somebody mentioned that the field was a bit smaller this year and, when I thought about it, they were right. 'It costs too much money these days,' was this person's theory. Then, I realised who'd travelled with me. I had three helpers, a team manager, a team owner and two mechanics. Seven people, just to look after one rider. I'm not daft enough to believe that every team should have exactly the same resources, but I knew that something wasn't right. My team Montesa had more money than the rest of the paddock put together and because I was winning champion-ships we attracted the biggest sponsors. There wasn't much the FIM (Fédération Internationale de Motocyclisme), the governing body, could do about that side of things, but what they could do was to change the rules a bit to even things up, to make sure the dominant riders weren't protected.

Reducing the number of assistants was one of the first things they did. That didn't make any difference to me but in some people's eyes it was essential in creating more of an even playing field. Next, they began playing around with the starting order and that's when things really began to change. Until now, it had always been the reverse order of the World Championship standings, which meant that the person in last place set off first. This is what I mean about the dominant rider being protected. The FIM had to take this assurance away and so instead of having a reverse-order system, they brought in a ballot for the first ten. This had an immediate and positive effect and is when I went from losing once or twice in a championship to seven or eight times. At the end of the day, the best always wins, but that has to be demon-strated. Otherwise, what's the point? I was still the best, but the results were now more representative of how good everybody else really was. It was back to being a competition again as opposed to a succession. I think the FIM have to be congratulated for acting as quickly as they did.

I'm not entirely sure why, but in early 2003 Montesa decided to enter me into the Spanish Championship again. I think my year off must have reminded Montesa how important it was to them as a company, both in terms of national pride and sponsorship, and once again I was more than happy to take part. Over the past year I'd been spending more and more time in Spain and had even bought a little house over there in Vallirana, just outside Barcelona. I still have it now, as a matter of fact.

The Spanish riders obviously hadn't forgotten about my victory in 2001 and when word got out that I'd be competing again they immediately made their feelings known. I thought this was a shame as I believe an international rider adds something to a national championship. That's just my opinion, though, and the Spanish riders obviously thought differently. Very differently, in fact.

The first round of the 2003 Spanish Championship took place in Jaén, which is in the south of the country, and in protest at me taking part all the Spanish factory riders, apart from those in the Montesa team, decided to go on strike. This backfired on them all big time as the Spanish Federation suspended their licences for a month, meaning they'd all miss the first round of the World Championship. It was a disaster for trials in general, really, and made headlines for all the wrong reasons. It was an embarrassment.

On the plus side, I went on to win the Spanish round of the 2003 World Outdoor Championship and in doing so I won my own body weight in a very expensive brand of olive oil. I remember, after the round, getting up on to the scales wearing my gear and my helmet and they just kept pouring the olive oil on. My team were absolutely delighted as each one of them ended up going home with about 5 litres of the stuff.

After winning the Spanish Championship again, much to the delight of the Spanish factory riders, I cracked on with the rest of the Worlds. This was definitely the beginning of the end for me and, as well as the rule changes kicking in, everyone seemed to have upped their game a bit. Riders who'd never won a World Championship round before were now pinching the odd one, but my teammate, Takahisa Fujinami, was the biggest surprise. He'd obviously had enough of coming second to me and he was a completely different rider in 2003. He was well up for it!

In the World Indoor Championship there'd been an even bigger shift, and after losing the opening round in Sheffield for the first time since 1997 I obviously feared the worst. By the time the championship ended I'd won just two rounds and had finished as runner-up. The man who took my crown was the extremely talented Spaniard who'd finished third in 2002 and the lad who'd had a crack at riding the British Championship, Adam Raga. He and Takahisa were the riders I feared the most. And admired the most, to be fair.

I'm almost talking like I didn't win anything in 2003 and that's obviously not the case. It had been a very strange season, though, and once again there'd been an accident or two. The worst of these actually happened to my dad during one of the Andorran rounds of the World Outdoor Championship and resulted in him breaking his collarbone. We'd been rushing to the finish down a big mountain road and after overcooking the brakes on a corner Dad hit the barrier and went flying. Cousin John was with us at the time and he was the first person to get to him. Dad couldn't move his arm but was on his feet trying to lift up his bike.

'What are you doing?' asked John. 'You can't move your arm.'

'I'll be fine. Just put my hand on the handlebars for me. You'll have to start my bike.'

'Sorry, but you're not going anywhere, Mart.'

'What? Not the doctor!'

'I'm afraid so. You're done.'

Poor Dad was absolutely gutted. He was also furious with himself.

I think that accident affected me a lot more than I first realised. Dad had always been like Superman to me and, although he definitely had a vulnerable side, he very rarely showed it. He was also getting on a bit now and it almost felt like I was putting him in danger. If only we weren't flipping late all the time! Even so, Dad wasn't the first member of the team apart from me to cop an unfortunate one in 2003. That particular honour went to James.

We were in Kiefersfelden in Germany and once again we were running late. This would have been about a month before Andorra and we were on our way to the last two sections, which were quite close to the paddock. There were people and bikes absolutely everywhere and James and I were on a mission. Because he's such a competent rider

James would often ride alongside me and he'd always have a big rucksack with him full of food, drink and spare gear. He was actually a few hundred yards in front of me at this point and as he was flying down this road he somehow managed to crash into a motorbike. What an impact! James ended up on his back in the middle of the road, his bike on the left-hand side, and the bike he'd crashed into went flying into the barrier on the right. James's bike came out of it worst, then James and then the other bike.

When I eventually managed to get to James he was still lying on his rucksack in the middle of the road. Just then, I heard a bike come screeching to a halt behind me and when I looked around it was Dad.

'Are you all right, Jim?' said Dad, pushing his way through.

'Yeah, I'm okay, Uncle Mart. I've just had a bit of a crash.'

'Well, we haven't got any time at the moment,' said Dad. 'We'll come back and get you in a bit.'

I feel ashamed saying this now but me and my dad left Cousin James lying in the middle of a road in Germany with a rucksack on his back and not knowing what day of the week it was. I think it's safe to say it wasn't our finest hour. We did keep our word, though, and the moment I'd finished the final section me and Dad were back up that road as fast as we could go. James was exactly where we'd left him, although he had a lot fewer people around him now and from a distance he looked like a bit of roadkill. It was the end to a rubbish day, though, and I think I came fourth in the end. Fuji had absolutely smoked it and he was on half the points I was.

By the time I'd finished whinging I'm afraid there wasn't a

lot of sympathy left for poor James. In fact, he had to remind us what had happened to him when we were back at the hotel. He was obviously still a bit sore and when we got out of the truck we just left him to get on with it.

'Hey! Give us a hand,' he shouted. 'I've just been involved in an accident!'

'Yes, all right. Go and give him a hand will you, Dad?'

By the time it got to the last round of the World Outdoor Championship I was on 276 points and Fuji was on 266. It certainly wasn't a case of whoever wins, wins, but I couldn't afford any disasters, that's for sure. Fuji had won six rounds so far to my four, so you can see how much things had changed. In 2002 I'd won over twice as many rounds as the nearest man and the year before that I'd won almost everything. Luckily for me, Fuji still tended to drop out of the top three when he didn't win, whereas I was always there or thereabouts. That's why it was so close. Had he managed to be a bit more consistent he could have wrapped it up by this point, but that was probably down to a lack of experience more than anything else, and maybe nerves. I think I was a bit more level-headed, which is probably what got me over the line. There'd been a lot of tiebreakers, though, so from a spectator's point of view it couldn't have been better.

The final round took place at La Cabrera in Spain, although it was classed as a European round as opposed to a Spanish one. I remember the first couple of sections were quite difficult and so it certainly wasn't going to be a high-scoring trial; nor could it have been considered my ideal venue. Adam Raga ended up winning the trial on his Gas Gas and to be honest he made it look easy. I came third behind Marc Freixa and Fuji was fourth. I think the pressure definitely got to Fuji in Spain. There were two rounds at La Cabrera and if he'd won both the chances are he'd have won the championship. This must have been playing on his mind big time because on the first day he'd come a disappointing fifth and with me finishing second behind Raga it was game over bar a disaster. He just couldn't follow a win up with a win, that was his problem. He's not the first to suffer from that, though, and he won't be the last.

As opposed to riding for a win I was riding for the World Championship and there was a lot to consider. But I'm not saying I would have beaten Adam Raga in La Cabrera. After all, he was in imperious form. It was the first time in a while that I'd had to ride tactically and once again this was miles better for the spectators. Although the World Outdoor Championship hadn't exactly gone to the wire, it had only been won on the final day and so that held everyone's interest.

I obviously didn't know it at the time, but this would be my last World Outdoor Championship title. Actually, perhaps I did know, deep down. There's a photo of me and Nicola in a clinch at the end of the last day and I'm blubbing my eyes out. We Lampkins don't usually cry in public, but for some reason my emotions got the better of me. I certainly had no thoughts of retiring, though, and was relishing the prospect of competing in a much closer field. To be honest, I can't really remember why I blubbed. I think I was just relieved.

Apart from just securing the World Outdoor Championship, the highlight of that weekend was seeing my Uncle Arthur, who had turned up unexpectedly. He had a habit of doing this and the first time I remember it happening was at Pateley Bridge in 1993 at the British round of the World Outdoor Championship. Arthur doesn't like crowds, it's as simple as that, and shortly before I started at Pateley Bridge he appeared out of nowhere and said, 'If you finish in the top ten, I'll give you a hundred quid.' After that he disappeared, just like the man off Mr Benn. One minute he was there, the next he was gone.

I ended up finishing ninth in Pateley Bridge (the prospect of that hundred quid never left me) and so the following Monday I made my way down to the family engineering firm for a bit of a gloat. To be fair, Arthur was waiting with the hundred quid and he was full of congratulations. Sid was, too, but there was no way he was handing over any brass. I think he thought Arthur had lost his marbles. Two years later, Arthur arrived at Hawkstone Park to wish me luck and when I went to find him afterwards I was told he'd already gone.

'He set off before the trial started,' said Dad. 'He can't have been here for more than fifteen minutes. I asked him to stay but he said there were too many folk about.'

That's Uncle Arthur for you. He drives 150 miles to wish me luck in a trial and then sets off before I do!

Anyway, the day before the first round in La Cabrera I was practising near the paddock when all of a sudden this enormous Honda Pan-European rolled up. Much to my amazement, and that of Dad, John, James, Mum, Nicola and everyone else, the man riding this monster of a bike was Uncle Arthur. He'd just got up one morning and decided to set off. The Lampkins and the Hemingways don't live

Bunny-hopping some trusting soul outside the Cartier Tent at Goodwood.
It's a time of year I always look forward to.

Filming with Ross Noble back in 2009. He got the Trials bug bigtime and I'm pleased
to say we still ride together now. He's actually not too bad!

Sometimes no matter how hard you try it just doesn't work out.

Always loved riding in Japan at the home of Montesa Honda.

The Scottish Six Days Trial is the ultimate test and is one of the main reasons I do what I do. Here I am holding the winner's trophy in 2012.

The Sheffield Arena Trial 2012, which was my farewell competition. Here I am with a few of my competitors, all of whom I'm happy to call friends.

Victory at the 2016 Scottish Six Days Trial, pictured here with my team–mate, James Dabill. I think the smiles say it all.

Totally focussed and totally in love with what I do.

My final year at the Erzberg Rodeo. It's one of the toughest events I've ever competed in.

The Red Bull Tundra Trial in 2014. It may not have been a competition,
but it was still tough.

The Red Bull Tundra Trial again, which took place in north Finland.
It's one of my favourite projects with Red Bull – so far!

The Red Bull Manchester City Trial that was organised by Dad and Jake.
A heroic achievement for all concerned and a great advert for our sport.

Training for the wheelie. I shudder to think how many hours I put in but it was only
ever possible once my mate Blackie got involved.

Achieving the impossible! Still the subject of the occasional nightmare, but it was worth it.

The Red Bull Italy project in 2017. I spent two whole days looking at this rollercoaster before I plucked up the courage to go for it!

in each other's pockets, but we always keep an eye on what we're all doing. Apparently, Arthur damn near turned back when he got to the Channel Tunnel and found out how expensive it was! Thankfully, he managed to cough up the £5.50 or whatever it was, but Dad gave him an absolute ton of grief for riding down on his own. It's not the safest trip to make and Arthur had done it without stopping. After I'd finished practising, me and Dad put the Pan-European in the back of the truck and took the keys off it.

'He's not riding home on his own,' said Dad. 'Like it or not, he's coming home with me and your mum in the truck.'

I think Arthur pretended to be a bit vexed at first, but he soon came around. Having him there was an honour for me and there's a really nice photo of him standing at the last section of the last round underneath a great big Union Jack with 'KING DOUG' written across it. It should have said King Arthur, really! After that Arthur got hold of this Union Jack and walked around with it draped over his shoulders.

The thing is, if it hadn't been for Uncle Arthur, I probably wouldn't have taken up trials; the same applies to Dad and Uncle Sid. Arthur had been the pioneer; the one who'd started tinkering with Grandad's BSA Blue Star 400 and who'd obsessed about buying his own bike as a young lad. He was the one who'd been a big TV star in the 1960s and who'd won everything there was to win in trials, both here and abroad.

For some reason, there were a lot of people following us that year – friends of Mum and Dad's, mainly, in motorhomes and camper vans – so after the final day we all went and had a right good knees-up.

Shortly after I was confirmed as world champion Amos came and had a word with my dad.

'Fuji's in his motorhome, Mart, and he's in a bit of a state. This is the fifth year in a row he's finished runner-up.'

'Do you reckon Doug should go and see him?' suggested Dad.

'Yes, I think that would be a good idea.'

When Dad asked me to go and see Fuji I was a bit shocked.

'What should I say to him?' I asked.

'Just make sure he's okay,' said Dad. 'Tell him what he's done right.'

It was a bit of a tricky moment, really. I was obviously elated at winning the championship, yet there was Fuji, a broken man. How the heck do you handle something like that?

After knocking on his motorhome door, I stuck my head round and asked if I could come in. The poor lad was sobbing his eyes out uncontrollably. Even so, he still managed to pull himself together and came straight over and congratulated me. I told him how well he'd done and that he'd really pushed me, but I stopped short of telling him what I thought he needed to do to put it right. I was feeling benevolent, but I wasn't daft. He'd given absolutely everything and in my opinion the only thing he was guilty of was trying a bit too hard. That's what desperation does to you. The only way Fuji was ever going to beat me was if he pulled back a bit and managed to keep his emotions in check. But after seeing him in his motorhome, I'd have put money on that never happening. Never in a million years. It was going to go one of two ways, though: either he'd carry on as he was, like I secretly thought and hoped he would; or he'd look at me and think, *Right you smug Yorkshire prat. I'm going to kick your bloody arse next year!*

I'd watched this lad progress over the years and, to be fair to him, nobody worked harder to try to improve. Nobody! When I first joined Montesa Honda he was riding quite a different bike and had a very strange set-up. I remember it sloped backward a little bit and it didn't make any sense to me. There were even certain sections he couldn't ride because of how his bike was set up but I didn't say anything. He had to work it out for himself and he had plenty of people around him who could help. It was a puzzle really. After a while he started watching what I was doing and about 15 minutes before practice he'd suddenly start appearing with exactly the same set-up as me: the same settings and the same engine mapping – everything! This was after he'd gone off on a tangent and tried something completely different, which he always did. It wasn't just the set-up, though. Fuji was taking information from all angles, just like he should have been, and despite coming second to me five years on the bounce he'd definitely been making progress. The closer he got to me, the less I wanted him to know, and in 2003 I'd had to remind myself that the team came first.

CHAPTER 12

Some Low Cloud and a
Few Stinging Nettles

Instead of being either discouraged or intimidated by the emergence of the likes of Adam Raga and Fuji, like I thought I might have been at one point, I became quite fired up by it. By the time 2004 came around I was hungrier than ever and had worked really hard in the close season. If you look at my results after 2003 it might seem like I rolled the gas off a bit, but, as I said, that's just not the case. I wasn't doing anything differently. I still had the same team behind me and despite my advancing years I was still one of the best riders in the world. That was the big difference, though. Before that I'd been *the* best in the world and despite the rule changes I'd proved it.

By the middle of the 2004 season Fuji had won five rounds and I'd won one. Talk about a reality check! For the first time since 1996 I was playing catch-up and to be honest it felt strange. Without wanting to sound arrogant I'd spent a lot more time winning than I had losing in my World Championship career, so the emotions I was used to experiencing, both before and after a round, had suddenly flipped. It was something I was going to have to get used to, though, as for the rest of that season if Fuji wasn't beating me, he was pushing me all the way. There were no excuses from my end, by the way. He'd obviously upped his game and was a carbon copy of how I'd been in 2003, i.e. if he didn't win a round, he was there or thereabouts.

As we approached the final two rounds of the 2004 championship, which took place in Switzerland, Fuji had a decent lead and unless something ridiculous happened he was going to be world champion. He'd won an impressive eight rounds so far and I'd won just two, so there was no questioning his dominance. The lad had come good at last.

I'd had the whole of August to try to get used to the idea of being toppled and by the time we got to Switzerland I thought I had. I was wrong, though. You see, what had actually got me through the summer break wasn't an acceptance of the inevitable. It was the notion that Fuji might lose his nerve at the last minute and hand the title to me. That might sound a bit harsh to some people, especially after his history of coming second, but I was there to win. I'd always been there to win.

By the time Fuji set off on that first round in Switzerland it was clear that he knew exactly what he was doing. He was at the front passing riders and was obviously going for a top five, which is all he needed. In fact, he was playing it exactly as I would have. There were no chinks in his armour now;

no nerves or erratic behaviour. He was as solid as a rock and from the moment I saw him set off on the penultimate day I knew he was going to be world champion. I ended up winning both days quite comfortably, but it still wasn't enough.

The journey back home to England was bizarre. Dad, James, Mum and Nicola were all there and for the last seven years it had been a journey I'd always looked forward to, for obvious reasons. Like the emotions I'd felt at all but two of the rounds this year, it was a sharp contrast to what we were used to and despite there being five of us in the wagon I don't think we said as many as five words to each other during the entire journey. We were all in mourning, I suppose. Not only for the loss of the World Championship, but also the atmosphere it had created and the effect it had on all our lives. It was a hard one to give up and no mistake, and unfortunately we didn't have the luxury of having something external to blame. At least that would have given us something to talk about and it might even have softened the blow a little bit. As it was, we just had to try to accept the fact that I was no longer deemed to be the best trials rider in the world.

We Lampkin men are not known for being romantic. In fact, out of all of us, I'd say the only one who's capable of showing any kind of sensitivity, or who has any kind of romance in his soul, is our John – the big girl's blouse! He's Silsden's answer to Noël Coward in that respect and most probably wears a dressing gown underneath his overalls. Nope. There's no moonlight and roses where I'm from, thank you very much. Just some low cloud and a few stinging nettles.

It's always been the same. Grandad Lampkin was too level-headed and too practical to be a romantic. Leaving London during the Second World War on a motorbike with your wife, your children and all your worldly possessions in a sidecar does that to you. Arthur, Sid and Dad were just the same, apparently, and I don't think Dad ever got my mum a birthday card or anything. It's not that he didn't care. Of course he did. He just liked to show his appreciation in other ways, like letting Mum watch him strip a bike down or something. Dad used to ask Nicola to get Mum's birthday presents for him. 'Get Issy a present will you Nicola?' he'd say. 'Sommert she'd like.'

I always said to Nicola that for as long as I was world champion, marriage would be out of the question. The excuse being that I'd have too much on. This worked like an absolute dream for the first few years and although we often talked about getting hitched I kept on winning. I dread to think how many World Championships I'd have won if I wasn't being threatened with marriage. Two, maybe? In all seriousness, marriage had been on the cards since about 2002 and as well as talking about it we'd even made a few tentative plans. Well, Nicola had. Then, when I won the World Championship in 2003, I thought, *She's suffered long enough now, the poor old thing.* So I decided to pop the question.

Nicola always said that if I ever asked her to marry me it should be somewhere romantic, like a beach or a lay-by in France. With that in mind, when Nicola confirmed that she'd like to accompany me to the FIM prize-giving ceremony for the 2003 season in Dubai, I thought it would be the ideal location.

As we were in our hotel room getting ready to go down to the ceremony I had to pop out for a bit to do some press. On the way back up I thought, *This is it, Dougie. You may as well get it over and done with.* I hadn't brought the ring with me because I might have had problems getting it through customs, and as Nicola wasn't keen on me getting down on one knee I thought it was going to be a doddle. I hadn't even asked her dad, which I thought might have been a mistake, but once I'd decided to do it, that was that.

When I got back to the hotel room Nicola was about three hours into getting ready and so with at least an hour to go I knew I had plenty of time. I was nervous, though, and the words I'd rehearsed in the lift, 'Nicola, will you marry me?' were no longer on the tip of my tongue.

'You're looking shifty,' said Nicola as I walked back in. 'Why are you fiddling with your dicky?'

For some reason words failed me and, as I stood there like a lemon trying to remember my name, Nicola twigged what was happening. She wasn't happy, though.

'If you're thinking of asking me what I think you're going to ask me you can stop right there,' she ordered. 'I told you I wanted it to happen somewhere nice.'

This brought me straight back to life.

'This is nice. We're in Dubai for heaven's sake.'

'Yes, but we're in a hotel room,' observed Nicola. 'What's more, if you ask me now I'll have to go down to a great big posh event trying to look like I haven't been crying.'

It was no use, it had to be now.

'Nicola,' I said. 'Will you marry me?'

'Yes, I will.'

'Right then,' I said. 'Because I haven't got the ring and because I haven't asked your dad, I don't want you to tell anybody.'

'WHAT?'

Poor Nicola. Despite having agreed to marry one of Silsden's most eligible bachelors, she had to sit there all night without telling a soul. She was bursting to get on her phone or make an announcement on the stage, but I wouldn't let her. I wanted to do it properly!

The following morning at about 5am I had to disappear off to an event somewhere and Nicola was due to fly back to the UK a few hours after. She later admitted to me that on the plane home she'd sat next to a Sri Lankan woman and while in the throes of having a big girlie conversation she'd spilled the beans about getting hitched to yours truly. She said it made her feel miles better and once I was back from my event we wasted no time in telling the family. I didn't ask her dad's permission in the end. He's dead laid-back and I think I just forgot.

The wedding itself took place on 26 October 2004 at Ripley Castle near Harrogate. The only things I was required to do for the wedding, apart from turn up and say 'I do', were to organise the honeymoon and get fitted for a suit. The honeymoon was a doddle to organise because all I did was contact the bloke who used to sort all my travel. Picking up the phone and saying, 'Five days in the Maldives please' was the extent of my efforts. Apart from paying for it, of course. Actually, I did arrange a surprise for Nicola at our wedding, so I'm not a complete lost cause. She'd looked at getting some fireworks for the evening do, but had decided they were a waste of money. Once she'd gone out of the room I called the people back and said, 'Whatever she was looking at, we'll have.' Do you know, I think that may have restored her faith slightly? If it was ever there to start with.

For our honeymoon we stayed at a beautiful hotel and spa place called the Banyan Tree, but it was a long way to go for five days. We flew economy, of course, which I think helped Nicola appreciate the luxury on offer all the more. You see, I think of everything.

The reason we could only stay five days in the Maldives was because I was due to spend the following ten days in Birmingham doing demonstrations at the motorcycle show. Twice as long as our honeymoon! That was a long slog, I can tell you. After about eight days being there, Nicola called me up one afternoon. 'Are you on your own?' she said, as I stood in the middle of Birmingham NEC surrounded by approximately twenty thousand people.

'Not exactly,' I replied. 'Why, what's up?'

'I'm pregnant,' said Nicola. And she had a go at me about making announcements in inappropriate places! I was absolutely over the moon when she told me and those last few demonstrations I did were dynamite.

Towards the end of 2004, just as the disappointment of being beaten had started to abate, I was asked to go to Spain to test the new bike that Fuji and I would be riding in 2005. The test took place in a private training area near Manresa, which is near Barcelona, and I remember there were a lot of people from Honda Racing in attendance. It was a proper Japanese delegation. Bearing in mind they'd only brought one bike with them, which both Fuji and I were due to test, this made me a little nervous. Either they were as pleased as punch with their new creation and wanted to celebrate the prospect of yet more Montesa Honda World Championships or they were expecting trouble. The looks on their faces made me suspect it was the latter and this was all but confirmed when I saw the bike. It had a tall four-stroke engine on it and to be honest it looked like a bit of a lump. Amos rode it first and when he came back, apart from looking crestfallen, I could tell that the last thing in the world he wanted to do was hand it over to me.

'Be careful, Dougie,' he said. 'I'm afraid it's not very good at the moment.'

Not very good? What an understatement! No word of a lie, that was the worst bike I'd ridden since I was a teenager, and by a very long way. For a start, it was heavy, very heavy, and, as well as having no noticeable power, the suspension was dreadful. The clutch, too, was like something off a sit-down lawnmower and as well as vibrating it kept on slipping all the time.

Normally, unless I'm absolutely knackered or have injured myself, I hate getting off a bike, but in this instance I couldn't wait. Straight away, the Honda Racing people were on to me looking for information, but I couldn't really speak. I was dumbstruck. They wanted to start going through a comparison sheet linking this to the previous two-stroke bike, but I didn't know where to start. Fuji and I had won multiple World Championships on the two-stroke, and as far as I was concerned it was one of the best things I'd ever ridden. Not *the* best, but one of. This, on the other hand, was one of the worst, if not *the* worst. Once I'd managed to regain the power of speech they were going to need more than a sheet!

'Any positives?' asked Amos.

'Not one,' I replied. 'That is an absolute lump. We've got a bit of work to do, Amos.'

Now I was the one dishing out the understatements.

I handed the bike to Fuji next and he immediately started adjusting the levers and handlebars. 'Don't bother about that now,' I said. 'Just go and have ten minutes on it. We're in big trouble.'

I don't know if Fuji remembers this but after about 15 minutes there was no sign of him and so Amos and I went back to the van to get a drink. As we arrived we noticed that the new bike was leaning up against Fuji's van and there, on the back step, was Fuji. He was crying his eyes out. Even after a few minutes he'd obviously realised that there was no way he was going to be able to defend his World Championship and that must have been devastating for him. It was obviously hard for me too, as I was desperate to win back the championship, but to have the opportunity of retaining it taken away from you – something you've fought tooth and nail to win and over a number of years – is the ultimate kick in the teeth.

The following day we had a crisis meeting with Montesa Honda and the members of the Honda Racing team and to this day it's one of the most sombre events I've ever attended. There wasn't a great deal anyone could say, really. Because of some impending rule changes that would eventually see the sport phasing out two-stroke engines, Montesa Honda had decided to make an early commitment to four-stroke engines. It was clearly a long-term strategy and because none of the other teams or manufacturers had done much about it, the chances are it would eventually pay off. When, though? None of this had been communicated to us beforehand so it had come as a massive shock. One minute we're a team with a great bike, happy staff, bags of success and two riders vying for both World Championships, and the next we're like a bunch of depressives on pushbikes. Poor Fuji was at his wits' end. After all, with the decision coming from Honda, a Japanese company, and with Fuji being the first Japanese rider ever to win the World Outdoor Championship, it must have felt like a right kick in the teeth. Why now? It was obviously a team decision and at the end of the day, nobody's bigger than the team.

The following week we started testing and we didn't stop testing for about two months. It was relentless. There were people from Honda Racing in Japan actually flying to and from Spain carrying engines as hand luggage! How times have changed. This was happening two or three times a week sometimes, so the airfares must have been astronomical. Needs must, though, and to be fair to Honda they worked their backsides off trying to develop the bike and did everything they could to help us catch up.

One thing that actually improved because of this situation (the only thing, in fact) was my relationship with Fuji. We'd always been on good terms as teammates but because we were also rivals there'd naturally been a bit of a barrier between us. I suppose there had to be, really. Now, because of all the testing, we were spending almost every waking hour together, and because the competitive barrier had been removed we were able to build a relationship, a relationship that was based around a common goal.

By the time Christmas came along the bike was still a million miles away, so as soon as it was over Fuji and I decamped to Spain again to continue testing. All I could think about while all this was going on was the impending first round of the 2005 World Indoor Championship. In 2004, Sheffield had been the only round I'd won in the Indoor and in eight years I'd only lost there once. In a couple of weeks' time, unless Adam Raga, Albert Cabestany, Jeroni Fajardo, who I went on to team-manage at Vertigo in 2016 and 2017, and Marc Freixa all came down with flu, I would be doubling that tally and on a bike that didn't have the power to pull the skin off a rice pudding. Sure enough, by the time Sheffield came along I practically had to put the bike on my shoulders and carry it through the sections. It was awful. I should explain that Fuji and I were riding semi-prepared bikes for the Indoor Championship as it just wasn't feasible to take the bikes that were in development out of the factory. They were works in progress and had to remain put. This meant that as soon as each indoor round had finished, Fuji and I would fly to Spain to begin testing again. It was almost as if the World Indoor Championship had been sacrificed in an attempt to save the Outdoor and I suppose that made sense. To be fair to Fuji and me, we actually did okay in some of the rounds, and despite never being in contention we managed plenty of thirds between us and I even scraped a second. God only knows how that happened!

After a few months we'd managed to build the power up quite a bit and by the time the outdoor season came around the clutch had improved and we'd made a lot of progress on the suspension. The suspension was down to Amos mainly, but everybody had a hand in it. We were a team, a very tight team, and that was definitely a second positive from that period. Just a few months before, we'd had a bike that I honestly wouldn't have given you a pound of spuds for. Now, we had something that was bordering on being competitive. It wasn't a championship-winning bike. Not yet. It was no longer a lump, though, and that was down to all of us. It was the ultimate team effort.

The first round of the 2005 World Outdoor Championship took place in Portugal, in and around a town called Pampilhosa da Serra. It's quite a nice trial to be fair and right out of the blue I actually ended up winning! What a boost that was. It was yet another of those days when I could have walked on water. In fact, you could have blindfolded me and put me on a Raleigh Chopper and I'd still have won. I was temporarily invincible! Those days were happening less and less now, but I appreciated them more than ever. Montesa Honda had been through some very dark days over the past months and this was exactly what we needed. Was it a bit of a fluke? Yes, of course it was. I only won by a whisker, but at the end of the day, they all count. We were also under no illusions as to how the season would probably pan out, though, so we took it for what it was. I remember the chief executive of Repsol phoning me after the round and congratulating me on the win. I think he thought we were going to go on and win the championship, but I didn't have the heart to tell him the truth.

Funnily enough, round two took place in Tarragona, which is where the Repsol refinery is, and for some reason either they or Montesa thought it would be a good idea to get all seven of my World Championship-winning bikes together. They even shipped the Beta ones over from England and it's the first and only time all seven bikes have been in the same place at the same time. A friend of the family called Eric Kitchen took a photograph of me with the bikes and unless he's asking more than a quid it should be in this book somewhere.

Despite the celebrations from the first trial, and the bikes being in attendance, I'm afraid I had a shocker in Tarragona, and I mean a shocker! Tarragona's on the coast and some-body had had the bright idea of building a section or two within the rocks next to the sea. This would have been fine if the waves hadn't started to break, but once they did it became farcical. The first section was okay, to be fair, but once we got on to the second the waves started lashing in, and despite us attempting to dodge them they were a bit too unpredictable. All that actually happened was that me and the bike got wet, but the moment that happened the bike stopped dead.

'What's up?' asked Amos.

'I've no idea,' I replied. 'I think it must have been that last wave.'

We were obviously being timed for the trial so it was important that we sorted it out quickly. The thing is, we had no idea what the problem was. I could tell by the look on Amos's face that he was worried and so was I. The bike was completely dead and nobody could get a peep out of it.

'We'll have to get it back to the truck,' said Amos.

'But that's about three or four kilometres away.'

'We've got no choice.'

Amos was right. The mechanical resources were obviously limited at the sections, so with the bike in a coma we'd just have to cart it back. My minders that year were my dad and my cousin Ben, and Ben ended up putting his foot on my footrest and pushing me back. He's a strong lad is Ben and it hardly took him any time at all.

Once there, we got the bike into the wagon and from then on it was chaos. The people from Honda Racing were calling the head office in Japan and while they were shouting into their phones, Amos and the mechanics were trying to concentrate. The reason the Honda lads were shouting was because we weren't getting any data and, with no data, we couldn't find a solution. Until then I'd never had to retire from a trial before and I remember sitting in the corner at the back of the wagon in a state of disbelief. Minor things went wrong all the time in trials, but major mechanical issues were about as rare as hen's teeth.

A man called Mr Masuda was the top dog from Honda Racing that day and after an hour or so he came over to me looking ever so slightly deflated. 'Mr Lampkin-san. Very sorry. No moto.' I thought, *Oh heck!* Apart from injuring myself or coming down with something, this was the worst-case scenario. No bike! The wagon was an absolute mess. There were parts everywhere and the bike was still wired up to about six different machines. My chief mechanic at the time was a guy called Oscar Alonso and, despite what Mr Masuda had said, he and Amos were still tinkering about.

'What do you reckon's up, Amos?' I asked.

'It must be the salt water,' he said. 'We just don't know what it's done. It's not a common problem!'

'Well, keep trying if you would,' I said to him. 'We've got nothing to lose.'

A few minutes later, and without warning, Amos jumped on the bench, mounted the bike and tried to kick-start it. He did this over and over again and it was obviously out of sheer frustration. I remember everybody looking at each other, as if to say, 'Well, I wasn't expecting that!' Nobody was daft enough to tell him to stop, so while Amos carried on kick-starting, the rest of us just stood there looking slightly uncomfortable. It's best not to get involved when a Mediterranean man is losing his marbles!

After about 40 or 50 attempts Amos started to tire and, just as I was about to call the men in white coats, he got a murmur from the engine. What a flaming surprise that was! Rejuvenated by the murmur, Amos started kicking again, this time harder than ever. Slowly but surely the engine started coming back to life. Even more encouraged, Amos kicked for all he was worth, until eventually he got overexcited and fell off. After that Oscar had a bash and five minutes later it was running.

'Get the plastics back on,' said Oscar. 'And let's get him out.'

The Japanese lads were wanting to double-check everything before we went out but they stood no chance. We were off, and that was it!

'DO NOT STOP THIS BIKE UNTIL THE END OF THE LAST SECTION!' ordered Amos.

Because we didn't have much time they'd stuck everything back on with gaffer tape, so if you weren't aware what had happened you'd have been forgiven for thinking it was some kind of bodge job. I suppose it was, in a way. I'm not sure how but I managed to finish fifth in that trial and by the end of it I was absolutely knackered. We all were.

The only person who was still really down after the first two rounds was Fuji and at the time I almost wished that he'd had the win in Portugal instead of me. He'd finished fifth in that trial, which we thought was far more representative of how we were faring as a team. So, at the time I remember thinking that it would have been nice for him to win a race. A consolation, if you like.

By the time I arrived in Alès for the two French rounds, I had one other issue to contend with. Actually, I think I might have worded that incorrectly, as the 'issue' in question was the imminent birth of mine and Nicola's first child. I was actually on a bit of a high at this point, as in addition to the new arrival I'd also managed to fluke a second win in Duluth, so I was actually lying second in the championship. Not bad for a blind lad on a Chopper!

The two French rounds were in June, which was roughly halfway through the season, and the idea was that after the second round I'd fly back to England and, providing Nicola hadn't started without me, be present at the birth.

The majority of the two rounds took place in and around a small racing circuit and after walking the sections beforehand it looked like it had the makings of being a good trial. Last year's French rounds had taken place in Valdeblore, which is just north of Nice, and Alès is about 250 miles west.

I'm not sure if it was the hot weather that affected my judgement, but during the second section on the first day I had to fly up this banking that had a large rock on top of it but because I hadn't given it enough wellie I wasn't able to crest the rock and went backward. Unfortunately, neither my dad nor Ben was able to catch the bike and on the way down it bossed me slightly and I ended up falling on to a big sharp rock hip first. I knew from the moment I opened my eyes that it had been a bad one because there were people absolutely everywhere. Worse still, I couldn't move my leg. It was totally dead. I'd never broken my hip before but at the time I was sure that's what I'd done.

Despite this, rather than getting into the ambulance, which was what everyone was suggesting (well, everyone apart from my dad!), I decided to try to ride to each of the remaining sections with Ben who had the punch card. As long as I arrived at each one he could get me stamped and so even though I wasn't able to ride the sections at least I'd get a result. As they punched the last section, which put me in 12th, the ambulance was already waiting for me and so I stepped off my bike and straight on to a stretcher. By this time, I was in all kinds of flipping agony and on arriving at the hospital I immediately had a series of X-rays all down my left side. I was completely black and blue! To this day, it's one of the biggest crashes I've ever had and after the X-rays the first thing the doctor said was that there was no way I'd be able to ride tomorrow.

'There's an awful lot of damage, Mr Lampkin,' said the French doctor. Actually, he spoke better English than me.

'How do you mean?' I asked. 'Have I broken anything?'

'We're not sure yet. The bruising is very severe so at the moment we can't actually determine the extent of the damage.'

'What if it is just bruising?' I asked.

'If that's the case you can go, but I'm afraid you can't ride.'

A couple of hours later the doctor confirmed that it was in fact just bruising, so although I was still in a massive amount of pain I was free to go. If you leave hospital during the World Championship and have a trial the following day, the only way you can ride is if you have a piece of paper from the doctor. In fact, even if you can't ride you still have to get a piece of paper. The piece of paper I got obviously said 'No' on it, so I wasn't in the best of moods.

With Nicola back in Yorkshire I had my mum and dad, Ben and team manager Miguel with me at the hospital and as we left to go back to the paddock the doctor handed Miguel this piece of paper.

'Somebody from the FIM will ask for this,' the doctor said to Miguel, who just nodded.

Once we were back at the paddock, which was quite late, we were expecting to receive a visit from the FIM, but it didn't happen.

'Do you think we're supposed to hand it in?' said Dad.

'Absolutely not,' said Miguel defiantly. 'The doctor definitely said that the FIM would ask for it, so unless that happens, I'm saying nothing.'

'Best to keep our options open, eh Miguel?' said Dad knowingly.

'Definitely, Mart!'

When I woke up the following morning I could hardly move. Because of the pain I'd had to sleep on the sofa in the back of the truck which is where I'd plonked myself after getting back from the hospital. After about half an hour of trying, Dad and Ben eventually managed to get me on my feet, and after taking another handful of painkillers I decided to take a walk around the paddock. The first person I met was Miguel and after seeing me hobble over to him he obviously feared the worst.

'I'm sorry, Dougie,' he said. 'You're obviously not up to riding. What a pity.'

To be honest, I'd actually forgotten about the trial for a second (it must have been the painkillers) and when Miguel said 'What a pity' I thought to myself, *Hey! I've just walked across the paddock.* I think my dad must have sensed this because he immediately asked me how I was feeling. Not in a concerned way, but in a 'Are you well enough to ride?' way.

'Do you reckon you're up to riding a couple of sections?' said Dad.

'Yeah, probably,' I replied. I could hardly bloody walk but why not? As long as they kept filling me with painkillers. It'd help take my mind off things!

'Has anyone asked for that piece of paper yet, Miguel?' I asked my increasingly enthusiastic team manager.

'No, nobody,' he said. 'They're all here, though. They must have forgotten.'

'I'll tell you what,' I said. 'Let's have a go.'

I was going to be in pain whatever I was doing, so it may as well be something I enjoyed. Also, I was getting paid to ride, not stand around doing nothing. And what about everyone else? If I did nowt, so did they. In the end, I wasn't able to attempt every section and I definitely gave the second one a wide berth! I ended up finishing sixth, though, which wasn't bad, and out of a field of thirty.

When I got back into the wagon I actually felt okay and when I lay back on the sofa I had the makings of a self-satisfied grin on my face.

'Good effort that, Dougie,' said Dad, stepping into the wagon. 'You must be pleased.'

I was about to reply and say that I was quite pleased, when suddenly the painkillers started wearing off. 'Bloody hell, Dad,' I said. 'It's starting to hurt again!' I think the adrenalin had also had quite a numbing effect and that was also starting to disappear. I was at my wits' end.

'Never mind that,' said Dad, handing me some ice. 'We've got to get home. There's a baby on the way.'

'What, you mean she's gone into labour?'

'No, no, no! She might be soon, though.'

Despite us all having flights booked for the following day, we decided to set off by truck instead. Dad said it would be quicker in the long run and with Nicola now being close to her due date we had no time to lose. By the time we got to Calais it was all quiet on the western front. Then, just as we were boarding the ferry, I got a call. It was Sarah, Cousin James's wife. She was Nicola's midwife and the first thing she did was ask where we were.

'We're in Calais,' I said. 'Just boarded. Where are you? Is Nicola okay?'

'Yes, she's fine. She's gone into labour, though, and we're on our way to the hospital. When you get to Dover, tell Mart to put his foot down.'

'Dad,' I shouted. 'As soon as we're off you'll have to floor it. Baby's on its way.'

To be fair to Dad he did exactly that but by the time we got to Bradford he was taking it to extremes. Whenever a car indicated to turn right, instead of waiting until they'd turned he'd kerb it. To an onlooker it must have looked like he'd stolen it! It was a seven-and-a-half-ton Mercedes truck, for heaven's sake, and he was driving it like a Subaru.

When we eventually screeched to a halt outside the front doors of the hospital it's a wonder we weren't being tailed by the police. Dad, Mum and Ben all jumped out and as they ran towards the doors they quickly realised that they were missing somebody. Me! Despite Dad driving through the night at an average speed of about a hundred miles an hour I'd stiffened up like a good'un and, even though Nicola and our unborn baby were just a few yards away, it may as well have been a hundred miles.

'Hang on, I can hardly bloody move,' I protested. 'I think my joints need oiling.'

After flatly refusing the offer of a wheelchair, which I think had been done just to wind me up, I dragged myself through reception and on towards the maternity ward. We'd travelled over 1,500 kilometres in about 16 hours but the last hundred yards were definitely the hardest.

When I finally reached the delivery room things had

slowed down a little. After asking Nicola how she was I remember thinking, *That bed looks bloody comfy.* I stopped short of asking her to shove up a bit, but I was tempted. I was also desperate to have some gas and air, but after being told how expensive it was by one of the doctors I settled for a chair instead. Could I get comfy? Could I heck. After trying two different chairs the nurse got annoyed and so in the end I just slumped against the wall. What a pair we must have looked. There's Nicola hogging the bed and pretending to be in agony and me slumped next to her, developing rigor mortis. I can't see *Hello!* magazine paying much for that one, can you?

A few hours later our son Alfie was born and so I hobbled off to call Dad. All of a sudden the crash, the pain and even the World Championship was kicked well and truly into touch. We Lampkins might be competitive so-and-sos, but family always comes first and the fact that my own had just grown by a third was a very humbling experience. Nobody loves winning more than I do, but watching a child come into the world, a child that you've helped to create, is on a different scale.

That's what I thought at the time. The next morning I couldn't wait to get back to work!

You remember earlier I said that at the start of the season I wished Fuji had won in Portugal? Well, in hindsight, I'm bloody glad he didn't because he went on to completely defy the odds that season and, as well as winning three rounds – in Japan, the USA and Italy – he also bagged a further eight podiums. The win in Japan, which was the first of his three, was obviously very special for him and I think it probably played a part in him performing as well as he did for the rest of the season. Bearing in mind we were the only team riding a four-stroke bike, and a bike that was very much in development throughout the entire season, that was an astonishing set of results and even though he finished the World Championship as runner-up, I think that in performance terms it's the best of his career so far. I know the saying goes that nobody remembers second, but I've got to take my hat off to Fuji. Had he been on the old bike he'd have stuffed the flaming lot of us.

The highlight of my own World Championship campaign, in which I finished third overall, behind winner Adam Raga and Fuji, was winning the British round of the championship, which took place at Hawkstone Park. Dad and Jake were running the event and I remember the crowd that year was absolutely massive. There were thousands there and that definitely gave me a lift. By this time, which was three rounds before the end of the World Championship, the bike had started performing quite nicely and, despite not being the finished article, it was light years ahead of where it had been at the start of the season. Adam Raga won those last three rounds and was crowned the new world champion. A very worthy one, I might add, despite what I said about Fuji stuffing us all. At my age, I'm allowed to contradict myself occasionally.

In truth, they were both tremendous and although the season wasn't the most successful I ever had, it was certainly one of the most eventful. I think the older I get, the more philosophical I become about this period. Had I written this book at the end of 2005 it would have been a very different story and this particular chapter would have been full of angst, regret and possibly even a few swear words. My head's a little bit clearer these days and despite all the obvious disappointments I can see now how it fits with regard to where I am today. I think this was when I first began to realise that I was never going to be world champion again. The thing is, there's a big difference between beginning to realise something and actually accepting it, and until the day came when I was able to do both I was just going to carry on. Had somebody suggested to me that this was it, I'd have told them to go away or words to that effect. But with the likes of Adam Raga now up there, not to mention a certain Toni Bou, it was inevitable.

Actually, there was one other highlight for me during the 2005 season (apart from becoming a dad, of course) and it's the perfect way to finish the chapter. We've got to go back to June and the first of the two American rounds. These took place in Duluth and the story involves my dad, Amos and a lost peak.

Duluth is in Minnesota by the way, on the shores of Lake Superior, and with much of the trial taking place either in or around a river, it suited me down to the ground.

I remember there were a lot of queues at the start of this round and so right from the off we were under pressure. The sections were also quite close together, and because the roads weren't brilliant my dad could afford to abandon his bike and do some of it on foot.

After completing the first section Dad ran up to Amos in a bit of a panic.

'Hey, Amos,' he said. 'I've lost the peak to my helmet. You've got to help me find it.'

'What the bloody hell are you talking about, Mart?' said Amos. But before Amos could say anything else Dad darted off back to his bike.

After I'd completed the second section the same thing happened again.

'Amos. Hey, Amos! I've lost the peak to my helmet. Have you found it yet? You haven't even looked, have you? I'm going to look like a right silly bugger if I don't find it.'

Once again, because of the time constraints, Dad ran off before Amos could answer.

'What's up with Dad?' I asked him.

'Oh nothing,' he said. 'He says he's lost the peak to his helmet, that's all.'

'Eh? How do you lose the peak to your helmet?'

'Don't worry,' said Amos reassuringly. 'I'll help him find it.'

By the end of the next section Dad had become desperate and once again it was Amos who bore the brunt.

'Amos! Hey, Amos! Have you found the peak to my flipping helmet yet? Come on lad, at least help me look. I've never lost the peak to my helmet before.'

We were obviously trying to ride a trial, not look for the peak of a helmet. Even so, Amos was able to put Dad out of his misery.

'Martin,' he said slowly. 'You – have – your – helmet – on – the – wrong – way – around!'

Dad wasn't at all impressed.

'Eh? Don't be daft! That's imposs—'

Suddenly, Dad started to realise that Amos might be right and slowly but surely he began taking off his helmet. When he finally saw the missing peak, he was absolutely horrified.

'Oh, bloody hell!' he said.

The thing is, if you try putting a trials helmet on back to front it's the most awkward and uncomfortable feeling ever. It's just not meant to happen. How on earth Dad didn't realise I have no idea, but he must have lasted the best part of two hours.

'I am *never* going to live this down,' said Dad. Just then, he went into damage limitation mode. 'Hang on,' he said. 'Where's our Doug and our Ben? You don't have to tell them, Amos. Don't tell our Dougie and our Ben!'

'Sorry, Mart,' said Amos. 'But I'm afraid I'm going to have to.'

'You absolute . . .'

The journey back home was wonderfully long, about fifteen hours door to door, and every ten minutes or so one of us would shout, 'Hey, Mart, where's yer peak?'

'Oh, shut up!'

That was definitely the highlight of my year.

CHAPTER 13

There You Go Dad,
I've Matched You

In 2006 the bike continued to improve, whereas I continued to slide. Not drastically, but enough for it to become a bit of a distraction. Subconsciously, I think I'd started analysing my performances a lot more around this time, which meant that as well as losing a bit of confidence I wasn't entirely focused. From 1996 to 2003 I'd had tunnel vision and it was almost impossible to distract me. Now, my head was everywhere and I still hadn't come to terms with the fact that I was no longer top dog. I knew it, but I didn't accept it. It was a cruel irony, in a way, but that's sport for you. I think the only person who really noticed it was me. At first, at least. As I said, the decline was gradual, so despite me being aware that things were on the slide, I was still spending most of my time on the podium.

In June 2006 we arrived in La Châtre in France for

round five of the World Outdoor Championship. When we had a look at the course the night before it was bone dry and apparently it hadn't rained for about two weeks. This obviously suited the Spanish lads down to the ground, so I knew it was going to be a tough weekend. Then, the following morning, the heavens opened and, as my young Mediterranean friends were all panicking and cursing the continuing rain clouds, I was rubbing my hands together! Not only did I prefer riding in the wet (I'd had plenty of practice living in North Yorkshire), but that four-stroke Montesa Honda could dig holes through mud like I don't know what, so I knew I was on to a good'un. The problem was, so was Fuji. He also had a four-stroke mud-cutting machine and because he was trailing me in the championship at the time, I knew he'd be up for it.

By the time the round started it was still tipping it down, but after the first lap I was lying sixth on 41 behind Raga, Bou, Fuji, Cabestany and Fajardo. Would you believe it? Every single Spanish lad who'd complained about the rain had bettered me, as had my teammate, so I was going to have to pull my finger out and look lively.

On the second lap I put in an 11, which was bang-on, even though I do say so myself. That put me on 52. Despite motorsport's answer to One Direction all improving on their previous scores, the only one who caused me any real trouble was Fuji with a 14. This meant that he also finished the round on 52, but my outstanding 11 trumped him. I didn't know it then, or perhaps I did, deep down, but this was to be my last ever Grand Prix win. My first had taken place at Hoghton Tower in 1994 and in between that and the one here I'd managed a further 97 wins, giving me a grand total of 99. People often ask if it bothers me finishing on one below a hundred, but I always make the point that if I'd finished on a hundred I'd have wanted 101. That's the one big drawback of being a permanently competitive individual. You're never satisfied!

Just two points behind Fuji and me in La Châtre was the 19-year-old Spanish upstart Toni Bou. Funnily enough, Toni was riding a Beta that year and had been since his World Championship debut back in 2003. In that, and in many other ways, he reminded me of me, except he was shorter, uglier and far less talented. The lad had promise, though, and when Montesa Honda signed him up from Beta, just as they had me six years previously, I knew exactly what Marc Colomer must have felt like. I must admit, I'd had more pleasurable experiences.

Ever since he arrived on the scene we riders had all been watching Toni Bou with an increasing mixture of disbelief, amazement, jealousy and awe. This lad could do anything, or so it seemed, and with regard to the Montesa Honda situation it was a case of history repeating itself. He was very much the future of the sport, whereas I was about to become part of its history. Mind you, if I'd been in charge of Montesa Honda I'd obviously have done exactly the same thing. It's all about the team, remember?

When we started testing for the 2007 season Toni was given one of my spare bikes and right from the get-go he was dynamite. Toni actually calls himself Dynamite Bou, the big-head, and never has a sportsman been more aptly named. It's perfect for him. It was suggested at the time, although not by me, that Fuji and I had done all the donkey work with regard to developing the bike and Toni had simply turned up and reaped the benefits. That's true in the sense that the bike was about ready for him and, yes, Fuji and I had done the majority of the work. That could have happened to anybody, though, and had the bike been as it was when we first got it there's a very good chance he'd still have won on it. Toni 'Dynamite' Bou really is that good and, although my days with Montesa Honda were now numbered, I was happy that I was being replaced by such a big talent. The biggest our sport's ever known.

Toni ended up winning a more than impressive nine of the eleven rounds in 2007, giving him the championship by a good margin. I finished a distant fifth I'm afraid, and I'd been warned in June that I'd probably be getting the push some-where along the way. Sure enough, about halfway through the summer break, Montesa Honda told me that as of the end of the season I'd be surplus to requirements. Looking back, I'd actually been warned about this long before June, but it was only after I got the push that I remembered. Colin Edwards, the two-time world superbike champion, had been through a similar thing with Honda a few years previously and, as soon as he stopped winning for them, he was out. 'Nobody is bigger than Honda, Dougie,' he'd said to me, and he was right.

As with the people at Beta, I'd been great friends with everyone at Montesa Honda and for that reason, as much as any other, it was going to be a very hard pill to swallow. One minute I was part of a team – a team full of friends whom I'd enjoyed several years of success with – and the next I was on my own. They were still there, of course, except now they were concentrating on Toni and Fuji. That was the worst bit, I think.

One thing I wasn't ready to do, despite being on a downward spiral with regard to success, was retire. Miguel, my team manager at Montesa Honda, had suggested this as an option after they'd told me I was no longer needed, and I remember me and my dad looking at him as if to say, 'Are you off your head?' As far as I was concerned I was still living the dream. Winning was obviously important, but so was riding a motorbike. Take that away and I'd be left with nothing. I even still enjoyed training, for heaven's sake!

Thanks mainly to Miguel's suggestion of retirement, I began to appreciate the sport again. Naturally, I'd become obsessed with being successful and after getting used to it that had always been my focus. Okay, so I wasn't going to be world champion again. In fact, given the options that were open to me, I was unlikely to get on the podium again. It was time to take stock and after sitting down with Dad I was actually happy with what I was left with: I had a sport that I adored, an enthusiasm that would have served an 18-year-old well, and enough talent and experience to potentially keep me within at least the middle, or even the upper echelons of the sport. There was also a lot less pressure now, so, providing I could find a team that would have me, I thought I'd have a laugh for a couple of years and at the same time maybe bring along some of the younger lads. That was the idea, anyway. All I had to do now was find a team.

After first winning the Scott Trial in 1994 I took 12 years off, for the simple reason I didn't want to injure myself. Being a timed event obviously adds pressure and as a consequence you tend to suffer more injuries. These were obviously my World Championship years and although I'd have been fit enough to ride the Scott, I just couldn't take the chance.

The first year I came back was 2006 and, after winning it fairly comfortably, I decided to have another go in 2007. Bearing in mind the World Championship had just finished, this was going to be my last hurrah with Montesa Honda and a chance to finish on a high. For me, at least. None of the bigwigs at Montesa really cared about the Scott Trial and because I was an outgoing rider, and because the new bike they were developing had a magnesium engine which cost an arm and a leg, I wasn't allowed to use a factory bike. I was disappointed by this as I obviously wanted to give myself the best possible chance of winning, but in the end they came up with an alternative.

At the time we had a female rider at Montesa called Laia Sanz. She was already a seven-time world champion but because she rode a bike with a slightly lower spec it was suggested I use one of hers. Fortunately, Laia agreed to this and the following week it arrived. It was a four-stroke bike that absolutely flew and, as well as having an absolutely cracking day on it, I won the trial by a decent margin. I don't think I'd enjoyed myself as much in ages. The bike did start rattling a bit towards the end, which gave me a worry. I remember it had a really fancy titanium front-to-back exhaust system and by the time we got to the 70th section the brackets had started coming loose and some of them had even fallen off. If the trial had lasted another two or three sections we might have been in trouble. As it was, it was all good, but I'm afraid Laia's bike was never the same again, that is for sure. To be fair, not many bikes are after the Scott. It's the bikes that always take the punishment. Actually, that's complete and utter rubbish, because when I won the Scott Trial on a Gas Gas in 2013, I ended up chopping my little toe off. Some of you might need a sick bucket for this, so if you've got a dicky tummy I suggest you flip a few pages.

I'd been having a really good day and by the time I was on the leg back in I had a right good lead. It wasn't unassailable, not by any stretch of the imagination, but I knew my observation had been good so providing I kept my head down and didn't become too taken by the scenery – which is stunning, by the way – I'd have a good chance of matching Dad's record of winning the Scott Trial and the Scottish Six Days in the same year, twice. If it happened, I'd be straight over to him!

I forget which section it happened on (there are over 70, after all) but it was a hillside that curved around some large limestone rocks and as I went past these rocks I rode into one. It's standard at trials to have a look at a section before you ride it, whereas at the Scott Trial you have a little look to see where the flags are going and just guess the rest, especially towards the end of the day. By then, there are very few marks to follow so it can be quite precarious. It's the same for everyone, though.

I remember riding into a little gap that was next to one of these limestone rocks and after turning slightly left I gave it a massive handful to take me through. As I accelerated, I could feel my foot getting caught by this rock and, despite me giving it loads, it actually slowed me right down. As

my foot became free again I remember feeling this winc-
ing pain. It was agony and, at first, I felt quite faint. I'd
completed the section, though, and with no more than 45
minutes to an hour to go, and the last petrol check coming
up, I decided to crack on. We were riding through a lot of
water by this point and because it was nice and cold I started
dragging my foot through it. This numbed the pain slightly,
but my foot felt absolutely sodden and I honestly couldn't
tell if it was water or blood. It definitely felt funny, though.

Shortly before the final petrol check my cousin Ben came
alongside me. It was strange that he'd caught me up as I'd
been a fair way ahead, so I must have been slowing down
quite a bit.

'What's up with you?' he asked.

'How do you mean?'

'You're weaving all over the place. What's up?'

'I've done something to my foot. It happened a couple of
sections ago. To be honest I don't feel too good.'

We were still riding at this point so I asked James if I
could hang on to the back of him. This was great as I could
watch him do the sections and he was going at a pace that
I could keep up with. I felt terrible, though, and as well as
being in all kinds of pain I was beginning to feel tired and
also slightly disorientated. Fortunately, the finish wasn't far
away. I still felt appalling, though, so the moment I finished
the last section I went straight to the van. The first thing I
did was take off my helmet and I remember my neck was
absolutely killing me. Not as much as my foot, but it was a
lot worse than it usually was. Because of the angle you ride
at, your neck is often quite sore after a trial, but this was on

a different scale. After opening the back doors, I sat down and just lay back. Thank God that was over with, I remember saying to myself. A few minutes later Dad appeared and started asking me how I'd got on.

'How were your points?'

'Fine, I think. Would you mind taking my left boot off, Dad?' I said. 'My foot's absolutely killing me.'

Dad being Dad, he grabbed my boot and started trying to yank it off like you would a pair of muddy wellies.

'Dad, Dad!' I cried. 'You'll have to be a bit more careful than that. I think I've done something to it.'

My God, that stung a bit. Dad didn't really do sensitive and at one point I thought we were going to have to cut the damn thing off.

'Please Dad,' I pleaded. 'Just slide it off as slowly as you can.'

As the boot came over my ankle I realised that the liquid I'd felt since going over the moor had been blood after all. It was absolutely everywhere.

'What the hell have you done?' asked Dad.

'I don't know yet,' I replied. 'You're going to have to take my sock off, Dad.'

The whole sock was blood red and it was dripping all over the place. Dad wasn't keen on taking it off but he had no choice.

'Slowly Dad!' I begged, as he grabbed the hem.

'Don't worry! Right, are you ready? Slowly does it.'

I'm afraid I couldn't watch this and once he'd taken the sock off I remember Dad saying, 'Aaaah. I think we might have a little problem here.'

At this point I made the ridiculous decision to look

downward and the sight that greeted me was like something out of a very graphic horror film. The foot, which was swollen and obviously covered in blood, seemed to have a toe missing.

'I can't see my little toe!' I said in a panic.

'Don't worry, it's still here,' said Dad, grimacing. 'Just!'

After closer inspection it seemed my little toe was hanging on by a bit of skin.

'Oh heck,' I said. 'What are we going to do about that?' I was remarkably calm for some reason. Perhaps I was in shock?

Before Dad could answer, a man from the St John Ambulance arrived.

After having a quick look, he recoiled and took a few steps backward.

'That's a little bit out of my league I'm afraid, gents,' he said, grimacing like Dad had. 'I can dress it, but you'll have to go to hospital.'

'What do you think, Dad?' I said. 'Should I stay for the presentation?'

'It's up to you, Doug,' said Dad. 'What does the ambulance man think?'

'If I were you I'd get straight to hospital,' he advised. 'After all, you have just severed part of a limb!'

Good point.

My time during the trial had been good and my observation excellent, so I knew I was in with a good chance of winning. The pain was still bad, but not being there to collect the trophy had I won would be a heck of a lot worse.

'I'll tell you what,' I said. 'You dress it and as soon as the presentation's over I'll go straight to the hospital.'

'It's entirely up to you,' said St John.

If Dad had thought I should have gone to hospital he'd have said so and the fact that he didn't say anything made me feel better.

'Right then,' I said. 'Dad. Once he's done, will you drive us to the presentation?'

'Well, you're obviously not driving!'

The presentation took place at Richmondshire Cricket Club, which is in the middle of Richmond, and when they announced that I'd won the trial I was absolutely delighted.

'There you go, Dad,' I said, shaking his hand. 'I've matched you. I've won it four times.'

'Aye you have that,' he said, smiling. I could tell he was as proud as anything.

The cheer as I made my way on to the stage was huge and just before I started to make my speech Cousin James shouted, 'All right, Doug, you can stop limping now.' That got a laugh.

I'm not that good at making speeches at the best of times, but with my foot throbbing like a jackhammer it was even shorter than usual.

'Thanks very much,' was about all I managed, so I really whipped the crowd up into a frenzy.

As soon as I was off the stage we went straight to the nearest hospital and, after taking one look at me, the doctor decided to keep me in.

'Can I ask when you did this?' asked one of the nurses.

'Oh, about six hours ago,' I answered honestly. A little bit too honestly.

'Six hours! You should have had this seen to straight away, Mr Lampkin. I just hope we can still save it.'

I must admit this worried me quite a bit, but it was my own fault. I had to look on the bright side, though. I'd won the trial and even if the toe went, I'd still have four left.

In the end they operated on me that night and after cleaning it all up they tried forcing the toe back on. Unfortunately, the bone had been crushed so badly they couldn't save it, so as opposed to having a little toe on the end of my left foot I've got something smaller that just looks a bit like one. It gets in the way sometimes so in hindsight they should have just taken it off.

I bet you're dead glad I told you that story! The things you do for a win, eh?

Funnily enough, one of the first telephone calls I received after leaving Montesa Honda was from Lapo Bianchi at Beta. Hearing his voice again was strange at first as we hadn't left on the best of terms and despite what had happened with Montesa I honestly had no idea why he was calling.

'How are you, Dougie?'

'I'm good thanks,' I said slightly suspiciously. 'How are you?'

After we'd exchanged a few pleasantries and Lapo had commiserated with me about Montesa, he said, 'How would you feel about having another go?'

Since I'd left, Beta had had quite a few different riders and, apart from a few podiums and a couple of wins with a young Toni Bou, they hadn't had a great deal of success. Then, when Toni went to Montesa, they'd started focusing more on the enduro market, but according to Lapo they wanted to concentrate on both. Although I wasn't as success-ful as I used to be, I was still a popular rider on the circuit and with such a strong association with Beta it made sense for them to ask me back. That's not arrogance. As their most recent world champion I was ideal, and when Lapo asked me I bit his hand off. I knew we weren't going to be that competitive, but when Lapo made me the offer and told me I was still one of the family, it felt like I was coming home. I was certainly coming full circle. John was also the Beta importer still, so with him and me still being as thick as thieves, there weren't many negatives.

One thing I noticed immediately when I went back to Beta was the difference in pressure. Success had been almost obligatory at Montesa Honda and in order to maintain that success they'd needed to apply pressure almost constantly. You only realise what that does to you once you're away from it and after a few weeks at Beta I felt like a different man. I'm not saying I didn't miss the pressure a bit. I did. There was also pressure at Beta, of course. I may have been a favourite with the fans and at the factory, but I was also there to help the company progress. The difference was that, in addition to Beta not having a Honda breathing down their necks, they measured their success differently. If Montesa Honda hadn't won the World Championship it would have been an absolute disaster, whereas if Beta, Gas Gas or any of the other manufacturers had won just one of them it would have been classed as a triumph. I don't suppose much has changed today, really. For the last ten years Repsol Montesa, as they're now known, have won everything with Toni Bou and if they suddenly stopped winning, even for a year, there'd be a massive inquest. When you're that big it's impossible to be happy with less.

Funnily enough, I did have an early scare in my second spell at Beta and it involved a little bit of déjà vu.

When I started testing with them they brought along the four-stroke bike they'd been working on and, just like the Montesa 250, it was miles away.

'Sorry lads!' I said. 'I'm not going through that again! Not at the moment, anyway. It's the two-stroke or nothing for me.'

As it was, the two-stroke also took a fair bit of adapting and it had definitely suffered due to the number of different riders it had had on it. It was a good clubman bike, but it wasn't at the top level. The power was absolutely first class, which was typical of Beta, but the clutch was a bit iffy, as was the suspension, so there was definitely a bit of work to be done.

My new teammate at Beta was the aforementioned Jeroni Fajardo and I spent quite a lot of time helping him. That was another difference at Beta: instead of there being any competitive barriers between the two riders, they had a number-one rider and a junior. This meant that we were all in it together and everyone helped everyone else. In that respect, it was more like Montesa had been while we'd been testing the four-stroke. That was fine with me and the atmosphere it helped to create was excellent.

In terms of results, I think the best way of describing my first season back with Beta would be 'peppering around the podium'. It was fourths and sixths mainly and, despite being there or thereabouts, the difference between me and the regular top three was marked. If I was ever going to get on the podium again, which was probably the extent of my ambitions at Beta, I'd need a repeat of what had happened in Portugal in 2005 and a bit more.

By this time the rules had changed and you were only allowed one minder. This too was like going full circle as it was just me and my dad again. But as time went on it became clear that our attitudes had changed. Dad was a bit older, as was I, and because we'd achieved everything we set out to, and more, the fire in our bellies had lost a few flames. Now, instead of looking at the sections and saying, 'It's a bit rough early on but you'll walk it, Doug,' as Dad used to, he would call me over and say, 'I'm not sure I like the look of this, Doug.' With the sections getting bigger (or was it us getting older and smaller?), our confidence was definitely on the wane, and instead of concentrating on what we *could* do, like we should have been, we'd started concentrating on what we couldn't do, and the first thing we did now when we looked at a section before a round was to work out where I might come a cropper. I'm all for self-preservation, but at the end of the day I was a professional trials rider and my first consideration shouldn't have been how I was going to avoid an accident. It should have been how I was going to clear the section. It'd been a long time since Dad had minded me alone and I think he was nervous as to whether he could still do it. He could, of course, but not like he used to. That summed us up perfectly at that point. We could still do it, but not like we used to.

CHAPTER 14

As Mad as a Lord March Hare

Early 2008 saw the birth of not only our youngest son Fraiser, who arrived in April without any of the hoo-ha we had when Alfie was born, but what has become my post-competitive career, although I certainly didn't know it at the time. Incidentally, Alfie weighed in at a hefty nine pounds when he was born, and Fraiser was only a few ounces less. Not surprisingly, Nicola still winces whenever it's mentioned. I suppose the initial seed for what happened after I gave up competing in the World Outdoor Championship – i.e. the Red Bull stunts such as Dougie's Wheelie and the Tundra Trial – had been planted when Red Bull first contacted me back in 2000 about a helmet deal. Although they weren't the ones who came up with the idea of doing stunts (that, believe it or not, came from a member of the British aristocracy who I'll come on to in a moment), they were certainly keen on shaking things up a bit and some of the suggestions they made about staging events were creative to say the least.

The person who first suggested I transfer my skills on a motorbike from trials to pure entertainment was Lord March, owner of Goodwood House and the man behind the Goodwood Revival and the Goodwood Festival of Speed. He called me up one day in early 2008 and asked me if I'd like to take part in the Festival of Speed. Bearing in mind I rarely went above 10 miles an hour, I was somewhat taken aback by this. But the Goodwood Festival of Speed is one of the biggest events in the motorsport calendar, so I was definitely up for a chat. When I asked Lord March what he wanted me to do at the festival I thought it was a wind-up.

'I want you to ride your motorbike around Goodwood House,' he said.

'How do you mean?' I asked. 'You mean around the grounds?'

'Yes, them too. But first I want you to ride around the inside of the house. The rooms and the staircases. Even the roof.'

At first, I thought, *Lord or not, this bloke's off his rocker.* After all, everything inside Goodwood House was probably antique and worth a fortune. Did he really want a great northern lump like me tearing through his ballroom and up his staircases on a trials bike?

It appeared he did!

After agreeing in principle to Lord March's idea and then suggesting that he might like to have a sit-down in a darkened room for a while, Jake arranged to go down and meet him. Once there, Lord March took Jake around Goodwood House and showed him where he'd like me to ride.

'For a start, I want him to ride up this staircase, through

that door and around my private photographic studio,' said Lord March.

It should be 'March Hare' really, as in, mad as a!

According to Jake the stair carpet, which was on runners, was obviously antique, so he suggested taking it up beforehand.

'I don't think that'll be necessary,' said Lord March.

'Okay, well, what about all the vases?' said Jake.

Apparently, there were vases everywhere and some of them were even older than my Uncle Arthur. They weren't quite as valuable, though.

'No, no. That's the whole point,' explained Lord March. 'I want Dougie to ride around Goodwood House in its natural state.'

In truth, Lord March wasn't mad at all. He just liked a laugh and a bit of a challenge and he knew exactly what he was doing. At the end of the day, trials bikes only weigh about 70 kilograms and because the tyres are dead soft there shouldn't be any damage. Providing, of course, I didn't hit anything! I obviously couldn't guarantee that, but Lord March didn't seem bothered and so that June, Jake and I made our way down to Goodwood in my van with a bike in the back and a whacking great insurance policy.

Timing-wise, this couldn't have been better. My competitive career had obviously peaked and to be honest with you I wasn't sure what I was going to do. Perhaps riding around stately homes and across people's roofs was where my future lay? If so, why not? It was better than working for a living.

To promote the fact that I would be appearing at the 2008 Goodwood Festival of Speed, which was taking place in July, and to promote Goodwood itself and what it had to offer, Lord March had asked me to come down beforehand and shoot a promotional video with me riding around the estate. All of it! The resulting film was entitled *Dougie Lampkin v Goodwood House* and featured me, Lord March, Lord March's butler, Chris Barrie (from *Red Dwarf* and *The Brittas Empire*) and two scrawny-looking car lads called Jenson Button and Lewis Hamilton. They were at Goodwood filming a promotional video for the new McLaren road car and Lord March had roped them in. The story, such as it was, had me trying to find Jenson and Lewis and in doing so I explored Goodwood House, the grounds, the racecourse, the hotel, the golf course and the old circuit on my trusty trials bike.

One of the first scenes I remember filming was me coming down a staircase on my front wheel with Sir Stirling Moss, who had a cameo role, stood at the bottom. Believe me, that was a very surreal moment! Next, after the butler had opened the door for me, I rode into one of the living rooms and rested my front wheel on a sofa where somebody was reading a newspaper. The person reading the paper just ignored me, as they wanted to give the impression that it was normal for me to be riding a bike around the house.

The people who were in charge of looking after the house (they must have been the housekeepers) weren't quite as laid-back as Lord March and every time I went near something valuable they all turned away in horror. Lord March, on the other hand, who I'm pleased to say has since become a good friend of mine, just stood there beaming. He was in his element!

It was the roof next and after doing wheelies from one end to the other, the butler suddenly appears with a bottle of champagne and a glass on a silver tray.

'A glass of champagne, sir?' he says.

'Yes please,' says I and after having a quick sip I carry on.

The only thing that was in danger of spoiling the film was that Lord March and I both had a few lines to speak and although he's obviously a born thespian, I am certainly not. To be fair to Lord March, he has quite a few different lines in the film and after watching it back again he's quite convincing. I, on the other hand, have just one line and despite having to repeat it several times it doesn't get any better.

The line was, 'Where are they?', as in Jenson and Lewis, which I deliver to Lord March and other people in various different locations. I sound like a Dalek.

Me: 'Where – are – they?'

Lord March: 'I've no idea, Dougie?'

After riding around the grounds and terrifying the gardener, we changed location and went down to the racecourse. On the way down there, some absolute idiot suggested that I ride across the roof of the main grandstand at the racecourse and some even bigger idiot, i.e. me, agreed. For some reason, I'd assumed that it would be similar to riding on the roof at Goodwood House, but I was wrong. Very wrong! The main grandstand at Goodwood racecourse is about 60 metres high and just as I was setting off I had a bit of a panic attack. I was shaking like a leaf and I thought, *I've got to park this for a minute.* After getting off the bike, everyone involved with the film started appearing at the escape hatch to see what was wrong.

'Are you okay, mate?' asked Jake.

'I will be in a second,' I said. 'I've just got an attack of the shakes.'

'This hasn't happened before,' said my concerned manager.

'I've never ridden sixty metres in the air before!' I replied.

After asking for a drink, a can of Red Bull arrived, which, given the circumstances, was exactly what I needed. After downing it in one I took a deep breath, got back on the bike and set off again. When the director eventually shouted 'Cut' I was so relieved. I'm not normally scared of heights. You can't be if you're a trials rider. This was on a different scale, though, and it was like riding my bike on the wing of a massive aircraft.

By the way, don't get any ideas, Red Bull. The answer's no!

Next up was the Goodwood Hotel. I was supposed to deliver my line to the manager, but instead of using the real manager they managed to persuade Chris Barrie to replace him. I have absolutely no idea what he was doing there but at least he could act. This was obviously the comedy section because as I ride off around the hotel looking for Jenson and Lewis, shouting 'Where – are – they?', Chris chases me and tries to chuck me out.

There's a scene in this section where a woman is having a massage and after charging in on my bike I pull my front wheel up and rest it on her shoulder. I'm not sure what the director was thinking here. It's a bit of an invasion of privacy if you ask me and makes me look a bit suspect!

After that we're off to the pool area. After riding around the swimming pool and jumping some of the loungers, I hide in the sauna. Then, when Chris Barrie finds me, I ride out straight into the swimming pool. Just me, though. Not the bike!

Comedy section over, it was off to the Goodwood circuit next which is where they hold the Goodwood Revival, another massive event. This is where Jenson and Lewis had been based all day, so once they'd finished filming for McLaren they were ready for the main event. After riding around the circuit for a bit and climbing over a few Land Rovers, I eventually find Lewis and Jenson, who are supposedly being interviewed. After doing wheelies around them for a minute or so they get up and shake my hand as if they'd been expecting me. I bet they were thinking, *Who the heck's this berk?* Anyway, the lads did reasonably well considering they drove cars for a living and after that it was 'a wrap', as I believe they say in the film industry. I don't think Jenson and Lewis were too keen on appearing in our video, as the moment the director said 'Cut' they were off in their helicopters, never to be seen again. How the other half live.

Just before we filmed this last bit I'd been doing massive front-wheel wheelies right up to the McLaren road car and the mechanics were all crapping themselves. 'If Ron Dennis sees this he'll sack us all!' one of them shouted. 'Give over,' I reassured them. 'It's only a car.'

The only bit that didn't make it into the final cut was the golf section, which went down like a lead balloon in some quarters and caused quite a bit of trouble. They've got a fabulous golf course at Goodwood and after we'd finished filming at the racecourse we went up there to do the same. Being a keen golfer, I was naturally very respectful of the course but not everybody appreciated my efforts and a few days later Lord March received a letter. Peter Alliss's daughter had been working at Goodwood at the time and had obviously reported my exploits to her father. He, in turn, had written a letter to Lord March conveying his disgust at there being a motorcycle on the golf course and requesting that all the relevant scenes be removed from the final film. To be fair, I actually agreed with Peter Alliss. It was a bad idea and all he did was flag it up. It was another claim to fame, though. How many people do you know who've been reprimanded by the great Peter Alliss? It's one to tell the grandkids.

About a month later we chipped up again for the festival itself, but this time, instead of riding everywhere and over everything, I was only required to repeat what I'd done on the roof and perform a few tricks in the grounds.

Since 2008 I've done every year at Goodwood and it's become a very important date in my calendar. I've done demonstrations down there and as well as riding on the roof of the house most years (not the racecourse!), which is right in front of the crowd, I've even ridden during the ball, which is held on the Saturday night. Lord March usually comes up with the ideas and providing I think they're doable, and it doesn't involve me having to act, I'll give it a go. Riding at the ball is a right laugh, though, and because it's dead posh and I'm not, it's the only way I can get an invite. I even rode my bike on a stage to music during the ball one year, which was interesting. Motorbike dancing. Now there's an idea.

The only time my presence has resulted in some actual damage – damage that Lord March is aware of, at least – was in 2010 when I was riding around his private lawn. This area is always taken by Cartier and it's probably the poshest part of the Goodwood Festival. Usually, Lord March has me bunny-hopping over a few people. It's a bit dangerous, I suppose, as a lot of them are tanked up, but at Goodwood anything goes. As I was riding over these posh people I suddenly spied this really ornate wall on the far side of the lawn and it gave me an idea. I know, I thought, I can bunny-hop off that over the garden. That'll wow 'em!

Best laid plans and all that.

As I rode up on to this wall it just disintegrated and the next thing I knew I was lying in a flowerbed wondering what the hell had happened. That wall had probably been there for centuries and I'd just destroyed it. At least it gave them all a good laugh. Luckily, Lord March also saw the funny side and so instead of being escorted off the premises with a builder's invoice in my top pocket I went off to find Nicola and the boys, who'd been invited as guests of Lord March. I eventually found Nicola in the champagne tent (where else?) and asked her where the boys were.

'I'm not sure,' she said. 'They were here a minute ago.'

Bearing in mind we were in the poshest part of Goodwood, and with the poshest people, I was a little bit nervous and, as I looked around to see where they were, I suddenly saw some human-shaped things in a nearby tree. It was them!

'Oh my God,' I said, putting my head in my hands. My children were actually climbing a tree next to the Cartier Lawn at Goodwood! I couldn't believe it.

As I made my way over to extract them from the tree I realised that they weren't alone. At first, I thought it must have been Lord March up there with them, but as I got closer I realised it was two other children. There was also a man standing at the bottom of the tree, so he must have been telling them off. Oh, the embarrassment! When I got to about 20 feet from the tree I realised that the man seemed quite familiar. Then, when I was about 10 feet away, I realised that it was actually Bear Grylls!

'Erm, is everything okay?' I said.

'Ah, these two must be yours,' said Mr Grylls.

'That's right,' I said. 'Are you trying to get them all down?'

'No! I'm teaching them how to climb. My two are up there with them.'

I thought, *Well, if the Chief Scout's okay with it, so am I.*

I just left them to it.

It was a bizarre situation, though, if you think about it. The wife was in the champagne tent knocking them back, I was on a trials bike jumping over aristocrats and destroying ornate walls and my two children were in a tree being taught to climb by Bear Grylls! You couldn't make it up. It was just a normal day in the Lampkin household, really.

Almost everything I've done since that first appearance at Goodwood, whether it be riding through a new shopping centre in Kuwait or around the Red Bull Formula 1 factory (that one's had over 10 million views on YouTube), is a result of Lord March's invitation. Well, at least we've got someone to blame!

Another thing that happened as a result of my exploits at Goodwood was doing *Top Gear Live*, which I did for a few years with the classic line-up of Clarkson, May and Hammond. I'm not sure if it's still going, but it used to be a rolling roadshow and went to Dublin, Birmingham and London, and we did about a week at each. Before setting off on this tour, everyone would spend weeks rehearsing and everything was done to absolute military precision. Part of my involvement in the show was a skit with the JCB demonstration team and involved me being chased around the arenas by a machine they'd made for the military. It weighed about 10 tons this thing and was absolutely enormous! There were scrap cars all over the shop and I had to ride over these cars before the JCB flattened them. It was obviously very well-rehearsed, but I always managed to scale them just before they were flattened. It's actually quite exciting and the kids especially absolutely loved it. The pièce de résistance of this part of the show involved me jumping off the bonnet of one of these scrap cars and into the front bucket of this monster before riding on to the bonnet, then the roof and then jumping off. Easy! Everyone had earpieces in, so if you needed to speed up or were doing anything wrong, the organisers could tell you.

The first time we ever did this in front of an audience was at Ally Pally in London. All the press were there and so everyone was a bit nervous. The first five minutes went perfectly and literally half a second after I rode off these scrap cars the JCB would flatten them. By the time we got to the finale I was buzzing as the noise from the crowd had been immense. But, as I went to jump into the bucket of the JCB, I suddenly realised that it wasn't slowing down like it should have. I was committed, though, and there was no abort button to press. Instead of landing in the JCB's bucket before scaling it heroically and then soaking up the applause,

I fell off and landed on the floor. My bike made it into the bucket okay, but all you could see was the front wheel dangling out. The next thing I remember, as I tried to get my bearings, was hearing voices.

'Dougie. Dougie. Are you there, Dougie? Speak to us. Speak to us, Dougie.'

It was the choreographer.

I obviously couldn't answer him verbally as the radios were one-way, so instead I stood up, climbed on to the bonnet of the car and then jumped into the bucket. It was like something out of *The Professionals*. Just then, I could hear the choreographer in my earpiece.

'Oh my God,' he said. 'It looks like we're going to carry on!'

Too flaming right we were.

The crowd were going absolutely bonkers by this point and I felt like Superman. After picking up my bike I kick-started it before giving the driver of the JCB a heroic thumbs-up. He must have been absolutely papping himself as he obviously thought he'd killed me. The look on his face was a picture. Sheer relief! Afterwards, we did some interviews with the press and they all thought it was part of the show. I wasn't going to tell them otherwise. I was in all kinds of pain, though. I didn't really feel much at the time of the accident (I was too busy being heroic), but by the time we spoke to the press my back and ribs were killing me and the following morning they were black and blue. I didn't say anything, though. You can't when you're being brilliant. You just have to crack on.

The *Top Gear* presenters were great fun but the only

one who was really a bike man was James May. He used to arrive on a different bike almost every day and we used to talk for hours about them. Despite being aware of just how popular the TV show was, I was still surprised by the number of people these shows attracted. There were literally tens of thousands of people every single day and the buzz it created was just incredible. It was a privilege to be part of something as big and successful as that, but it was also a great opportunity. After all, how often do we trials riders get to promote our sport in front of new audiences? We're not exactly swimming in opportunities, are we? That's one of the best things about Goodwood and the relationship with Red Bull. The stunts I do with Red Bull are seen by millions of people all around the world, people who would never normally watch a trial or might not even be aware of the sport. You've got to keep flying the flag! The fact that I can make a living out of it is obviously a massive bonus, but it's not why I do it. I do it because it makes me look good occasionally.

In terms of my trial riding, by the time 2009 came along I wasn't enjoying training any more and for the first time in my life I felt like I was making up the numbers. I also had other interests now. As well as mixing things up with a bit of extreme enduro, my relationship with Red Bull was going great guns and because of Goodwood I was being invited to ride in all kinds of strange places. I was, without doubt, the elder statesman of motorcycle trials and the opportunities that this was now throwing at me were new and exciting. As a former world champion, I also missed being the centre of attention. There's no two ways about it. And with Red Bull and Goodwood, in particular, that was given to me in spades. I was allowed to rest on my laurels for a change and enjoy my past successes. In the World Championship you were only ever as good as your last win.

There were two highlights during my last two years with Beta and they came in the shape of two podium finishes: one at Carlisle in May 2009, where I got two 20s and finished behind Toni Bou and Adam Raga; and one at Fort William in 2010, where I got 38 points and finished second behind Toni Bou. Who else? The god of trials was certainly on my side that day. I'm not saying it was a fluke exactly, but I definitely had a little bit of luck along the way. And why not? We seniors deserve a bit of a windfall occasionally.

Towards the end of 2010 Beta started asking me what I wanted to do. They were keen for me to do less trials and more extreme enduro, but despite what I've just said about being the elder statesman there was still a part of me that wanted to continue riding the World Championship. This was obviously misguided, but to be honest, I just couldn't let go. Ninety per cent of me wanted to go and soak up the applause at Goodwood and work on some challenges with Red Bull, but that 10 per cent of me that wanted to carry on competing in trials was still as gobby as hell and a bit of extreme enduro just wasn't good enough.

Over the years I'd read about dozens of sportspeople finding it difficult to retire and, to be honest, I'd always assumed it was more about money than anything else. They'd carried on the lifestyle after the money had gone and this was the result. Now, I knew differently. Success is a drug, there's no two ways about it, and even if there's just a morsel of a chance of you regaining some of that former glory, it's very difficult to turn down. Consequently, when I was approached by Adam Raga about working with him at Gas Gas at the end of 2010, three years after rejoining Beta, I couldn't resist. I think Lapo Bianchi had been on the verge of letting me go, so when I got a call from the owner of Gas Gas saying, 'We've got a three-year plan and I want you to come to Spain as soon as possible,' I was there – as soon as possible!

It's hard to overestimate the effect it has when somebody calls you up and tells you that you're wanted, especially when you're on the verge of being let go. It was obvious that history was repeating itself again, but because Gas Gas weren't Beta or Montesa Honda there was no baggage, so I had to say yes.

When Jake and I went for lunch with them all a couple of weeks later they treated me like a king and I fully admit that I loved absolutely every second of it. The elder statesman was still considered to be a potential force by some people and who was I to argue? Isn't it funny how much control your ego has over you?

By the way, one of the main reasons Gas Gas had taken me on, which became apparent over the lunch, was because they wanted me to help Adam Raga improve as a trials rider. They also suggested that I become the team manager of the trials team, so the agreement itself was multidimensional. It was fresh and it was new. Just what I needed.

I was back at the Scottish Six Days (SSDT) in 2011, leading the trial on my new Gas Gas, when, on the Thursday, I tried to jump a gap on one of the sections. In hindsight, this was a really bad idea and after failing to clear the gap I ended up landing awkwardly. At first, I thought I was okay, but when I tried putting pressure on my left ankle I realised straight away that I was anything but. I'd obviously done it a lot of damage and when I tried walking on it I fell flat on my backside. I tried carrying on, but it was no good and on the Friday, after trying everything under the sun, I had to retire. To this day, it's the biggest mistake I've ever made at a trial and it was the first time I'd had to retire at a big event. I cannot begin to tell you how distraught I was. I was leading my all-time favourite event, so to do something so careless was, in my eyes, almost unforgivable. Needless to say, I absolutely hate riding that section now and the sigh of relief that I breathe after completing it could inflate a bouncy castle.

Shortly after that I went to the opening round of the World Outdoor Championship in Germany and I was still really struggling. In fact, I shouldn't have been there at all. Subsequently, I ended up missing the French round and when I arrived in Pobladura de las Regueras for the Spanish round I was told in no uncertain terms that I wouldn't be riding.

'Look at you. You're not fit,' said Dad.

He was right. I was there out of desperation, really.

'Come on Doug,' he said. 'I think it's time to let go. Don't you?'

It obviously wasn't the end I'd been hoping for, but in hindsight it was probably a godsend. That noisy 10 per cent that had been keeping me in competition had been showing no signs of quietening down and I fully admit now that it needed shutting up once and for all. I could still do a bit of extreme enduro if I fancied getting my hands dirty and I could always compete in the Scott and the Scottish Six Days. Providing I didn't end up knackering my ankle!

The British round of the 2011 World Outdoor Championship, which was being staged by the dynamic duo – Dad and Jake as they were also known – took place in Fort William and even though I was still badly injured it was suggested, by Dad I think, that I might want to think about taking part as a bit of a swansong. Fort William is obviously where the SSDT starts and finishes and, as that was really my home as far as trials was concerned, I thought, *Why not?* Once they'd finished strapping my ankle up just prior to the start I tried walking on it and I must have looked like Frankenstein's monster.

'Are you all right, Doug?' asked Dad. 'You reckon you're good to go?'

'Of course I am, Dad,' I said. 'Providing they can find a big enough boot.'

Looking back, I'm so glad I took part in that round at Fort William and although I only came eighth, which I was sickened with at the time, that wasn't really the point. It was symbolic and for a far more significant reason than the one I've just mentioned above. It only actually occurred to me when me and Dad walked away from the last section, but this had been about us and the hundreds of trials and thousands upon thousands of miles we'd travelled together.

There's a video on YouTube of me riding the fourth section of the first lap at Fort William and Dad's loving every single minute of it. I'd almost forgotten how loud he could be when he was minding for me. It was impossible not to hear him.

'Thirty left, so nice and high. Yes, nice there. Fifteen. We're in it. WE'RE IN IT!'

He was like a foghorn.

This wasn't just my swansong. It was Dad's too. He'd been there at the start and he was there right at the very end. That's what mattered that day. Not the location or where I finished. That was immaterial. I was with my dad.

CHAPTER 15

No Cheating, Dougie!

One of the hardest things I've ever done in my life is cycle from Chorley to Nice for charity, which I did in August 2013. A very good friend of mine called Paul Dixon had lost a child the previous year at just 16 weeks of age and he wanted to raise some money for the hospice where he'd died. Poor little Harry had been born with a terminal illness and when he passed away everyone was absolutely devastated. Paul, who I'd ridden club trials with when I was a kid, had been a mad keen cyclist most of his life and he'd been badgering Jake and me to go with him for ages. Because of the absence of an engine I'd always declined Paul's offer, but when he approached us about doing a ride to Nice for the hospice, we were naturally a bit more responsive. Actually, that's not strictly true. The first time Paul asked Jake about it he said it was to celebrate his fortieth birthday and so Jake had said that we'd meet him in Nice after flying there by easyJet! A few weeks later his wife had told Jake that he wanted to raise some money too and so after that we took a different view. In hindsight I wish I'd just handed him a blank cheque and told him to do his worst!

We started training for the ride in October 2012 and would meet once a week in Settle. After knackering ourselves for an hour or two we'd then find a pub and have fish and chips or a burger and pile back on what we'd just lost. We started off doing about 30 or 40 miles and then built it up gradually. The distance from Chorley to Nice is about a thousand miles if you go the sensible route, but Paul wanted to go via the Alps and through Geneva. This was going to turn it from being an eight- or nine-day trip into a twelve-day trip, and despite being relatively fit I'd started having nightmares about it. Big nightmares!

As well as going the silly route, Paul also wanted us all to travel with a pair of flip-flops and a bag each but Jake was having none of it. We were going with a support crew or we weren't going at all. In the end two friends of ours, Ian Weatherill and Simon Sharp at Hope Technology, who are a bike component manufacturer based in Barnoldswick, lent us a van and a member of staff called Nick Owen (who would eventually come and work for me) to follow us down there, and once that was sorted out I felt a bit better about things. They also gave us a bike each which was absolutely tremendous, so we were in danger of actually doing this if we weren't careful!

By the time we were ready to set off we'd raised over £30,000. That was obviously a cracking achievement but it was still dependent on the task that lay ahead of us. If anything was going to keep us going, though, that was definitely it and I don't mind admitting that for the first few days I had to call on that fact more than once.

The route itself went through Belgium and then down the east side of France, and each day had been planned out meticulously as to exactly how many miles we rode and where we stayed. Somebody had said to us all that if we could get through the first four or five days we'd walk it from then on. What they didn't say was how bad the first four or five days were going to be! Riding through Belgium was an absolute nightmare because, as well as doing about 120 miles a day on some of the most boring roads in Europe, it was also chucking it down most of the time. I remember us all hiding behind a wall at about 2pm one day, trying to shelter from the rain, and then all of a sudden Jake appears with the itinerary. He was the man with the plan, by the way, and so we were all following him.

'If we carry on at the same pace we have been, we'll get to our hotel at about 6pm.'

Now, bearing in mind we'd been riding since 8am, this went down like the proverbial lead balloon.

'We can't!' I said.

'Sorry, but we have to,' said Jake.

That four hours was purgatory. There's no other word for it.

The following day we were riding into a headwind and so while Jake wasn't looking I dropped back behind the van. The slipstream was exactly what I needed and for about 200 metres I hardly pedalled at all. It didn't take him long to suss me out, though, and as soon as he found me I got a dressing-down.

'No cheating, Dougie!' said Chairman Jake.

'It's not really cheating,' I said. 'I'm just taking advantage of a turbulent flow!'

'Get back in front of this van, now!'

'Yes boss.'

It was a good try.

We had a Facebook page which was being updated daily with photos and a blog, so Jake made sure we did everything absolutely by the book.

'We're open to scrutiny,' he said. 'And I don't want any repercussions.'

Typical manager. Belt and braces! He was right, though. If we were going to do it, we were going to do it properly, and so once I'd been reprimanded that became the norm. When we stopped of an evening, if we had to drive a bit to the hotel we'd always start off again at exactly the same point where we'd stopped. We never gained so much as a metre.

By the time we got into northern France things hadn't changed much, really. The roads were long and flat and whenever we came to the brow of a hill hoping for something a bit different we seemed to be invariably disappointed. Also, I'm not sure if grit is poisonous or not but I must have eaten a ton of the stuff on the first few days. It's not pleasant.

Sure enough, after about five days of unbridled purgatory the pain began to lift a bit and by the time we got to Lake Geneva some of us were in danger of actually enjoying ourselves, me included. Unfortunately, and this was probably inevitable given our collective characters, this change in fortunes lulled us into a false sense of security, and as we approached the beautiful town of Val d'Isère, I was ready for a sherbet. The following morning, after polishing off a few bottles of wine and several crates of beer, we emerged from the hotel feeling a little bit worse for wear. Jake didn't, though. He hadn't had a drop and had been warning us about the consequences of our actions all evening.

'You do realise we've still got three days to go,' he said. 'That's hundreds of miles.'

'It's only a couple,' I said, raising a glass. 'We'll be fine.'

We weren't fine. Were we heck as like.

The first few miles that day were a mountain road and I swear to God that as we were attempting to scale this thing we were overtaken by an old woman riding one of those electric bikes. That was probably one of the most demoralising moments of my entire life and it haunted me for the rest of the journey.

Later that day the drive shaft broke in the van, which meant we no longer had a support vehicle. This was a very strange feeling, really, and then when it started piddling down we all feared the worst. There were an awful lot of other cyclists around and because the weather was so bad they'd all packed up for the day and were passing us in their support vehicles! The road was like a river at this point and they must have thought we were lunatics. When we eventually got to our hotel, which was crap by the way, I got on with washing everyone else's riding gear while Jake wrote the blog and posted the photos. That's right. Dougie Lampkin MBE – 12-time world trials champion and Crown Prince of Silsden – had to wash everyone's mucky riding gear every single day. How the not-very-mighty had fallen!

By the time we got to the last day I think we'd all become quite emotional. It had been one hell of a journey and because we'd all been as naive and as rubbish as each other at the start we'd become a proper team. There'd been no bickering or cross words. Just laughs and camaraderie. We'd bonded, if you like, and those 12 days on the road had given us all a very similar experience. What surprised me most was the enormous sense of achievement I felt. It was unlike anything I'd experienced before, even winning a World Championship, and all I can put that down to is the fact that it was something I wasn't sure I could do. I didn't even own a pushbike when we first agreed to do it and had never really ridden one as an adult. Ten months later and I was just a few miles away from Nice having cycled over a thousand with some pals. Who'd have thought it?

As we rode into Nice the atmosphere among the riders was celebratory to say the least. Our families had all flown over to meet us, and as we reminisced about the previous 12 days and routinely took the rise out of each other, we totally forgot that it was all about to come to an end. In fact, I think we'd all have happily gone on for a few days. We were due to finish the trip on the Promenade des Anglais, which runs along the seafront in Nice, and when we finally turned on to it and realised where we were everyone fell silent. Our families were just a few hundred metres away but as much as we were looking forward to seeing them they weren't what we were thinking about. We were thinking about young Harry and we were thinking about what we'd achieved together. It had come about because of a tragedy – the worst tragedy that can befall a parent – yet it had all been so massively positive.

I wanted to hold on to that feeling for a bit which is why I slowed down. I honestly didn't want it to end.

Because of the number of cars on the road we decided to ride the last few metres on the pavement and scattered a few locals and tourists. I enjoyed that bit.

Our families and friends gave us all a very warm welcome and seeing them all brought us back to reality. Okay, maybe I did want to go home! In the end, we only had two or three hours together before commitments back in England or wherever started pulling people away. Jake was hammered after just two beers. That's what I remember most about the end!

So, did I carry on cycling?

Well, what do you think?

No, of course I didn't. It's too knackering. I like an engine on my bikes.

About two months after returning from Nice, just as the feeling in my legs was starting to return, the subject of one or two heated conversations between Nicola and me began to rear its ugly head again. Basically, Nicola wanted a dog. I think she was after an ally, really, as living in a house with three males can't be easy. When she first suggested it to the boys they were all over the idea and so the next step had been to try to persuade me.

'No flaming way are we getting a dog,' was my response. And although it went down like a lead balloon, I stuck to my guns.

'But I want a bit of company,' argued Nicola. 'You're always away and with the boys at school I'm on my own a lot. I want something to walk.'

'N – O spells no! We're not having a dog, Nicola, and that's final.'

Despite being mild-mannered I can actually be quite masterful when I want to be.

I've never been a fan of dogs, though, and as much as Nicola and the boys wanted one, I just couldn't get my head around the idea. Whenever I've been away for a few days I look forward to coming home and the last thing I wanted to see when I opened the front door is a four-legged licking machine lolloping towards me. Nicola's bad enough!

Unbeknown to me, my dear wife had taken about as much notice of my strict doggy ban as I took of her whenever she moaned about me leaving the toilet seat up. Fair do's. So, while I was going about my business and not thinking about dogs, she was on the internet researching the perfect one. God only knows how she arrived at the decision, but she told me later on that after doing some research she'd found out that the perfect dog for a family like ours was a Hungarian Vizsla. What on earth she meant by 'a family like ours' I've absolutely no idea, but without further ado she went back online and started finding some breeders. I was blissfully unaware of all this, of course, and when Nicola told my mum what she had planned, it was game over. For me, that is.

My mother is a dog fanatic and when Nicola voiced her concerns to Mum about what I'd said about having a dog, Mum dismissed this outright. 'Don't take any notice of Dougie. It's nothing to do with him. If you want a dog Nicola, get one!'

'Okay then, I will!'

This was sister power in action and within a few days Nicola had set her sights on a puppy in the north of Scotland. The following week she and Mum arranged to have a look at this creature and on the way they phoned me. I was away testing in Spain at the time and when my phone went I assumed it was Nicola.

'What's up, love?'

'Dougie, it's your mother,' said the voice at the other end. 'We've got you on hands-free. Nicola and I are driving to Scotland.'

'Eh? What do you mean you're driving to Scotland?'

'Exactly that. We're driving to Scotland.'

'We're going to look at a dog,' said Nicola firmly.

'No you're not!' I said, even more firmly. 'I've told you a hundred times, Nicola. We are not having a dog!'

The silence that followed my command was deafening and I had a funny feeling that I might have overstepped the mark. My mother is a formidable woman and I knew that if I'd been there with her she'd have found a duck pond immediately.

'We're not asking you, Dougie,' Mum said slowly. And quite scarily, to be fair.

'We're telling you.'

Before I could say anything else (not that I would have) the phone went dead and, as I sat there whinging to myself, Mum and Nicola drove on to bonnie Scotland triumphant. They'd won, I'd lost and that was the end of it. A couple of weeks later we all piled into the van and went to collect this hound. When Nicola told me how much we were paying for her I almost drove into a bloody wall.

'HOW MUCH? Is a dog really worth that much money?' I asked her.

'This one is,' she said, being firm again. 'She's called Minnie, by the way.'

It wasn't as bad as her Louis Vuitton handbag, but it was bad enough. I didn't dare take it any further, though, because I knew she'd get Mum involved and that was the last thing I wanted. I might be brave, but I'm not stupid.

CHAPTER 16

What a Bloody
Stupid Idea, Doug!

Despite the following event taking place over a year ago, in September 2016, it's still the subject of about seven different nightmares for me and, once you've read the following two chapters and have hopefully watched the accompanying documentary, you'll understand why.

The thing I find hardest to understand, even now, isn't how I succeeded in wheelieing a customised trials bike around the entire Isle of Man TT course – all 37.7 miles of it – but how I came up with the idea in the first place. For a start, I'd always been notoriously bad at wheelieing and had never managed more than a few yards before. It was like somebody with a fear of heights suggesting they have a go at climbing Mount Everest. But, as bad as I was, nobody I knew had ever wheelied more than a few hundred yards before and so what on earth possessed me to even suggest attempting anything on one wheel, let alone the Isle of Man TT course, is completely beyond me. A momentary lapse of reason, you might say. But one that would have far-reaching consequences.

Since winning my last World Outdoor Championship in 2003, Red Bull had been presenting me with all kinds of opportunities. One of the most memorable was when they invited me to compete in the infamous Erzberg Rodeo, which features some five hundred motorbike riders and is one of the high points of the enduro calendar. The entire event, which takes place inside a huge quarry, is complete and utter mayhem and features drops and ascents that, as well as being hundreds of feet high, are almost vertical. When I took part in 2015 only seven of the five hundred riders completed the race and, as well as being one of the seven, I also beat five of them to the finish line. Not bad for an old man. But, in addition to inviting me to take part in events like the Erzberg, which I often fared well in, he said modestly, Red Bull had also started asking me to suggest some unusual places that I'd like to ride my bike. This is how the stunts and challenges came about, which have now become my calling card.

Over the years I've ridden across some amazing terrain: from the arctic landscape of northern Finland, which also included a specially built trials course made out of solid ice and set inside a giant igloo, to a four-day tour of Sri Lanka, where, as well as riding through the rushing waters of the world-famous Ravana Falls, which is one of Asia's widest waterfalls, I also rode across the rocky red cliffs of Ussangoda, which are 5,000 feet above sea level. Each time we embark on one of these trips a film is made to accompany it and, as is always the way with Red Bull, the production values are high enough to make some parts of Hollywood blush.

Each year we have to suggest four or five new, different ideas to Red Bull and the first time I mentioned the wheelie idea was back in 2010. We were at a brainstorming meeting where we were due to discuss these ideas and in the days leading up to it I'd been storming my brain trying to think of some. This time, I wanted to try something that the public could relate to. Something they might be able to do themselves. It still had to be impressive, mind you, and preferably somewhere iconic. The question was, what and where?

After hours of trying to think of something, I eventually went back to basics and asked myself a question: what's the first thing people do when they get a pushbike or a motorbike? The answer was, they do a wheelie. That, I'm afraid, was my sole idea for the meeting, to wheelie somewhere iconic, and when I got around to suggesting it the response was, not surprisingly, lukewarm. In fact, I don't think it even got shortlisted as a possibility, so when it was brought up again in a similar meeting about three years later, I got the shock of my life.

'Where are you up to with the wheelie idea?' said somebody from Red Bull. 'Have you had any more thoughts?'

There were lots of things I'd thought about during the last three years – motorbikes, mainly – but wheelieing hadn't been one of them.

'Oh, we've had one or two ideas,' I fibbed. 'Nothing we'd like to mention now, though.'

A few weeks later we had a follow-up meeting, this time with a few more people from Red Bull head office. Once again, the wheelie idea came up and as before the noises being made were favourable.

To be honest, I hadn't really thought beyond doing an actual wheelie, so as we were supposed to be brainstorming again, I started thinking aloud. And that's when it happened.

'I used to have a place on the Isle of Man,' I said, not really concentrating. 'Wouldn't it be amazing to wheelie the TT course?'

The moment the words left my lips the entire room suddenly came to life and, as I began to retreat slowly and regretfully into my leather chair, I knew I'd made a massive mistake. *Oh, my God*, I thought. *What the hell have I done?* I could tell by the look on everyone's faces that this was the idea they'd been looking for and before I could try to wriggle my way out of it they were already putting flesh on the bones.

'How far is the TT course?' somebody asked.

'Almost thirty-eight miles,' I replied.

'Is it possible to wheelie thirty-eight miles?' said the same voice.

'NO!' I replied resolutely. 'Absolutely not.'

'Well, how far is it possible to wheelie?' they asked. 'And, more importantly, how far can you wheelie?'

This was my big chance.

'How far can I wheelie?' I said humbly, praying that by pleading incompetence they might ditch the idea. 'Oh, heck,' I said, scratching my head. 'The most I could probably do is a few hundred yards.'

Unfortunately, this course of action backfired big time.

'Really,' said my executioner. 'It'd be a real challenge then?'

'Yes. Very!' I replied.

A few weeks later at the next meeting, my fate was finally sealed.

'We've mentioned the wheelie idea to head office in Austria,' said the person leading the meeting. 'And they'd like us to proceed.'

'Eh?'

This kind of challenge was, and is, manna from heaven to Red Bull and, as I sat there quietly having a minor heart attack, the rest of the room started chatting about the details. There was no turning back now, though. We were doing it.

After conducting a little bit of research, we discovered that a stunt rider named Dave Taylor had already attempted to wheelie the course back in the 1970s, but unfortunately for him he hadn't managed it. After doing a little bit more research, I managed to get in touch with Dave's family. Although the man himself had sadly died some years previously, his two sons were kind enough to talk me through their dad's attempt and I even got to have a look at the motorbike he used. Seeing some of the photographs from Dave's wheelie attempt certainly made everything feel very real, but at the same time they helped to highlight all the potential dangers and pitfalls. One photograph in particular had my stomach doing somersaults as it showed Dave going into a corner at an angle of about 45 degrees. That would be absolutely fine if you were on two wheels, but on one wheel it suggests that all is not well.

I remember having a conversation with Jake about this soon afterwards. He'd already been looking after me for about sixteen years and whenever a challenge had presented itself we'd always said the same thing: 'Let's make it happen.' Without wanting to sound big-headed, this had always served us pretty well. Now, more than ever, I needed to hear those words again, and at the same time seek some reassurance that I wasn't on the brink of making a fool of myself and undoing some of that good work we'd done.

'If I didn't think you could do it,' Jake assured me, 'I'd say so. Seriously, Dougie, it'll be fine.'

As reassuring as Jake's words were, they were very soon contradicted when I eventually got around to telling my dad about it.

'You're doing what?' he said, astonished. 'What a bloody stupid idea, Doug. You'll never do it. Couldn't you have chosen something a bit easier?'

'If it was easy, Dad, everyone would be doing it.'

'Yes, but nearly thirty-eight miles? That's a long way, Doug. And especially when you can't even wheelie.'

'Thanks for reminding me!'

As daft as he thought I was, I was going to need Dad's help and guidance more than ever. There was just one problem, though. Towards the end of 2014, just as he was preparing for the Sheffield indoor trial in January 2015, Dad had started experiencing some health problems and had gone to see a specialist. To cut a long story short, he was eventually diagnosed with bowel cancer in the spring of 2015 and ever since then he'd been having treatment.

Dad had broken the news to me by telephone while I was

working through some emails one day and as he said the words both of us started crying. 'I'll tell you what, Doug,' he eventually said. 'I'll call you back later.' After hanging up I just sat there in my office and cried. Nicola eventually arrived home with the boys and the moment she saw me she knew what had happened.

Although we'd managed to keep the news off the internet, word had got around in the paddock at trials and the number of messages and get-well-soon cards he received was just amazing. This was a testament not only to Dad's character and popularity, but also to the sport itself. It's a family and that was exactly what Dad needed.

Anyway, back to this ridiculous idea of wheelieing the Isle of Man TT course.

The original plan, which was finalised at a meeting early in 2016, was to spend a week on the Isle of Man and, as well as attempting the wheelie, the people at Red Bull would make a film to accompany it. The attempt had been scheduled for late September. Then, right out of the blue, somebody from the production company Red Bull had hired to film the event had the altogether unhelpful idea of broadcasting the attempt live on Red Bull TV. This immediately added an extra layer of horror to the proceedings and Jake and I tried our best to dissuade them.

'Who on earth would want to watch a motorbike travelling at twenty miles per hour for two hours?' we argued. 'It'd be like watching paint dry!'

To be honest, I thought we'd won this particular battle but when head office in Austria came back, they were resolute. 'Sorry,' they said. 'But it's got to be live.'

As far as they were concerned that was the only way we could prove conclusively that I'd succeeded. If I managed it, of course. Dave Taylor had tried several times and, although there had been rumours that he'd completed the course, nothing was ever documented. As it was, while filming Dave's sons for the documentary, one of them had confirmed to our director, Stu, that Dave hadn't managed to complete the challenge. This meant that we'd definitely be starting with a clean sheet of paper and, if I managed it, I would be the first. This only heightened the need for it to go live, however, and I could understand Austria's proviso. It didn't make it any less terrifying.

When the implications of doing the attempt live were fully explained to me, I very nearly passed out. I was, as I've said several times in this book, mortified! In truth, there were only two implications, but they were both large, and very black. The first one was that I'd only get one chance and the second was that the whole world would be watching.

'Live means live, Dougie,' said Jake.

The next dose of completely unwanted reality came in the form of a rundown of how many people would be involved and what kind of equipment. During our time in Sri Lanka there'd been a few cameras and, for a short time, a helicopter. Five or six people in all. The terrain was obviously quite challenging, but that was why we were there. I may have been on a different continent, but professionally I was well inside my comfort zone. This was a complete about-turn. The crew required to broadcast the event live would, so I was told, number about 120, with a further 60 people needed to close the mountain road. The gear would be transported in a total of seven articulated lorries and, as well as having two helicopters to film with on tap, there'd also be an aeroplane to bounce the signal off and about twenty additional ground vehicles. Once again, I could feel myself recoiling into the base of my chair when Jake told me this and when the daunting directory of men, women and machines had finally been read out, I raised my head and attempted to murmur a few words of enthusiasm.

'All that for a prat doing a wheelie?' I sobbed.

That, I'm afraid, was about all I could muster at the time and, as Jake continued talking, I remained slumped. I felt like the proverbial condemned man.

The penultimate nail in this one-wheeled coffin of mine was hammered in shortly after Jake had won permission to have the course closed down for the duration of the attempt. He called Red Bull to tell them the good news, but they immediately said they didn't want it.

'We don't want a sterile environment,' they said. 'It'll look awful. We want to do it with the roads open and with a rolling convoy.'

As with the decision to go live, I had to admit they had a point. A closed circuit with just one bike on it would have been boring to say the least. In the end we compromised, because as well as needing the left-hand lane to be clear – obviously – we'd also need to have the mountain road closed. Having lived on the Isle of Man for several years, I knew that it was almost constantly windy on Snaefell Mountain so we'd definitely need the whole road. Despite the compromise, Jake too started having sleepless nights at this point (I'd been having them for weeks), but it was about to get even worse.

Although I'm quite a realistic man, I obviously allow myself to dream from time to time and on the whole I'm generally quite optimistic. Because my brain was now constantly questioning the possibility of the challenge, I had to try to drag some of that confidence to the fore. Everybody associated with the attempt was being ultra-positive and, despite me being both the original instigator and the central character, I was in danger of being left behind. I did manage to find a little bit of positivity, but a minute or so after I got on my bike and first started training for the attempt, that disappeared into thin air.

Being a so-called 'trials legend' meant that it was always going to be unthinkable for me to attempt to wheelie on anything other than a traditional trials bike. But, without wishing to sound too defeatist, you really could not wish for a less suitable means of transport. Trials bikes are designed to overcome obstacles not travel long distances and as well as having no seat there's also nowhere for you to put your feet. Oh, yes, and they also have a fuel tank that's good for about 25 miles in a straight line. The moment I realised this, I picked up the phone to Jake. We were in massive trouble.

Unfortunately, while all this was going on the situation with my dad was becoming worse. Despite having chemotherapy, the cancer had stayed as it was. At first, we took this as a positive, and for a time we'd been hoping for a full recovery. The chemotherapy, however, was taking its toll on Dad's general well-being and, as well as not being able to get comfortable, he was almost always in pain. He was tired, too, and the only time he left the house was to visit Malcolm Wilson, who was his specialist at the Christie Hospital in Manchester. In February 2016, Dad had been in agony over the weekend and was due to visit Malcolm on the Monday. With his trolley bag packed he slowly climbed into my van and for the whole trip there he was in unbearable pain. As soon as Malcolm saw him he admitted Dad and he ended up staying there for about a week. During that stay, my boys Alfie and Fraiser came over to see him and that was the last time they saw their grandad.

The following week Dad headed back home while his next course of chemotherapy was being prepared, the plan being that he would wait for a week and regain some strength. During this time Nicola, the boys and I flew to Dubai to celebrate my fortieth birthday. We arrived in Dubai on the morning of my birthday, 23 March, and on the same evening my phone started to ring during dinner. It was my brother Harry and as I walked outside to talk to him I knew by his voice that it was bad news. He was struggling to get the words out, and when he finally managed to compose himself he told me that Dad had had another scan and that the bowel cancer had grown and was putting pressure on his body. What he said next was the most upsetting. 'Dad's decided he doesn't want any more treatment.' The moment he said that both Harry and I broke down, just as Dad and I had when he told me about the diagnosis.

When Harry went I headed back towards the restaurant, but I just couldn't bring myself to walk in. In the end I had to call Nicola who then rushed out to see me. Once again, she knew what had occurred. 'Let's go back to the room,' she said. 'I'll book us on the next flight home.' When we arrived back I went straight from the airport to the hospital, but because of the long flight and the fact I hadn't slept I struggled to hold myself together. Dad's pain was being managed and he was drifting in and out of consciousness. Over the next week or so, Mum, Harry and I spent most of our time at Dad's bedside. John would also visit during the evenings as he'd always had a very close relationship with Dad. It also gave us something else to talk about, apart from the obvious.

As the pain got worse it was suggested to Dad that we might move him to Manorlands Hospice in Keighley. He refused, though, on the grounds that it was where you went to die. That was typical of my dad! A few days later, though, he accepted the fact that he might be more comfortable there and so we made arrangements to have him moved. At Manorlands Dad had his own room and there was even a bed for Mum. During the mornings I would arrive, which would enable Mum to nip home and check on the animals, and as soon as he'd finished work Harry would come over for the evenings. During this time the level of medicine was being increased and so Dad slept most of the time. He wasn't in pain, though, which was the main thing.

On 2 April I arrived mid-morning as usual and at lunchtime Mum and I went for a bite to eat. Dad was sleeping away as normal and shortly after lunch Harry arrived unexpectedly. Work wasn't where he wanted to be and so he came straight over. It was good to see him. As it was, Harry had made a very good decision because just after we arrived back in Dad's room his breathing began to go quiet, and as we sat by his bedside he slowly slipped away. It was incredibly peaceful.

Eventually, once I'd said my goodbyes, I went outside to make some phone calls to family and friends. The first person I called was Nicola and the first thing I told her was not to tell Alfie and Fraiser. 'I'd like to tell them myself,' I said. After that I called the rest of the family, followed by Jake, who announced the news on social-media channels. When I arrived home, I went to tell the boys as planned. But, as I tried to speak, I'm afraid I just broke down. Alfie and Fraiser knew what was coming and together with Nicola we all had a hug and shed a few tears. Well, a few gallons!

Dad's funeral took place on 11 April and I'm told the number of people at the church in Silsden was massive. I was in a bit of a daze, I'm afraid, and had to try to hold myself together. Nothing can prepare you for something like that. Your emotions are all over the place. I just remember feeling incredibly sad.

CHAPTER 17

Dougie's Wheelie

About a week after Dad's funeral I started practising again. Before he passed away I'd managed to wheelie just under a mile and with the attempt taking place in just over five months I had a bit of work to do. I am definitely king of the understatement! A bit of work to do? With the course being 37.7 miles, I still had to find almost all of it. I hadn't even touched the sides.

Ever since I started riding competitively there'd always been a chance of me winning, regardless of the trial and regardless of who I was competing against. That chance of winning had obviously increased as I improved and, as you know, it had waned again as I got older. It had come full circle, if you like. The fact remained, though, that even as a young pretender or as an outsider who was considered to be past it, I still had a chance of doing the job, which is what got me up in the morning. Without that possibility, and after managing just under a mile in about five months' practice and with just over five to go, I didn't stand a cat in hell's chance.

Over the next month or so I carried on practising as usual, but at the same time I slowly sank into a pit of depression and abject despair. That may sound a bit dramatic, but it's the truth. I'd had glitches before, mentally. A few seeds of doubt, now and again. I'd even felt desperate once or twice and a bit miserable. All that had been temporary, though. A few clouds masking my confidence and ability. This was, or felt, totally permanent and by June I admit that I was having a full-on meltdown. The only person who could have prevented this from happening was Dad. Words cannot describe how much I miss him and, even if he'd not been able to solve the problem immediately, he'd definitely have known what to do. He wasn't just my father, he was my mentor and he'd guided me through every single section of every World Outdoor Championship I'd ever competed in. We were a partnership. *The* partnership. We were unortho-dox too and we always did things differently to everyone else. Or, rather, Dad did. As I've already said, he could be quite loud at times and although he didn't do it deliberately, some of the things he bellowed at me during these sections would have the crowds in stitches. He was famous for it and whenever he got a laugh I used to grin like a Cheshire cat. It could be downright distracting sometimes, but I wouldn't have changed it for the world. His favourite expressions were as follows: 'Use your knees', which is self-explanatory, 'You're perfect at the back', which was in reference to where my back wheel was situated, and 'Mek it 'ave it', which roughly translated means, 'Give it some wellie!'

One day, after a particularly punishing and unfruitful practice session, I sat in my garage looking at my bike and just willing my dad to tell me what to do. I kept asking myself, *What would he have said? What would he have done in a situation like this?* In truth, Dad wouldn't have got himself into a situation like this in the first place! He'd have gone for a game of golf instead. What the hell had I done?

The catalyst with regard to me going public with my meltdown, or at least telling Jake, was the forthcoming announcement of the wheelie, which was due to take place at the 2016 Goodwood Festival of Speed. Once it had been announced to the press, I was due to wheelie up Goodwood Hill where they hold the famous hill climb. The closer this got, the more I started to panic and by mid-June, roughly a month before the announcement, I couldn't take it any more.

'Jake, I need you to get me out of the wheelie. I can't do it.'

I think Jake thought I was joking at first, but only for a second. I'm usually extremely mild-mannered and the tone of my voice, according to Jake, was completely different.

'What do you mean? You can't get out of it now, Dougie. Everything's arranged. It'll be fine, mate. We'll make it happen.'

After everything I'd been through, I'm afraid it was going to take a lot more than a few words to bring me around and unless Jake, or anyone else for that matter, could teach me how to wheelie more than a mile in a few weeks, they'd be on a hiding to nowt. I could not be reasoned with.

'Look, Jake,' I said. 'You're my manager. I want you to call Red Bull and get me out of this challenge. Okay? Just do it, please.'

Notice how I said please. I never forget my manners.

After making it clear that my mind could not be changed under any circumstances whatsoever I hung up and then switched off my phone. I knew that Jake would be calling my friends and family and they'd all want a go at telling me it would be okay. It wouldn't, though.

The only person I could bring myself to talk to was Blackie Holden. And, luckily for Jake — and for me, as it turned out — Blackie was one of the first people he called. As well as being one of my oldest friends, Blackie was also very straight-talking and practical. I knew for a fact he wouldn't tell me that everything was going to be okay if it wasn't and when I eventually turned my phone back on and saw I had a missed call from him, I decided to call him back.

'I suppose Jake's been on to you,' I said.

'Never mind all that,' replied Blackie. 'Now listen to me. I've been looking at some photographs of Dave Taylor. You know he used to stand on his back axle when he did a wheelie?'

'Yes, I think that rings a bell.'

'Well, I think we should try that.'

The moment I heard the words 'back axle' I could suddenly picture Dave Taylor from the photos I'd seen and the reason it hadn't really registered was because, as far as I was concerned, it wasn't something I'd be able to do.

'Well, if you think it'll work, I'm up for giving it a go.'

Blackie's idea had instilled the tiniest bit of confidence in me. I'd almost forgotten what it felt like.

The following day Blackie grafted two large M10 bolts on to each end of my rear spindle. After that he put a hose leading from the rear brake caliper disc on the back wheel to the right handlebar, making that the rear brake. The brake didn't work that well, but it was good enough for me to give it a go and so off I went up to Coniston for a practice. There's a nice long private road up there and the moment I pulled that front wheel up I could immediately notice the difference. As well as feeling more comfortable, which was a massive relief, I also had some control. In fact, providing we could get the brake working better, this might actually be the solution.

Over the next week or so I practised like mad and managed to get up to a couple of miles. Progress was still too slow, though, so it was back to the drawing board. After doing some more research, Blackie came up with what was to be the final piece of the jigsaw.

'On his final attempt,' he said, 'Dave Taylor used a gyro on his front wheel.'

I forget when I first noticed it, but when the front wheel was spinning, everything felt fine. The moment it stopped, so did the wheelie. That was it then! The problem now, apart from wheelieing another 35.5 miles, was how the heck do we get one?

'Already sorted,' said Blackie. 'I've ordered the parts from a mountain-bike company. Once they've arrived they'll have to be re-spoked into the rim of the front wheel. I can't do that, though, so we'll have to send them off.'

The bloke who was fitting the gyro was based miles away, but when the parts finally arrived Blackie drove them over to him and waited. I think the bloke thought he might have a few days but he was out of luck. The sooner he got it finished, the sooner he'd get rid of Blackie!

Once we had the wheel back, Blackie took the bike up to Hope Technology at Barnoldswick and they replaced the large bolts on the spindle with two pedals. This was the icing on the cake with regard to the whole positioning issue, so now that was sorted out once and for all we had to work out how we were going to power the gyro. It was obviously going to be a battery, a 36-volt to be exact, but the question was, where would it go? In the end we just taped it to the frame and decided to work out the final position later. Time was running out and I had to get practising.

When I first took the modified bike up to the private road in Coniston I was absolutely bricking it. It really did feel like it was make or break and, despite being confident of making progress that afternoon, I was still conscious of the fact that the effect of the gyro still might not be enough to enable me to wheelie such a long distance. Fortunately, after just five minutes I knew for a fact that the gyro was indeed the link to possible success, and for the first time since I came up with this ridiculous bloody idea I actually thought that I might be in with a chance of doing it.

After calling Red Bull and telling them about the breakthrough, they booked the circuit at Croft for more practice. They were absolutely cock-a-hoop with the progress Blackie and I had made and said that whatever we needed to make it work, I just had to say. Well, the first thing we needed was my rear brake sorting out, so before we all set off for Croft we took the bike back to Hope Technology. Bearing in mind this was the first time the rear brake had been worked on properly, and was a bit of an unknown quantity, it could have taken ages. In the end, Blackie and Simon Sharp, who was the co-owner of Hope and who sadly passed away before the attempt was made, had a conversation that was so ridiculously technical that I couldn't make hide nor hair of it. Within a day or two, though, the issue was sorted. I pride myself on being quite mechanically minded, but when those two started talking about leverage and piston sizes, I was completely out of my depth.

With a nice new brake fitted on to my rear pedal and a front wheel that wouldn't stop spinning, off we went to Croft to do some serious practice. When it came to conditions and terrain, this wasn't going to replicate the TT course. Croft's quite flat and, as well as being a lot wider than a normal road, there was none of the usual traffic. It allowed me to get used to the bike, however. And, more importantly, it allowed me to practise the core requirement of the challenge, which was to wheelie over a long distance. I think I managed four or five laps at a time, which is about 10 miles. Not bad, bearing in mind that prior to that I'd barely done two.

When I drove away from Croft after the first day I think I actually cracked a smile for the first time since before Dad passed away. He'd still have thought I was bonkers for giving this a go, but I know for a fact that had he been with me at Croft he'd have realised that there was a chance I might succeed, and for a man who didn't like to fail he'd have been all over it like a rash.

'We can do this, Doug,' he'd have said. 'I still reckon you're a berk for trying, but let's get back here first thing and crack on with some practice. Ten laps on the bounce tomorrow, okay?'

While I was competing in the World Championships I think my confidence had come from two different sources: 80 per cent of it had come from my own ability, but the other 20 had come from my dad. Even though he wasn't there I had to keep thinking about him and I had to keep reminding myself what he'd have said to me.

Despite the progress there was still a massive amount of work to do and any bookmaker with half a brain would have felt comfortable offering odds of at least 25/1 on me succeeding. I knew all that. I also knew that we had some hurdles on the design front, such as where to put the extra fuel tank and where to put the battery for the gyro. This was a challenge, though, and challenges are meant to be challenging! All I could do was crack on, but at least I felt able to do so.

With Blackie and the lads at Hope working on the afore-mentioned design issues, I decided to clear my diary and devote every waking hour of every day to wheelieing. There's a road quite close to me that's very long and very quiet first thing, so I knew that as long as I got up early, I'd have a good few hours in which to practise. At this point I had about six weeks until the attempt, and although that might sound a lot I'd still only wheelied less than a third of the required distance and on fairly flat private roads and circuits.

I'd arrive at this road at about 4.30am and would wheelie the length of it several times. It leads to a dead end and because it's no wider than a track I was having to turn around on a sixpence. That was good practice, though, as was the width of the track, and once I'd perfected the U-turn I was flying. Well, not flying, exactly. I rarely fly!

Once it got light some of the local farmers would roll up for a chat and although they didn't know the exact details of what I was doing, I think they could sense by the sheer repetition that I was making progress. I remember the gyro stopped working one day and one of the farmers gave me a lift back home on the back of his cattle truck. He was on his way to Skipton auction mart and dropped me at the door. It wasn't just farmers who took an interest, though. I'd have walkers offering me cups of tea from flasks and everyone who saw me waved. It wasn't always easy to wave back, but providing I didn't think I was going to go arse over tit, I'd even wave to them mid-wheelie. How's that for skill and common courtesy? I think most of them thought I was off my top, but I didn't mind. Some of the sunrises I saw were absolutely breathtaking and as things progressed I actually looked forward to going up there.

Apart from Carl Fogarty, who gets a nosebleed going out of Blackburn and claims to be allergic to God's Own County, I think most of us know that the Yorkshire Dales is a very special place. When the only living creatures on the entire landscape are you and a few animals, it's even more amazing. Also, because he'd only been gone a few months, I was still thinking about my dad a lot. Bearing in mind he was a proud Dalesman himself and absolutely loved the area, there was no better place for this to happen. Had he been there with me he'd have been scratching his head on the side of the road, saying, 'I can't believe it, Doug. You can actually wheelie!'

One thing this road helped to familiarise me with was a bit of traffic. It might only have been the odd tractor perhaps, or even a few sheep, but it took away the isolation and made me more aware of my surroundings. Once that had become the norm, I was in a much better position. Distance-wise, I was doing at least 30 or 40 miles every morning, and after getting back home at about 8.30am Blackie would be on the phone asking me how I'd got on and giving me updates as to how things were at his end. Apart from sorting out the big stuff like the fuel tank and the battery, etc., they were also testing out different brake pads and different tyres, just in case anything could be improved on. It was a constant process of elimination, really, but because we no longer had any major issues it was all about refinement as opposed to fixing a specific problem. And, because I was now making steady progress, the mood in the camp was brilliant. We all knew the odds, don't get me wrong, but all we needed was a sniff of a chance. Now we had that we were all feeding off it big time.

'How did you get on this morning then?' Blackie would say. 'Hit any sheep?'

'Nope. Forty-four miles this morning. Only touched down three times. Used a stack of petrol, though!'

'Never mind the petrol! Forty miles? That's brilliant, that is.'

After that Blackie would rush off to tell the people at Hope Technology and by the time I arrived there in the afternoon you'd have thought I'd completed the challenge! Between them and Red Bull, I don't think I've ever met, let alone worked with, such a positive bunch of people before. I hate using sayings like 'can-do attitude' but this lot had it in spades. Given what had happened with my dad, and with the challenge itself, this helped me an awful lot. A bit of infectious enthusiasm goes a long way and it was exactly what I needed.

One afternoon in early September I said goodbye to Nicola and went to Cadwell Park in Lincolnshire where I was due to practise. I'd been an absolute bloody nightmare to live with these past few months and she had been amazing. When things had been really bad she knew there was nothing she could say to bring me around. It was something that had to take its own course and fortunately Blackie had found a way out. Nicola was always there for me, though, and she always let me know. Looking back, that was probably what kept me going. Her patience was incredible.

Anyway, enough of all that soppy rubbish. She's been punching well above her weight for years now and no doubt considers herself to be a very lucky woman.

The reason I've mentioned my trip to Cadwell Park, which I made with Nick Owen, is because apart from the fact we had a jolly old time, it was the first time I wheelied the full distance without my front wheel going down. Nick and I came home with very, very big smiles on our faces that night, I can tell you. I'd just answered the penultimate question that was being asked of me for this challenge: can you wheelie for 37.7 miles without your front wheel coming down? The final question, and the biggest of them all, was could I do the same thing again on the TT course with people lining the streets, two helicopters following me, several outriders, a massive pick-up directly in front of me carrying my manager, a presenter for Red Bull TV and a cameraman, and a massive worldwide audience?

Do you know, when I drove on to that ferry from

Liverpool about five days before the attempt, I actually reckoned I could do it.

Apart from the challenge itself, the task that presented me with the most difficulty during the final push was getting Blackie to the Isle of Man. Since his accident in Spain he'd hardly been out of North Yorkshire, but out of everybody who'd been involved in the project he was the person I needed there most. He really didn't want to go, though, and every time I thought I'd talked him into it, he'd change his mind and say no again. I could understand his reluctance. After all, there's a fair bit more to consider when you're in a wheelchair. Especially when you're going away. Blackie had his own routine and was nervous about being taken out of it.

The day before we were due to set off I managed to talk Blackie around once again, but about half an hour into the journey he started panicking.

'I've changed my mind,' he said. 'I can't go. You're going to have to let me out. Don't worry. I'll get our lass to come and pick me up.'

Normally I'd fly to the Isle of Man as I absolutely hate taking the ferry. This wasn't going to be an option, though, as I knew that if I wanted Blackie there I'd have to take him myself. This was a big sacrifice for me and I was damned if I was going to get on that ferry alone.

I managed to keep Blackie talking all the way to Liverpool, but by the time we arrived at the terminal he was still resolute.

'I'm sorry, mate, but I just can't do it. You're going to have to let me out.'

'Okay then,' I said finally. 'I'll just pull in over here.'

Instead of pulling in I put my foot down and drove straight through check-in.

'What do you think you're doing?' shouted Blackie.

'Taking you to the Isle of Man. I'm sorry, Blackie, but I need you there. There's nothing you can do about it now. In a minute's time we'll be on that ferry and it'll be anchors up!'

That was the first time I'd ever kidnapped anyone and although I wouldn't make a habit of it, it was actually quite exciting. I'd rather not repeat what Blackie said to me on the ferry. Suffice to say, it wasn't that complimentary and at one point I think he even questioned my parenthood. He came around, though, and once he got among the crew and started sensing the excitement and anticipation, he was fine. I think he was still a bit self-conscious about people lifting him into cars and things, but at the end of the day nobody gave a monkeys and, once Blackie realised that everyone was just doing a job, he started to get stuck in. We were a team and he was a very big part of it. I knew he'd come around eventually. He still hasn't thanked me for kidnapping him, though.

We arrived in the Isle of Man about five days before the attempt and, while Blackie was becoming more and more relaxed, I was becoming more and more agitated. All of a sudden everything was very real and after driving the course on the afternoon I arrived, I was reminded of the difference between those final two questions I mentioned: wheelieing the distance and wheelieing the course itself. I'd been back to the island several times in the build-up to the wheelie, but it had never felt real then. There was always something in the back of my mind saying it wouldn't happen, or rather hoping it wouldn't. Now, with the full crew in attendance and with everyone running around like headless chickens, it was definitely happening.

Or was it?

The weather forecast for the day of the wheelie, Saturday 24 September, was absolutely appalling and a couple of days before I started hearing rumours that we might have to postpone the wheelie. Or, at worst, even cancel it. I haven't mentioned this yet but just before a race or a competitive event, I go into what Jake calls 'race mode'. Anyone else would probably call it 'pain-in-the-arse mode' as I stop talking to folk and start biting people's heads off. I never do it on purpose. It's just part of my mental preparation and anyone who knows me will always try to avoid me at this point.

Prior to a race, pain-in-the-arse mode would normally start a few hours before. With the wheelie, though, it started a full two days before! Or, when I first started hearing rumours about the postponement. Getting my head around the course itself was bad enough. I'm afraid this just pushed me over the edge.

The morning before the day of the attempt I came down for breakfast having not slept a wink. In fact, I don't think I'd slept more than about six hours in the last three nights. That's in total, by the way. I remember coming into the breakfast room and as I entered everyone suddenly fell silent. They obviously knew the state I was in and they were all walking on eggshells. I was fit to burst and if anyone had said 'Good morning, Dougie' I'd probably have tried drowning them in cornflakes.

Just after breakfast Jake called me into a meeting with Red Bull and they told me they were going to have to postpone the wheelie until the Sunday.

'I'll decide whether or not we postpone the fucking wheelie,' I said.

I would never usually talk like that, even in race mode, but these were extenuating circumstances. I had no control. And, what's more, I didn't like it one bit.

They'd already asked the police and the council about moving it to Monday, which is when the weather was supposed to be much better, but that had been denied. Monday was a normal business day and so it was Sunday or not at all.

The following morning, which was supposed to have been the day of the wheelie, the weather had become torrential. Heavy rain and gale-force winds were the order of the day and after driving up onto the mountain to take a proper measurement, the figures we came away with were frightening: a base wind of 34mph with gusts of up to 50mph. There was no way in the world I'd have been able to wheelie in those conditions. In fact, the only positive would have been that if the gyro had failed the wind might have kept the front wheel spinning! I needed a little bit more than that though, and although I didn't admit it, I knew the decision had been the right one.

I came down to breakfast once again on the Sunday morning having slept about four hours. It was an improvement but I was still knackered. Once again, the entire team were walking on eggshells and once again I was at breaking point. The weather had improved marginally and we were good to go, but a mixture of nervousness, anticipation and sleep deprivation had turned me into a bit of a headcase, and as well as drowning them in cornflakes, if anyone had tried talking to me I'd have force-fed them black pudding. Anyone except Blackie, that is. As I sat down at my table he came rolling into the breakfast room and, after parking himself opposite me, he said, 'Get us a cup of tea and a couple of poached eggs would you, Doug?' The whole room froze. I scowled at him, as if to say, 'How dare you talk to me the morning of the wheelie?' Blackie didn't care, though.

'Well I can't bloody do it, can I?' he said. And so, I got up and did as I was told!

To be honest, that helped to break the ice a bit and it enabled me to pull my head out of my backside. It needed doing.

I only found this out later on, thank God, but Red Bull had said to Jake that if my front wheel went down at any point – even for a split second – that was it. I'd have failed and it would be abandon wheelie. I had it in my head that even if my front wheel did go down I'd carry on to the end and it would be classed as a brave attempt. Not abject and immediate failure! When Jake told me this afterwards I was gobstruck. Red Bull had told him that if I did drop the front wheel he'd have to stop the wheelie, get out of the pick-up and tell me about their decision. Needless to say, Jake wasn't relishing the prospect of having to do that and, although I didn't know it at the time, he was almost as nervous as I was.

To be fair to Jake, he'd shouldered almost as much of the burden as I had and when he'd turned up in the Isle of Man the day before Blackie and me he'd been as sick as a dog. This was purely down to stress but because it was so bad he'd had to call a doctor to give him something to get him back on track. He too had been coasting on fumes all week. Unlike me, he hadn't been able to act like a giant toddler who'd had his sweets nicked. He'd had to remain composed!

CHAPTER 18

A Bit of a Wobble

Once it had been confirmed that the wheelie could go ahead, I went back up to my hotel room to get ready and have a few minutes to myself. The next time I went out of that door again, that would be it. For the next few hours I'd have people, cameras and a whole lot of pressure to contend with. And a flaming wheelie, of course!

At about noon Jake gave me a knock and said it was time to go.

'I'll be down in two minutes,' I said.

I was sitting on the edge of my bed at the time and I could quite easily have just lain back and gone to sleep. Just for a couple of weeks! Instead, I grabbed my jacket, forced a smile on to my face, opened my bedroom door and marched down to the foyer. It was showtime.

When we got to the paddock I got on my bike and started practising. Wheelieing had become second nature to me now and whenever I got on a bike that was the first thing I thought about doing. I had definitely become Wheelie Man!

With an hour to go, the convoy started pulling up into the pit lane and that's when I could hear the helicopters. I remember my stomach lurching at this point and, as I looked around the paddock and in the pit lane, all I could see were people running about and shouting all kinds of instructions to each other. All this was for me. For me, and for what I was about to attempt. That was quite a lot to take in, really, hence the lurching stomach. The only blessing was that because everyone was so busy, I was left alone.

The convoy itself consisted of several outriders, some of whom had been instructed to ride about half a mile ahead of me and ensure that nobody turned on to the road from any of the smaller junctions; a pick-up truck which would drive directly in front of me and would have Jake on the back with Caroline, who was the presenter from Red Bull TV; and my own van following me with my engineer, Francesc, and Blackie on board. Blackie was my lucky mascot and I needed to have him there. Unlike the *Top Gear* show, I had a two-way radio this time, together with a cut-off wire that, should I fall off, would cut the engine dead. Every box had been ticked and I'm pretty sure we'd thought of absolutely everything. The only things we couldn't legislate for now were the weather, which seemed to be behaving itself but could obviously chuck in a surprise or two, and my ability to wheelie the course. Or at least that's what we thought. There'd be one other surprise early on that would almost bring everything to a halt.

When there was about half an hour to go the director tried calling me into position.

'Balls to that,' I said. 'I'll be up there just before I'm due to set off and not before.'

I was in pain-in-the-arse mode again.

Prior to setting off the only person I wanted to speak to was James, so he relayed my reply to Jake, and Jake to the director. I'd be in position, but it had to be when I was ready. When I eventually did roll on to the road just behind the pick-up I got a massive attack of the nerves. It was like being in Matlock again during that six-day trial. That was probably the first time I'd ever suffered badly from nerves and with any luck this would be the last. I was sick in Matlock, though. What if that happened now?

'Ladies and gentlemen, we're going live now to Douglas on the Isle of Man to watch Dougie Lampkin puke his guts up. There he goes! Well done, Doug. Get it all up.'

They'd remember me if I did that, that's for sure.

According to Jake, when I eventually pulled up in front of him I was as white as a sheet and as far as he could tell I wasn't breathing. I was, obviously! At this point he just said to himself, *What the bloody hell have we done?* Because I looked so ill he didn't think I'd do it, so he too went as white as a sheet. Fortunately, despite being as nervous as hell, I actually thought I *could* do it. I remember it as clear as day. I looked around at all the people in front of me – there must have been hundreds including the spectators – and after registering the sound of the helicopters once again I noticed James. Because there'd been a lot of surface water my feet had become wet and he was drying them for me. Just as he was doing that he looked up at me, smiled and said, 'We've got it.' That was it. I needed to be off now. I looked up and saw Jake raise his hands. He was counting down from ten to zero. When he got to five, I could see the pick-up start to move slightly, so put the bike into gear. Right then. At last, we were finally off.

I pulled my front wheel up about 50 metres before the start line and after changing gear I immediately started wobbling. This was the worst possible start and some of the language I came out with was appalling. After that, I just said, 'Calm down, Dougie', and then tried to regulate my breathing by taking a few deep breaths. After that I had another slight wobble and in between Bray Hill and the roundabout on Quarterbridge Road I don't think I took a single breath. This may sound slightly far-fetched, but because the external factors were taking up so much of my concentration it was almost as if I'd forgotten how to ride a motorbike. I needed to relax quickly and remember who I was and what I did for a flaming living!

Because of the two-way radio I was able to regulate the speed via Jake and once I'd finally settled down a bit we were travelling at 22–25 miles per hour. That may not sound like an awful lot but on one wheel it's plenty, and going into Union Mills and then over Braddan Bridge I at last felt quite settled. Actually, I think settled is the wrong word. Let's just say I was crapping myself slightly less than I had been going down Bray Hill and had remembered how to ride a motorbike and – more importantly – how to wheelie!

Incidentally, what I forgot to tell you earlier is that if I dropped the front wheel within 2 miles of the start I was able to go back and start again. Just once, mind you. Once I'd passed that 2-mile mark it was like having a safety net taken from under me. In a way, though, it was actually quite liberating – like having the stabilisers taken off your bike. When that happens, you're left feeling excited but ever so slightly terrified and that's exactly how I felt. I was well up for it, though.

About three miles further on, just as I was taking the right-hander through Ballacraine, I went past a massive open gateway and as I did I was hit by a huge gust of wind. As well as having a proper wobble I could feel my front wheel drop a bit and that was the first time I felt my heart skip a beat. I looked forward. I could tell that it hadn't gone unnoticed. Caroline was speaking furiously into her Red Bull microphone and Jake was doing the same into his. He had an iPad with him that was keeping track of all the out-riders, and that was the first time he'd felt able to take his eyes off me and check it. Talk about bad timing!

About 5 miles further on, just as we were coming into Kirk Michael, panic ensued. As a tight but notoriously busy road this was always going to be a hotspot for potential prob-lems. And, sure enough, just as we were making our way into the village one very large problem suddenly came into view: an oncoming single-decker bus had pulled out into the other lane – our lane! There was a van parked in front of it so the driver obviously thought he could overtake it. The thing is, the driver would have been well aware of the wheelie and of the fact that the opposite lane was closed. He'd also have seen the outriders flying through the village, so what the hell he thought he was doing I have no idea.

Because this bus driver had now obstructed part of the road it left very little room for us to manoeuvre. I'd be okay – just – as would the two outriders who were just behind me. The massive pick-up, however, that was carrying Jake and Caroline wasn't going to fit. Not on the road, anyway. All I could sense and hear as we approached this bus was increasing panic and a whole lot of shouting. Although I was trying to concentrate on what I was doing, I was well aware that disaster may be about to strike. The pick-up was only ever a few metres in front of me and if it had to stop suddenly I wouldn't stand a chance. Come to think of it, neither would Jake or Caroline. They'd have gone backward under the van that was following and I'd have ploughed head first into the pick-up. It doesn't bear thinking about.

In the end the only way the pick-up could avoid the bus was to mount the kerb. Fortunately, there were no pedestrians on the pavement at the time as if there had been the pick-up wouldn't have been able to mount the pavement so it would have been game over. Funnily enough – or, should I say, luckily enough – because it was a narrow pavement this was one of the only spots on the course where there weren't hundreds of people lining it, and so they were able to get through without mowing anyone down. Apparently James and Harry, who were both outriders, stopped and had a quick word with this bus driver. I think they must have sent him our thanks and best wishes.

It did dawn on me as we passed through Kirk Michael that me, Blackie, Jake, Caroline, Francesc and the outriders weren't the only ones who would have been papping themselves at that point. In fact, there were at least another hundred or so who'd have been experiencing exactly the same emotions. This was just a spike, though. A heightened version of how we'd all been feeling for the best part of a flaming week. That in itself has to be some kind of record. 'Congratulations, you've managed to give a hundred and twenty people a massive nervous breakdown!'

The next part of the course where I was anticipating an issue or two was the Ramsey Hairpin that leads up on to Snaefell Mountain. That part was also going to be a potential nightmare as it was the most exposed and the most breezy. First, though, I had to negotiate Ramsey. I hadn't had an attack of the nerves for ages by this point but as I started to scale May Hill I could feel them coming on again. This time I applied a bit of mind over matter and managed to cut them off before they got to me. Then, as I approached the hairpin, I calmly changed down and went wide. Perfect! Next up was Waterworks, which is where both lanes of the road were closed. If was going to experience any problems I assumed it was going to be somewhere between Guthrie's Memorial and Verandah. I was wrong. The moment I rode on to Gooseneck I felt an almighty gust of wind hit me from behind. This was the first time the wind had been following me which meant from now on, or at least until we'd turned direction again, there'd be more chance of a gust pushing me forward and so more chance of my front wheel dropping. When my front wheel dropped on Gooseneck it was within about 20 centimetres of hitting the road. Fortunately, Jake was looking at his iPad again, but Caroline wasn't. She was shouting into her microphone and once again I was aware that this latest fright would be shared by many. Perhaps millions.

Mark Webber, who was watching it at home, called me

up afterwards and told me that he watched the wheelie standing up and whenever I moved, so did he. His wife said he looked absolutely ridiculous. I'm not so sure, though. He was merely clinging on to the coat-tails of greatness.

Two minutes later exactly the same thing happened again, by which time my arms were starting to ache, as was my back. I can withstand quite a bit of pain but with over 10 miles still to go I wasn't sure if I'd be able to cope. Especially if I was having to battle to keep the wheel up. A couple of weeks earlier John McGuinness had said that as soon as I got out of Gooseneck I should get myself tucked into the left-hand side. 'You'll get out of the wind a bit there,' he said. I remember doing as I was told and the moment I got over to the left-hand side the wind increased tenfold! I actually managed to crack a smile at this point as I could picture Mr McGuinness watching me and wetting himself laughing.

About half a mile further on we decided to get Francesc to pull the van alongside me and act as a windbreaker. What we hadn't bargained for, however, was the fact that during the wheelie my head would be a lot higher and because it was above the van it didn't work quite as well as we'd hoped. I could see Blackie, though, which was nice. He looked a bit nervous.

The problem we had once the van had pulled alongside me was that I was now wheelieing in a space about 3 metres square. I couldn't alter my speed and I definitely couldn't wobble! One thing that occurred to me as we were passing over Mountain Mile was that Francesc, who was driving the van, is Spanish and as far as I know he'd never driven in England before, let alone on the wrong side of the road!

Who the hell had roped him into driving my bloody van? Actually, I think it was me. He seemed to be doing a good job, though, so I tried to think about something else.

While all this was going on Jake lost communication with the outriders for a while, and as we approached Windy Corner, which more than lives up to its name, there were an awful lot of squeaky bums on Snaefell Mountain. Like the Ramsey Hairpin, that turned out to be okay in the end but just as I went past Kate's Cottage going down to Creg-ny-Baa, yet another gust of wind hit me full-on from the left-hand side. I'd forgotten we'd changed direction and had been anticipating the gusts coming from behind. What a bugger! I had to stick out my right leg to stop me keeling over and that was the closest I'd come to failing. So far. It certainly woke me up and looking at things positively it was exactly what I needed going into that tight corner at Creg-ny-Baa. After that, we were back to one lane again. But, more importantly, I was just 3 miles or so from the finish.

By now the pain had become excruciating and the expression on my face was one continuous grimace. Jake had assumed I'd been in trouble since Gooseneck and he'd been right, in that I'd had problems keeping the wheel up at times and had not been enjoying myself especially. Another understatement there. Now, with the pain going up a notch and fatigue setting in, I was in a proper battle. If I had a wobble now, like the ones I'd had on Gooseneck and at Kate's Cottage, I wouldn't be able to hold it up. I just didn't have the strength. Jake knew what the state of play was and he admitted to me afterwards that he was expecting me to fold. Mark Webber also said that the moment he saw me grimacing he thought I was done. I didn't think I was done, but I was worried. What gave me strength was the eventual realisation, after Hillberry I think, that we only had a couple of miles to go. I hadn't thought about the finish much so far, and when I was reminded that there was in fact an end to all this it galvanised me and helped me give it one last push.

As well as the outriders, which were part of the convoy, there were also two camera bikes: one for the documentary and one stills photographer. Shortly after the road opened again, which meant we had oncoming traffic, both decided that they wanted to come alongside me for a while, but without the luxury of the extra lane they had to encroach on the little space I had. This was the first and only time that I really lost my temper during the attempt itself and my exact words were, 'Get those fucking bikes out of the way!' Jake then passed on my request to the chaps riding the camera bikes and they quickly pulled back. Normally I'm fine having my photo taken but I needed to concentrate! This bit coming up was the final potential banana skin. And, providing I got through it, barring any unforeseen disasters such as a dog running into the road or a bus driver doing a flipping U-turn, I should be home and dry.

The part of the course in question was where you go off the main road on to the old racetrack. After that you go around the roundabout and then down Governor's Dip. This was the only part of the course that had given me night-mares, and as I approached the old racetrack I had a horrible feeling they were going to come true. This part wasn't just difficult for me, it was difficult for the entire convoy, and being aware of this did me no good whatsoever. At the end of the day, though, there was nothing I could do for anyone else. I just had to concentrate on keeping my front wheel in the air. By the time I got to the roundabout, which had been closed off, the pick-up was that far ahead that it was out of vision and when I realised this I panicked for a second. Then, just as I rode on Governor's Dip, I saw it again and knew that all was well. The reason I panicked was because I'd become disorientated and I'd had an awful feeling I might take the wrong exit. That was almost impossible as the only ones open were Governor's Dip and the road I'd ridden on from. The mind can play funny tricks when you've been wheelieing for over an hour and a half.

As I assumed my position just behind the pick-up Jake told me the state of play. 'Half a mile to go, Dougie,' he said. 'That's half a mile. For God's sake, don't balls it up now!' As I came out of Governor's on to the main road, which was the home straight, there were people everywhere. 'Go on Dougie!' they were shouting. The police had closed off the final two junctions. I thought, *Get past these, Dougie, and you've done it*. Despite the police there was always a possibility of somebody driving through the roadblock and in that situation I'd have screamed 'Get out of the way!' and ridden on to the pavement.

Fortunately, everyone stayed put and as I passed the final junction I allowed myself to get a little bit excited. I should really have changed up into fifth here but there was no way I was going to chance missing a gear. My legs were shaking and it could well have spelled disaster. Because I hadn't changed I was revving like mad and for a moment Jake thought I was in trouble. Once he realised that I'd decided to ride the last half a mile in fourth gear he was able to relax a bit. I could see the finish now and the closer I got, the louder the crowd became. Shouts of encouragement were now turning into what sounded like screams of desperation and a few metres before the line the noise triggered something inside me. The best way of describing it would be an outpouring of emotion, and when I finally crossed the line I dropped my front wheel and began punching the air. Until now, I'd always managed to resist doing this, even when I'd won the World Championship. For the first time ever it seemed appropriate and I must have got 40 years' worth into about 20 seconds.

As well as an outpouring of emotion at the finish line, I also experienced a momentary outpouring of pain. God knows how but it seems I'd managed to all but ignore the increasing pain for the entire duration of the wheelie and the moment the front wheel went down it was like, 'Right then, Doug, it's my turn now. Get ready for hell!' I thought to myself, *You can bugger right off.* There was no way I was going to let this get to me now. I definitely felt it more than I had done on the bike, but for the moment I just had to push it away again. And I did. I knew it would be hell later, but I didn't care.

I'd been told beforehand that after the wheelie I had to ride into the paddock and park in front of two cameramen. One was for the documentary and the other for the live feed. When I came to a halt and took off my helmet I was immediately engulfed by a crowd of people. Blackie was the first person I saw who registered as being a friend of mine, so I bent down and gave him a hug. He was crying his eyes out. So, it appeared, was everyone else.

Hand on heart, this was the biggest achievement of my entire career. Winning 12 World Championships and 99 Grands Prix is obviously up there and, although it allows me to be talked about in the same breath as some incredibly talented riders, it's ultimately a culmination of my efforts. This, on the other hand, had been one extraordinarily monumental effort that in the last 11 months or so had taken me all the way to hell and back, and at the same time had awakened inside me pain and emotions that I never even knew, or indeed hoped, existed. What is it they say, though? The bigger the sacrifice, the greater the reward?

Because Red Bull TV were still live they wanted to get me to go straight to the studio for an interview, but when they came to fetch me I realised I couldn't move my legs. In the end, somebody had to help me, so that probably looked quite heroic. Or like I'd just wet myself. Either way, I'd temporarily lost the use of my legs and it took a good 10 minutes before I could walk again.

When I came out of the studio I saw that everyone associated with the attempt who wasn't still working, together with all my friends and family, had gathered in the paddock. Sorry, did I say attempt? This was now an achievement. A done deal. The sight that greeted me as I emerged was hilarious. Some of the outriders were on my bike trying to wheelie. None of them could, though. Not more than a few yards. I was half-tempted to go over and demonstrate but a sudden searing pain running through my back – and my legs, my ankles, my forearms, my hands, my shoulders, my neck and even my backside – stopped me just in time. The pain was back and this time there'd be no stopping it. What really made me laugh, though, was that everybody in that paddock had one thing in common. We were all absolutely knackered! I'd never seen as many visibly tired people before in my life. We were all happy, though.

A few months ago, Nicola said something quite insightful. She said: 'There are two Dougie Lampkins. There's Dougie Lampkin MBE, the man who enters World Championships and wheelies the Isle of Man, and there's Dougie Lampkin the home bird. The man who collects bikes and just wants to potter around with friends and family.' Nic's right, there are definitely two Dougie Lampkins and until that day on the Isle of Man the two had never met before. What brought them together wasn't the wheelie. It was the people who'd been involved. Those who I didn't know well at the start had become friends and those I did know well had become even closer. Also, almost everybody I cared for in the world had been involved in some shape or form, from James drying my boots at the start and being an outrider, to Fraiser and Alfie telling me that everything was going to be okay when I was on a downer. The only person who hadn't been there was obviously my dad. Without him, though, there would never have been a wheelie, as without him there wouldn't have been a Dougie.

This is for you Dad.

ACKNOWLEDGEMENTS

Competing in trials is very much a team effort and it appears that writing a book is no different.

First of all, I'd like to thank James Hogg for suggesting the book and helping me to write it, Ian Marshall at Simon and Schuster for publishing it, and Julie Vasey for giving James the original idea. Thanks guys. It's been a heck of a lot of fun.

Because I've got such an awful memory I've had to rely on one or two external sources for information regarding my career, and if it hadn't been for www.trialonline.org I'd have been well and truly stuffed! Charly Demathieu, who runs the site, knows more about our sport than anyone else on earth and so I'd personally like to thank him for documenting it all and saving me from having to pick dates and results out of thin air! You're truly the God of trials! I would also like to personally thank family friends and photographers Eric Kitchen and Andy Greig (Trialscentral) for allowing me to include some of their great images in the book.

Despite there being little or no danger involved in writing this book (apart from my head almost exploding!) my friends and colleagues at Red Bull have been extremely supportive and I'd like to thank each every one of them. I don't think they thought I could even read or write so it's come as a big surprise.

Next, I'd like to thank my amazing manager and great friend Jake Miller for building and extending my career more than I could ever imagine. Cheers mate. Here's to another twenty years working together!

A lot of the stories and bits of information in this book have come from me, but a lot haven't. So, if it hadn't been for the following people, *Trials and Error* would be a heck of a lot thinner and a lot less accurate! They are Blackie Holden, Cousin John, Auntie Janet, Uncle Arthur, Uncle Sid, my brother Harry and my wonderful Mum, Isobel. I reckon Dad would have been chuffed to bits with the result.

Last but certainly not least, I would like to thank my beautiful and incredibly patient wife, Nicola, and our two boys, Alfie and Fraiser. I don't want to build her up too much, but I honestly couldn't have got by without her these last twenty years. As kids go, I reckon we hit the jackpot with our two and I love you all.

INDEX